D1806951

Helen Davies is Principal Lecturer in English Studies at Teesside University. She is on the editorial board for the *Journal of Gender Studies*.

Claire O'Callaghan is a lecturer in English at Brunel University. She is on the Executive Committee of the Contemporary Women's Writing Association (CWWA) and is on the editorial board of the *Journal of Gender Studies*.

'*Gender and Austerity in Popular Culture* is an important development in our understanding of the ways in which the "austerity" politics of both the UK and the USA are deeply gendered. But what is also recognised here are the historical parallels in which policies demanding restraint in both personal and state spending had different forms for men and women. Thus in this highly original collection of essays the various authors consider distinct locations of the traditions through which women and men are asked to live out, and through, economic inequality. In all, a highly readable and valuable collection.'

Mary Evans, Centennial Professor at the Gender Institute,
London School of Economics

Library of Gender and Popular Culture

From *Mad Men* to gaming culture, performance art to steam-punk fashion, the presentation and representation of gender continues to saturate popular media. This new series seeks to explore the intersection of gender and popular culture, engaging with a variety of texts – drawn primarily from Art, Fashion, TV, Cinema, Cultural Studies and Media Studies – as a way of considering various models for understanding the complementary relationship between 'gender identities' and 'popular culture'. By considering race, ethnicity, class, and sexual identities across a range of cultural forms, each book in the series will adopt a critical stance towards issues surrounding the development of gender identities and popular and mass cultural 'products'.

For further information or enquiries, please contact the library series editors:

Claire Nally: claire.nally@northumbria.ac.uk
Angela Smith: angela.smith@sunderland.ac.uk

Advisory Board:

Dr Kate Ames, Central Queensland University, Australia

Prof Leslie Heywood, Binghampton University, USA

Dr Michael Higgins, Strathclyde University, UK

Prof Åsa Kroon, Örebro University, Sweden

Dr Niall Richardson, Sussex University, UK

Dr Jacki Willson, Central St Martins, University of Arts London, UK

**Library of Gender
& Popular Culture**

Published and forthcoming titles:

GENDER AND AUSTERITY IN POPULAR CULTURE

FEMININITY, MASCULINITY & RECESSION IN FILM & TELEVISION

EDITED BY HELEN DAVIES AND CLAIRE O'CALLAGHAN

I.B. TAURIS

LONDON · NEW YORK

Published in 2017 by
I.B.Tauris & Co. Ltd
London • New York
www.ibtauris.com

Library of Gender and Popular Culture 13

ISBN: 978 1 78453 664 0
eISBN: 978 1 78672 092 4
ePDF: 978 1 78673 092 3

A full CIP record for this book is available from the British Library
A full CIP record is available from the Library of Congress

Library of Congress Catalog Card Number: available

Printed and bound by CPI Group (UK) Ltd, Croydon, CR0 4YY

MIX
Paper from
responsible sources
FSC
www.fsc.org   FSC® C013604

Contents

Contents

Acknowledgements

We would like to thank all of the contributors to this collection for sharing their work with us and for all of the hard work that has gone into their chapters. We are especially grateful to Dr Claire Nally and Dr Angela Smith for all of their support and encouragement, and Anna Coatman, Lisa Goodrum and Sophie Campbell at I.B.Tauris for working with us through this project's lifecycle. We also thank Kate Reeves for her support in the production of our manuscript.

The Introduction to this collection is derived in part from two articles published in our special issue of the *Journal of Gender Studies*, 2014 (23:3), available online:

http://wwww.tandfonline.com/10.1080/09589236.2014.913824

http://wwww.tandfonline.com/10.1080/09589236.2014.928437

We wish to thank colleagues at Taylor & Francis for giving us permission to reproduce this material.

Contributors

Leanne Bibby is a part-time lecturer in English Literature at Leeds Beckett University, an academic communications tutor in Leeds Beckett's Skills for Learning Service, and a support worker in the University of Leeds's Disabled Students Assessment and Support Department. Her PhD was awarded by Leeds Beckett University in 2012. Her thesis examines the representation of intellectual women in the fiction of A. S. Byatt, arguing that her novels and stories reconstruct cultural histories as forms of mythology, with significant feminist implications for other re-narrations of women's historical experience. Leanne's research interests include contemporary fiction, women's writing, historical fiction and historiographic metafiction, feminist theory and activism, creative writing, popular literature, and publishing.

Diane Charlesworth is Senior Lecturer in Film, Television and Cultural Studies in the School of Film and Media at the University of Lincoln. Her research and teaching interests are stardom and celebrity studies, gender politics and British broadcasting history, ethics, law and regulation. She is currently undertaking a research project on the spaces for and traces of the female television personality in British public service broadcasting history. She has recently published articles in the journals *Celebrity Studies* and *Critical Studies in Television*.

Ruth Charnock is Lecturer in the College of Arts at the University of Lincoln. She specialises in modernist and contemporary literature (particularly contemporary American literature), feminism, popular culture, psychoanalysis and affect theory. She has published on Anaïs Nin, incest narratives and Joni Mitchell, and Angela Carter. Her current book project is entitled *Anaïs Nin: Shame and Sex in Contemporary Culture*.

Helen Davies is Principal Lecturer in English Studies at Teesside University. Her research interests include gender, sexuality and disability in Victorian and neo-Victorian fiction. Her publications include *Gender and Ventriloquism in Victorian and Neo-Victorian Fiction: Passionate Puppets* (2012) and *Neo-Victorian Freakery: The Cultural Afterlife of the Victorian Freak Show* (2015). She has published widely on Victorian and neo-Victorian fiction, and co-edited (with Claire O'Callaghan) a special issue of the *Journal of Gender Studies* entitled 'Feminisms, Academia, Austerity' (September 2014). She is a member of the editorial board for the *Journal of Gender Studies*.

Zach Finch is a PhD candidate with a concentration in Media, Cinema, and Digital Studies at the University of Wisconsin-Milwaukee. He is a graduate of the University of Wisconsin-Eau Claire and North Carolina State University. He is a contributor to, and the co-editor with Bob Nowlan, of *Directory of World Cinema: Scotland* (2015).

Stéphanie Genz is Senior Lecturer in Media Studies at Nottingham Trent University. She specialises in contemporary gender politics and theory, post-feminism and popular culture. Her book publications include *Postfeminist Gothic: Critical Interventions in Contemporary Theory* (2007), *Postfemininities in Popular Culture* (2009) and *Postfeminism: Cultural Texts and Theories* (2009).

Erin Wyble Newcomb earned her doctoral degree in Language and Literacy Education and Women's Studies from the Pennsylvania State University. Currently, she teaches English and Women's Studies at the State University of New York at New Paltz. Her courses include young adult literature, women in literature, feminist theories and women in popular culture. Her research focuses primarily on young adult literature, including recent chapters such as: 'The soul of the clone: Coming of age as a post-human in Nancy Farmer's *The House of the Scorpion*', 'Orson Scott Card's Ender's game: Authoring home in *Fairyland*' and '"Weak as women's magic": Empowering care work in Ursula Le Guin's *Tehanu*'. Her next project focuses on gender and disability in young adult literature in works by Ursula Le Guin and Merrie Haskell.

Claire O'Callaghan is a lecturer in English at Brunel University. Her research interests centre on gender and sexuality in contemporary literature and culture, feminist and queer theory, and neo-Victorianism. She has published widely on neo-Victorian fiction and film (including pieces on lad culture and female genital mutilation), the contemporary writers Sarah Waters and Emma Donoghue, and on feminisms more broadly. Her monograph on Waters is forthcoming in 2017. Claire is an editorial board member of the *Journal of Gender Studies* and on the Executive Committee of the Contemporary Women's Writing Association (CWWA).

Lauren Pikó is a doctoral candidate in the School of Philosophical and Historical Studies at the University of Melbourne. Her thesis is entitled 'Mirroring England? Milton Keynes, decline and the English landscape'. This work investigates the meanings of Milton Keynes from 1967 to 1992 in relation to declinism and national identity narratives, in order to integrate urban and planning histories with contemporary English cultural history. Other current research examines the spatial politics of British masculinities, travel writing, cultural attitudes to urban planning, and postwar urban heritage. Her work is funded by the Wyselaskie Scholarship in Modern British History.

Evan Smith is Vice-Chancellor's Postdoctoral Research Fellow in the School of International Studies at Flinders University, South Australia. He has published widely on the British left, anti-racism, the British immigration control system and the politics of youth culture. He is the co-author of *Race, Gender and the Body in British Immigration Control* (2014) and the co-editor of *Against the Grain: The British Far Left from 1956* (2014). His current research project is an exploration of the transnational links between the communist parties of Great Britain, Australia and South Africa in the era of decolonisation.

Series Editors' Foreword

In Britain, the 2015 general election debates included discussions of the particular effects of austerity on women. This collection explores many of the themes highlighted in these debates from a UK and US perspective, looking at the ways in which film, literature and television emerged as sites to negotiate, construct and reconstruct the politics of austerity and gender. As many of the books in this series show, representations of gender and sexuality in popular culture offer the potential for the generation of alternative or even progressive politics of identity, and this collection of essays adds a nuanced economic/political reading to these.

The global recession that began in 2007 and spread quickly from 2008 onwards has been seen as one of the deepest and longest lasting in history. Much has been written on this in relation to national and international political ramifications, economic repercussions and emergent 'anti-austerity' movements. This collection explores the recession through the lens of popular culture, focusing on gender and sexuality and exploring the politics of identity. It places the twenty-first-century recession in the context of previous periods of economic hardship, as represented through popular culture. Whilst the often-depressing conclusions of these chapters point to the limits of feminist potential in such times, they all offer the hope that popular culture can be used to galvanise feminist concerns and so, as with other books in this series, offer nuanced approaches that highlight the continuing shifts towards gender equality.

—Angela Smith and Claire Nally

Introduction: Boom and Bust? Gender and Austerity in Popular Culture

Helen Davies and Claire O'Callaghan

From October to December of 2008, the BBC screened an adaptation of Charles Dickens's *Little Dorrit*, a tale of a family dogged by debt and devastated by poor investments and unscrupulous bankers. The resonance of these themes in the context of the 'Great Recession' was not lost on cultural commentators. For instance, A. N. Wilson, writing in the *Daily Mail*, remarked:

> It is hard to think of a more appropriate time to retell the story of the small man ruined by the machinations of big finance. All the guilt and humiliations caused by bad debt are in this Victorian credit crunch story. If some of you had read *Little Dorrit* a year ago, you might have thought it was a melodrama: but in the light of what happened in Wall Street, Iceland, and our own banks, the terrible trail of sadness caused by bad debt seems all too plausible.
>
> (Wilson, 2008, p. 64)

The origins of the recent recession are in the United States; when the North American housing bubble burst in 2007, with a knock-on effect which lead to the bankruptcy of Lehman Brothers in 2008, the ramifications of irresponsible lending were felt around the world. Banking groups in the UK and Eurozone failed or teetered on the brink of collapse, and governments were compelled to pump money into the 'bad debts' of financial organisations. As Wilson's comments suggest, however, the vagaries of economic markets wreak dreadful material consequences upon people's lives, with the fiscal crisis bringing with it the repossession of homes, unemployment and poverty on both sides of the Atlantic. This edited collection is not about the politics of the economic downfall; instead, we are concerned with popular cultural responses to financial hardship, and the politics of identity – especially in relation to gender and sexuality, but also with regards to class, disability and race – which are reflected, constructed and negotiated in such representations. Wilson's gloss on the way in which a television programme can become a cautionary fable of financial ruin for our times indicates that popular culture reflects, responds to and is in dialogue with the Great Recession. Moreover, it makes transparent that anxieties about the cultural impact of economic hardship have historical precedence as well. In Wilson's terms, we can learn lessons about the contemporary social effects of recession via popular cultural forms, but we also have the opportunity to reflect upon the ways in which earlier times of financial hardship might echo our own cultural moment.

Gender and Austerity in Popular Culture: Femininity, Masculinity and Recession in Film and Television seeks to explore the diverse manifestations of the gendered politics of recession and 'austerity' in popular culture. The discourse and effects of austerity in the context of the current global recession have received considerable attention in terms of politics and economics, and has dominated the media and press. Indeed, as explained below, a significant strand of the debates surrounding the influence of austerity upon society have been gendered, with concerns expressed that we are in a 'man-cession', to fears being articulated that women's ongoing struggles are further hampered by austerity measures. Bringing together a selection of essays from international scholars, this edited collection examines the ways in which literature, film and television have become crucial sites through which politics of gender are represented, negotiated and (re)constructed in times of recession and austerity measures. The collection focuses on both UK and US recessionary contexts, and also engages with historicising concerns about austerity and gender. However, before discussing the content of the chapters in more detail, we offer below an overview of the key terms and themes which underpin this volume: the gendering of the recession; the concept of austerity and how this might relate to gendered power inequalities; the ideological significance of popular culture; and the role of (post)feminism in the context of the recession and austerity.

Austere Times for Feminism? Gendering the Recession

Perhaps inadvertently, Wilson's comment on the 'small *man* ruined by the machinations of big finance' (Wilson, 2008, p. 64; our emphasis) invokes a recurring theme in media coverage of the recession. Shortly after the ramifications of the economic crisis started to become apparent, commentators turned to debating the effect that this might have upon men. Initial response from North America suggested that a 'mancession' had taken hold; according to high-profile reports in the mainstream press, men were being disproportionately affected by job losses. For instance, the *New York Times* cited statistics from the Bureau of Labor Statistics which suggested that 82 per cent of job losses in the USA befell male workers and that such inequalities would 'put pressure' on traditional gender roles (Rampell, 2009, n.p.). Such rhetoric has spread across the Atlantic in recent years, with the *Telegraph* offering a headline in 2011 that 'Women Do Better Than Men' in the recession (Peacock, 2011, n.p.). The implications of such discourse for gender equality are troubling, as Diane Negra and Yvonne Tasker explain: 'Underpinning the compelling rhetoric of masculine crisis is not only the suggestion that men are the primary victims of recession – a thread within the reporting of unemployment figures – but also that equality is a concern to be reserved for times of plenty' (Negra and Tasker, 2014, loc. 208). Of course, feminist groups in both the USA and Europe have belied such claims by offering compelling evidence to suggest that it is women's lives – economically, politically and socially – that have been particularly affected by the recession and the attendant government policies of cuts and austerity measures.

In response to the economic crisis, political discourse on both sides of the Atlantic turned towards championing an 'age of austerity' to combat the recession. Indeed, David Cameron's Conservative conference speech in the spring of 2009 used the phrase no less than eight times. Cameron was able to make 'good' on his word in the formation of a coalition government between the Conservative and Liberal Democrat parties in May 2010, with the Tory leader as the new Prime Minister of the UK. This coalition government was responsible for a series of ongoing cuts to public spending in Britain, which included redundancies and pay caps for those working in the public sector and substantial alterations to the welfare state (involving, for instance, benefit caps, and the abolition of disability living allowance).[1]

In the context of the USA, The American Recovery and Reinvestment Act of 2009, signed into law by President Barack Obama on 17 February 2009, had the objectives of saving and creating jobs, and offering financial relief to sectors most affected by the recession such as education and health, in an attempt to stimulate the economy rather than to introduce austerity measures. Unsurprisingly, the extent to which such measures actually aided the recovery of the economy are controversial and are still being debated.[2] However, despite Obama's apparent rejection of austerity discourse at a national level, state and national government spending cuts did take place, as Randy Albelda summarises:

> From FY09 through FY11 [Financial years 2009–2011], 31 of the 50 states implemented cuts to health care services and/or restricted access to care and/or health insurance; 29 states cut funding to programmes that serve the elderly and disabled, mostly used by low-income individuals (and often provided by low-wage women workers); 34 states reduced funding for child care [...] and 44 states imposed a range of cost-reductions on state employees, the majority of whom are women, including compulsory unpaid leave [...], eliminating or not filling vacancies, and reduction in employee benefits.
>
> (Albelda, 2014, p. 95)

In the UK, despite Cameron's promise that 'we're all in this together', the brief examples of the austerity measures given above provide the framework for highlighting significant gendered inequalities in the age of cuts. The Fawcett Society, a UK based organisation which campaigns for 'women's equality and rights – at home, at work and in public life', published a policy briefing in March 2012 which offered a comprehensive account of the detrimental effect of austerity measures upon women's equality. 'The Impact of Austerity on Women' indicates that women make up 64 per cent of the entire public sector (2012, p. 6); they will thus be disproportionately affected by job losses in this area, with women on lower-income jobs and from Black and Ethnic groups being particularly vulnerable (2012, p. 7). The number of women on Job Seekers Allowance is at the highest figure for 17 years, and women who are single parents of children over the age of five must struggle with the shift from Income Support to Job Seekers Allowance, meaning that if they are unable to take any job they might be offered their benefits will be cut (2012, pp. 8–9). Women of or approaching pensionable age must work for longer but also face losing money from their pension scheme (2012, p. 12). As a recent article by the Feminist Fightback Collective has argued, cuts to public services and benefits are liable to impact women in particular as they still perform a disproportionate amount of domestic labour in the form of caring responsibilities: 'Shifting work into the home, where it is done "for free", is a convenient way of hiding the hard realities of austerity behind closed doors' (Feminist Fightback Collective, 2011, p. 77). Just after our completion of this book, the results of the May 2015 UK general election were announced, with a Conservative government headed by the then British Prime Minister, David Cameron now leading the country. Early signs of any abatement of the gendered effects of government spending cuts are not promising; the Chancellor of the Exchequer, George Osbourne, presented his Summer Budget to Parliament on 8 July 2015, and commentators have identified the ways in which cuts to tax credits will be particularly detrimental to working mothers.[3]

In response to US recessionary measures, comparable patterns have become apparent over the past couple of years; whilst men's employment initially dropped quickly, women's employment rates rapidly followed and have yet to rise, creating a broader inequality between men and women in terms of their place in work and the home. Randy Albelda's above summary of US cuts begins to highlight the particular impact upon women, which have the following broad consequences:

> Women are more likely to be poor than men and be the ones primarily taking care of children. Programme cuts toward low-income individuals and families disproportionately hurt

women and children. This recession has led to significant funding decreases to services and programmes that are considered essential for the economic security of many women and children. It is also responsible for the reduction in government workers, disproportionately women.

(Albelda, 2014, p. 95)

And, of course, not all women are equal. When issues of class, race and disability intersect with broader gendered inequalities, the irony of us being 'all in this together' only becomes all the more apparent on both sides of the Atlantic.

Typically, austerity is defined as a fiscal procedure associated with 'the George Osborne paradigm in which we live' (Elmhirst, 2010, n. p.). In Mark Blyth's definition, it is 'a form of voluntary deflation in which the economy adjusts through the reduction of wages, prices, and public spending to restore competitiveness, which is (supposedly) best achieved by cutting the state's budget, debts, and deficits' (Blyth, 2013, p. 2). In this sense, 'austerity' is a term synonymous with the credit crunch rhetoric of 'cuts'. But, as numerous commentators have pointed out, the definition and effects of these terms are not necessarily the same. Whereas 'cuts' refers to 'specific budgetary cuts leading to specific cuts in services' and 'austerity' denotes 'a general reduction in government spending' (Lanchester 2010, p. 5), austerity is also, as Rebecca Bramall argues, 'a complex ideological phenomenon' that produces and enables socio-cultural politics as well as financial policies (2013, p. 3). Bramall's important monograph, published in 2013, makes clear that the concept of austerity is bound up with cultural politics such as constructions of gender. In her analysis, 'in austerity culture, certain gendered subject positions are more visible, desirable and possible than others' (Bramall, 2013, p. 111). It is this emphasis on *gendered* 'socio-cultural politics' which our collection takes as its broad focus. As detailed above, if the recession brings debates about gendered power inequalities to the fore, and if the rhetoric of austerity privileges certain gendered representations over others, then the chapters in this book offer a selection of case studies taken from popular culture for exploring and interrogating the ideological messages concerning gender which are offered in times of financial hardship.

6

Feminism Goes Pop: Constructing Culture, Constructing (Post)Femininities

John Storey has observed that 'feminism has always recognized the importance of cultural struggle within the contested landscape of popular culture' (2012, p. 11), and we take the view that popular culture is a field in which representations of identity can be made and re-made. As Richard Dyer opines:

> How a group is represented, presented over again in cultural forms, how an image of a member of a group is taken as representative of that group [...] these all have to do with how members of groups see themselves and others like themselves, how they see their place in society, their right to the rights a society claims to ensure its citizens.
>
> (Dyer, 2002, p. 1)

Popular culture thus might reflect existing norms and values with regards to social identity, yet also has the potential to actively (re)construct such identities: 'We make culture and we are made by culture' (Storey, 2010, p.172). The power of popular culture for feminist commentators is in its role in 'the construction of everyday life' (Turner, 2003, p. 6); the role that representations of gender in film, television and literature perform in the consolidation and perpetuation of traditional gendered identities, but also the potential that popular culture might have in generating alternative or even progressive politics of identity. Considering this collection's focus on the relationship between economic hardship and gender in cultural representation, it is important to note that the study of popular culture has repeatedly noted its inextricable connection to capitalist concerns, as Tony Bennett's use of vocabulary here suggests:

> The field of popular culture is structured by the attempt of the ruling class to win hegemony and by forms of opposition to this endeavour. As such, it consists not simply of an imposed mass culture that is coincident with dominant ideology, nor simply of spontaneously oppositional cultures, but is rather an area of negotiation between the two within which [...] dominant, subordinate and oppositional cultural and ideological values and elements are 'mixed' in different permutations.
>
> (Bennett, 2009, p. 96)

Bennett's stance on popular culture echoes our own call to tease out the complex, ambivalent and often contradictory messages and implications of popular cultural representations of gender. But if matters of economic and class power relations have become an even more pressing issue in the age of austerity, then how are 'dominant, subordinate and oppositional' perspectives on constructions of gender also shifting with regards renewed scrutiny of market conditions?

It is in this light that postfeminism – with its emphasis on economic and personal achievement and empowerment of individual women at the expense of the apparent rejection of earlier feminist activities and campaigns (McRobbie, 2009, p. 1) – is of particular interest to exploring the impact of the recession on constructions of gender. For Angela McRobbie, and for Yvonne Tasker and Diane Negra, postfeminism is typified by an investment in conspicuous consumption, commodification, class privilege and earning power (McRobbie, 2009, pp. 1–2); Tasker and Negra, 2007, p. 2). And this focus upon a certain construction of femininity has been pervasive in the first decade of the twenty-first century, as Rebecca Munford and Melanie Waters have identified: 'postfeminism has become the lens through which contemporary discussions of the relationship between popular culture and feminism are most often refracted' (Munford and Waters, 2014, p. 13). Taking up the quandary of how the neoliberal messages of postfeminism have needed to adapt in the context of the Great Recession, Diane Negra and Yvonne Tasker's Introduction to their recent collection of essays claims that traits such as 'freedom to consume' and 'self-fashion[ing]' have adapted rather than been challenged in the current climate of recessionary popular culture: in the 'commodification of domestic femininities' it is 'female consumer resourcefulness' which is now privileged (Negra and Tasker, 2014, loc. 281).

Whilst we obviously share Negra and Tasker's concerns that popular cultural representations of recession and austerity might reconsolidate traditional gender roles – a theme which is debated throughout the essays in this book – we also take the perspective that such formulations might be undermined even as they are invoked. Popular cultural representation is often ideologically unstable, and thus perpetually available for reappropriation and re-presentation, and the chapters in this volume are always attuned to the ways in which even the most problematic depictions of gender, recession and austerity might be turned into vehicles for feminist critique.

Gender and Austerity in Popular Culture: Chapter Summaries

The first four chapters of the book explore the current economic crisis via the way in which representations of economic hardship set in and dating from previous decades (the Victorian era, the Edwardian period, the 1940s, and 1980s–1990s) have also had implications for thinking about representations and ideologies of gender and sexuality in popular culture in the present. The latter five chapters are concerned with the fraught negotiations of femininity and masculinity in the context of contemporary consumer culture, a terrain which is shaped by complex postfeminist values.

The collection begins with Helen Davies's 'A Big Neo-Victorian Society?: Gender, Austerity, and Conservative Family Values in *The Mill*'. Davies's analysis of David Cameron's Conservative Party conference speech of October 2009 and discussion of Cameron's subsequent rhetoric about the 'Big Society' reveals how, in recessionary times, a return to traditional gendered roles within the family is positioned as a balm for austere cuts to state support. Furthermore, certain roles of dependency – particularly surrounding disability – are depicted as feminised, and implicitly devalued, in the current economic climate. Cameron's privileging of 'neo-Victorian' values of private philanthropy forms an important parallel with the 'paternalistic' world of employment relations in the neo-Victorian Channel 4 series *The Mill* (2013–2014). Whilst themes of sexual exploitation, gender/ class power inequalities, and the shortfall of aid for people with disabilities offer a compelling critique of Conservative 'family values' in series one of *The Mill*, the context of economic crisis in series two offers a stark portrayal of the apparent limits of feminism in austere times. In both series, the consequences of the failure of maternal care serve as a cautionary tale for women who might attempt to usurp patriarchal authority.

Chapter 2, Claire O'Callaghan's 'The Downturn at Downton: Money and Masculinity in *Downton Abbey*', uses the gender politics of this highly popular series screened on ITV (2010–) as a lens through which to problematise broader claims about the 'man-cession'. Series three of *Downton Abbey* dramatises the consequences of Lord Robert Crawley's 'bad investment' of his wife's inheritance, a plotline which offers a pertinent parallel of the recent global financial crisis. Moreover, the representation of the economies put in place at Downton as a result provides a compelling echo of the austerity measures deployed by governments in response to the Great Recession. However, although women are largely the source of money at Downton, O'Callaghan's analysis exposes the various ways in which *Downton Abbey* persists in locating capitalism and economics as the preserve of masculinity, with damning consequences for the agency and independence of women. As O'Callaghan demonstrates, the show might depict the effects of austerity measures upon women, yet still relegates women to the traditional feminised role of passivity; the female characters of *Downton* are used as mere narrative devices to shore up masculinity in crisis, and to restore the patriarchal, capitalist status quo.

In Chapter 3, 'Wartime Housewives and Vintage Women: A. S. Byatt's *Ragnarok: The End of Gods* and Reframing Popular Nostalgia', Leanne Bibby elucidates a point of connection between literary fiction and popular culture in her discussion of Byatt's 2011 novel in the light of blogs written by women about 'vintage' femininity. Following Rebecca Bramall's work (Bramall, 2013), Bibby demonstrates how nostalgia and 'vintage' culture are imbricated in the cultural politics of austerity. Furthermore, she highlights how both Byatt's text and the blogs depict nostalgia as having considerable feminist potential by allowing women to take control of their own destinies by imaginatively engaging with 'myths' of femininity whilst simultaneously challenging their limitations. Bibby's concept of 'feminist mythopoeia' offers an important counterpoint to dismissals of nostalgia as uncritical of traditional gender roles, and thus demonstrates how austerity discourse can – perhaps inadvertently – produce subjects who are actively engaged with the politics of femininity.

Lauren Pikó and Evan Smith's '"Thatcher's Bloody Britain!": Unemployment and Gender in Neoliberal Britain in *The Young Ones* and *Men Behaving Badly*' explores the ways in which these two popular television series from the 1980s and 1990s reflected contemporary political discourse on the role of unemployment in the British economy. Considering that widespread unemployment has been a high-profile consequence of the

2008 financial crisis, Chapter 4 offers a reflection on how more recent debates about gender and unemployment were being represented and constructed in popular culture in the context of previous Conservative governments. In their analysis of *The Young Ones*, Pikó and Smith argue that the comedy series offered a serious critique of traditionally masculine roles by depicting characters who were unable to conform to the expectations of patriarchal occupations. However, whilst the precarious situation of young men under Thatcher's regime is exposed, Pikó and Smith indicate how the portrayal of women in the series tends towards marginalisation and misogyny. Although in many ways *Men Behaving Badly* invokes a framework of sexist 'lad' culture in its depiction of gender and sexuality, it does offer a forum for exploring significant anxieties about gendered experiences of unemployment.

Chapter 5 inaugurates the latter part of the collection, which considers constructions of gender in the contemporary climate of recession and austerity. In 'From Homebuyer Advisor to Angel of the Hearth: The Development of Kirstie Allsopp as the Female Face of Channel 4 "Squeezed Middle" Austerity Programming', Diane Charlesworth suggests that a consequence of austerity measures in television programming has been to offer a space for a female presenter's voice as one of authority on British television, taking Kirstie Allsopp as her case study. Charlesworth provides an overview of key constructions of Allsopp's personae as a presenter and explores how these have shifted in austere times, focusing in particular on her roles in *Kirstie's Homemade Home* (2009) and *Kirstie's Homemade Britain* (2011) and how these series deploy the austerity discourse of 'make-do and mend'. Whilst acknowledging Allsopp's class privilege, and the ways in which she has been criticised for reiterating traditional gendered values which seem inflected with postfeminist sensibilities, this chapter provides evidence to suggest that Allsopp's visibility and her willingness to debate pressures upon women in relation to home/work could be understood as having some feminist significance. The analysis of the series teases out the complex politics of gender, class and austerity in Allsopp's representation.

Zach Finch's '*The Walking Dead* and Gendering Zombie Austerity' identifies the significance of post-apocalyptic narratives in popular culture in the wake of the recent global financial crisis in terms of the apparent destruction of a previous world order, and profound uncertainty about what might come in its place. Within this terrain, zombies have emerged as an especially loaded trope for expressing anxiety about 'undead' debts, and frightening reanimations of certain economic policies such as austerity which seemingly refuse to be killed off. Chapter 6 thus positions HBO's *The Walking Dead* (2010–) as a notable representation of the ways in which cultures of austerity influence constructions of gender in popular culture. Finch notes how the series' production and business practices reflect austere times, and, furthermore, explores how the plotlines of the programme have a tendency to normalise white male leadership, upholding patriarchal privilege and relegating women to roles of passivity and dependency underpinned by casual misogyny. Nevertheless, this post-apocalyptic and conservative world order – enabled by austere conditions and values – is displayed as precarious and undesirable, perhaps pointing towards the redundancy of such ideologies for creating a 'new' civilisation.

In Chapter 7, 'Embodying Austerity: Food and Physicality in *The Hunger Games*', Erin Wyble Newcomb examines the relationship between austerity and consumption in Suzanne Collins's novel *The Hunger Games* (2010), which is played out – with disturbing ideological consequences – in media responses to Jennifer Lawrence's body in her role in the 2012 film adaptation. Lawrence's appearance was repeatedly criticised for failing to appear appropriately 'starved'. Deploying feminist understandings of the politics of cultural representation of women's bodies, Newcomb considers the idealisation of the 'starved' female body as an example of the gendering of austerity. She exposes how austere consumption is positioned as a feminine virtue, yet also discusses how Lawrence's body is in turn 'consumed' by her audiences in a metafilmic parallel of the spectacle of (capitalist) consumption in the Games in both the book and film.

Chapter 8, Ruth Charnock's '"I Want What Everyone Wants": Cruel Optimism in HBO's *Girls*', provides a detailed reading of 'One Man's Trash', episode five of the HBO series *Girls*, in the light of Lauren Berlant's concept of 'cruel optimism'; a fantasy of the good life, and its unattainability in the current economic, social and cultural climate. Charnock explains how *Girls* has been criticised by cultural commentators for failing to engage with twenty-first-century anxieties surrounding recession and austerity. However, she considers how the series' engagement with tropes of the 'Millennial' and 'Boomerang Generation' – both of which are marked by economic and social anxiety and precarity – does manifest an awareness of shifting aspirations and expectations in austere times. The interaction between Hannah and Dr Joshua in the episode is clearly marked by postfeminist gender politics, yet gendered and economic inequalities are brought to the forefront of their relationship as well. Charnock's analysis suggests that Hannah's desire for the material comforts of Joshua's life are critiqued as unrealistic and unobtainable, and a life beyond gendered austerity emerges as difficult to imagine.

The collection's final chapter, Stéphanie Genz's 'Baring the Recession: Sexual Sensationalism and Gender (A)politics in Contemporary Culture', explores the discourse of 'sexual sensationalism' in recessionary popular culture, for which she coins the term 'boob and bust politics'; in other words, a strategy of sexualised activism which seeks to address gendered inequalities in the context of the current economic crisis. Analysing notable instances of feminist reclamation of the topless female body as a form of political protest, Genz considers how such performances might trouble neoliberalism's emphasis on apolitical individualism. Using HBO's *Game of Thrones* (2011–) as an example of a television series which unites economic anxieties with the hypervisibility of sexuality, Genz's analysis exposes how a slippage occurs from the programme's 'sexist liberalism' to 'liberal sexism', enacting a naturalisation of sexual violence towards women and girls. Nevertheless, she also considers some instances of *Game of Thrones'* challenges of gender binaries, and discusses the potential for overt sexualisation to be understood as an exposé of patriarchal mechanisms.

Taken as a whole, then, the essays in this collection have the following aims:

- To explore the ways in which gender has been depicted and constructed in representations of recession and austerity in popular culture.
- To examine the ideological implications of austerity-inflected representations of femininity and masculinity in popular culture. To what extent does popular culture offer a forum for critiquing discourses of austerity and gender? In times of financial difficulty, does popular culture seek to challenge and/or offer alternative images of traditional gender roles, or are popular cultural responses conservative and reactionary?

13

- To discuss the ways in which discourses of austerity and gender intersect with other representations of cultural identities (including class, disability and race).

Although the essays in this collection often come to depressing conclusions with regards to the feminist potential of recessionary constructions of gender, these analyses clearly demonstrate that popular cultural representations have the potential to mobilise feminist concerns. Indeed, the arguments offered in the forthcoming chapters provide evidence that such representations do not just signify in a hegemonic way to audiences, but can also prompt critique and resistance. Recessionary conditions and attendant manifestations of austerity are hardly productive in themselves, but they can generate cultural debate and awareness which challenges social and political complacency about prevailing gendered inequalities.

Notes

1 For a summary of the Coalition government's welfare reforms and cuts, see Patrick Wintour, 'The Day Britain Changes: Welfare Reforms and Coalition Cuts Take Effect'. *Guardian*, 1 April 2013. Available from: <http://www.theguardian. com/politics/2013/mar/31/liberal-conservative-coalition-conservatives>.
2 See Michael Grunwald, '5 Years After Stimulus, Obama Says It Worked'. *Time*, 17 February 2014. Available from: <http://time.com/8362/economic-stimulus-recovery-act-anniversary-obama/>.
3 See Nicholas Watt and Frances Perraudin, 'Cuts to Tax Credit in Budget Hit Women Twice as Hard as Men, say Labour'. *Guardian*, 8 July 2015. Available from: <http://www.theguardian.com/uk-news/2015/jul/08/budget-child-tax-credit-cuts-affect-women-worse-men-labour-yvette-cooper>.

Bibliography

Albelda, Randy. (2014). 'Gender Impacts of the "Great Recession" in the United States'. In: Maria Karamessini and Jill Rubery (eds) *Women and Austerity: The Economic Crisis and the Future for Gender Equality*. London and New York: Routledge.

Bennett, Tony. (2009). 'Popular Culture and the Turn to Gramsci'. In: John Storey (ed.) *Cultural Theory and Popular Culture: A Reader*. 4th edition. London and New York: Routledge.

Blyth, Mark. (2013). *Austerity: The History of a Dangerous Idea*. Oxford: Oxford University Press.

Bramall, Rebecca. (2013). *The Cultural Politics of Austerity: Past and Present in Austere Times*. Basingstoke: Palgrave Macmillan.

Dyer, Richard. (2002). *The Matter of Images: Essays on Representation*. 2nd edition. London and New York: Routledge.

Elmhirst, Sophie. (2010). 'Word Games: Austerity'. *New Statesman*, 24 September. Available from: <http://www.newstatesman.com/ideas/2010/09/austerity-word-red-conference> [Accessed: 29 April 2015].

Fawcett Society. (2012). 'The Impact of Austerity on Women'. March. Available from: <http://www.fawcettsociety.org.uk/?attachment_id=407> [Accessed: 29 April 2015].

Feminist Fightback Collective. (2011). 'Cuts are a Feminist Issue'. *Soundings* 49, pp. 73–83.

Grunwald, Michael. (2014). '5 Years After Stimulus, Obama Says It Worked'. *Time*, 17 February. Available from: <http://time.com/8362/economic-stimulus-recovery-act-anniversary-obama/> [Accessed: 20 April 2015].

Lanchester, John. (2010). *Whoops! Why Everyone Owes Everyone and No One Can Pay*. London: Allen Lane.

McRobbie, Angela. (2009). *The Aftermath of Feminism: Gender, Culture and Social Change*. London: SAGE.

Munford, Rebecca, and Waters, Melanie. (2014). *Feminism and Popular Culture: Investigating the Postfeminist Mystique*. London and New York: I.B.Tauris.

Negra, Diane, and Tasker, Yvonne. (2014). 'Introduction: Gender and Recessionary Culture'. In: Diane Negra and Yvonne Tasker (eds) *Gendering the Recession: Media and Culture in An Age of Austerity*, Kindle edition. Durham, NC and New York: Duke University Press.

Peacock, Louisa. (2011) 'Women Do Better than Men as "Mancession" Hits'. *Telegraph*, 14 December. Available from: <http://www.telegraph.co.uk/finance/jobs/8954370/Women-do-better-than-men-as-mancession-hits.html> [Accessed: 13 March 2015].

Rampell, Catherine. (2009). 'As Layoffs Surge, Women may Pass Men in Job Force'. *New York Times*, 5 February. Available from: <http://www.nytimes.com/2009/02/06/business/06women.html?pagewanted=2&adxnnl=1&adxnnlx=1393524229-p4xsjpveZedyU6yFBTYfhw> [Accessed: 13 March 2015].

Storey, John. (2010). *Cultural Studies and the Study of Popular Culture*. 3rd edition. Edinburgh: Edinburgh University Press.

——— . (2012). *Cultural Theory and Popular Culture: An Introduction*. 6th edition. Harlow: Pearson Education.

Tasker, Yvonne, and Negra, Diane. (2007). 'Introduction: Feminist Politics and Postfeminist Culture'. In: Yvonne Tasker and Diane Negra (eds) *Interrogating*

Postfeminism: Gender and the Politics of Popular Culture. Durham, NC and London: Duke University Press.

Turner, Graeme. (2003). *British Cultural Studies: An Introduction*. 3rd edition. London: Routledge.

Watt, Nicholas, and Perraudin, Frances. (2015). 'Cuts to Tax Credits in Budget Hit Women Twice as Hard as Men, say Labour'. *Guardian*, 8 July. Available from: <http://www.theguardian.com/uk-news/2015/jul/08/budget-child-tax-credit-cuts-affect-women-worse-men-labour-yvette-cooper> [Accessed: 1 September 2015].

Wilson, A. N. (2008). 'Credit Crunch Classic'. *Daily Mail*, 25 October, pp. 64–66.

Wintour, Patrick. (2013). 'The Day Britain Changes: Welfare Reforms and Coalition Cuts Take Effect'. *Guardian*, 1 April. Available from: <http://www.theguardian.com/politics/2013/mar/31/liberal-conservative-coalition-conservatives> [Accessed: 20 April 2015].

1

A Big Neo-Victorian Society?: Gender, Austerity and Conservative Family Values in *The Mill*

Helen Davies

Judith Johnston and Catherine Waters's discussion of the term 'neo-Victorianism' highlights the way in which this appellation for contemporary culture's engagements with the nineteenth century implies a sense of nostalgia for that which has gone before:

> The term 'Neo' when used in conjunction with a political movement, implies a desire to return to the political beliefs of that movement's past [...] and a desire for the reinstatement of earlier, and often conservative, values as opposed to more radical change. Margaret Thatcher's Neo-Victorianism – her call for a return to 'Victorian values' – might be interpreted in this way.
> (Johnston and Waters, 2008, pp. 10–11)

Debates as to whether neo-Victorianism is a genre typified by a conservative idealisation of the nineteenth century, or is more clearly committed to politically progressive challenges to the social power inequalities of this historical era have been a central feature of neo-Victorian criticism.[1] In short, both impulses can be at play in neo-Victorian cultural productions, and often simultaneously.[2] However, whilst Margaret Thatcher's ideological investment in nostalgia for 'Victorian values' has received some notable attention in extant neo-Victorian criticism,[3] the extension and development of this 'neo-Victorian' rhetoric in David Cameron's Conservative–Liberal Democrat coalition government – particularly with regards to the austerity measures outlined to combat the recent UK recession – deserves further scrutiny. In what ways might Cameron's recent discourse on family values, social responsibility and Victorian-inflected philanthropy in his concept of 'the Big Society' become manifest in contemporary and popular cultural representations of the nineteenth century?

Beginning in summer 2013, with the second series screening the following year, Channel 4's neo-Victorian drama *The Mill* tells the story of a family of mill owners and their workers employed at Quarry Bank Mill in Cheshire during the 1830s. The historical Quarry Bank Mill offers an invaluable insight into the lives of its employees, for a detailed and substantial archive of 'over a hundred years' worth of documentation, thousands of original mill records, personal correspondence, [and] thousands of artefacts' is preserved on site (Hanson, 2014, p. viii). It was this material which formed the basis of the fictionalised version of the community surrounding Quarry Bank Mill in the television series. David Hanson's book about the original Mill acknowledges the necessary process of condensation, adaptation and reimagining which attended the development of these sources into *The Mill*'s screenplay:

> In the retelling of these stories it is sometimes for the benefit of the writer and ultimately, therefore, to the benefit of the viewer, that characters and events are slipped from their historically accurate moorings, to a place of greater immediacy and relevance.
>
> (Hanson, 2014, p. xi)

That historical adaptations reflect the concerns of the cultural moment in which they are produced is evidently something of a truism, yet the ways in which the plotlines of *The Mill* engage with the current 'age of austerity' in Britain was highlighted in several press reviews of the series. Remarking upon series one, episode one's depressing emphasis on the exploitation of impoverished workers and the 'wet smacking of gruel into indentured child worker's grubby [...] hands', Ceri Radford summarised the opening of the series as 'history as misery memoir, the anti-Downton Abbey' (Radford, 2013, n.p.). Whilst Radford does not elucidate the differences between

The Mill and *Downton Abbey* as two examples of historical drama, her comment implies that the latter offers idealised escapism from the gritty realities of poverty and class conflict, realities depicted in *The Mill* which are as relevant to contemporary austere Britain as they are to the nine-teenth century.[4] Charlotte Runcie's review of the beginning of the second series of *The Mill* makes such analogies more transparent: '*The Mill* [...] is *Benefits Street* for the 1830s, except there are no benefits – unless you count the workhouse (which doesn't seem to benefit anyone) or a kindly neighbour bringing round a load of bread every now and then' (Runcie, 2014, n.p.). Considering the outpouring of self-righteous indignation and hatred towards the perceived 'scroungers' upon the taxpayer which attended the screening of *Benefits Street* on Channel 4 in January 2014,[5] Runcie's remark notes that the absence of a Welfare State in the nineteenth century had dire consequences in times of unemployment and financial hardship. *The Mill* depicts the conditions of the workhouse as unbearably cruel and squalid, and community charity as precarious in the face of the need for self-preservation. The miserable fates of the series' characters represent 'some grotesque failure of pre-Welfare State Britain. It made the modern bedroom tax seem almost like a cuddly indulgence' (Runcie, 2014, n.p.) This review, though damning of the 'gloomy and po-faced' tone of the series (Runcie, 2014, n.p.), casts *The Mill's* rendering of austere times in the nineteenth century as simultaneously a justification of the current benefit system in contemporary Britain *and* a refutation that the Coalition's austerity measures – such as Bedroom Tax[6] – are quite as stringent by com-parison. Put another way, in Runcie's assessment, *The Mill* might critique austerity measures such as benefit cuts, but it also seems to affirm certain aspects of Conservative policy which have ideological implications for the 'private' space of the home and family. And, of course, the spheres of home and family are gendered; women have been and continue to be associated with the role of child-rearing and domestic care-giving in a variety of ways, a cornerstone of their marginalisation from the world of work and subject to patriarchal authority and oppression in both the traditional family unit and society beyond.

It is this broad tension between *The Mill's* critique and simultaneous support of contemporary policies of austerity, and the ways in which these influence cultural constructions of gender, that this chapter explores. I seek to read the series through the lens of the British Coalition government's policies on austerity and 'family values', and to consider the ways in which *The Mill* represents the pressures placed upon women in times of economic hardship. I begin with an extended analysis of David Cameron's rhetoric in his speech delivered at the Conservative party conference at Manchester on 8 October 2009. Although given when Cameron was leader of the Conservative Party rather than the Prime Minister, the speech offers a significant overview of his vision for austerity measures which would begin to take shape as policy when his Coalition government came to power in May 2010. Importantly for my purposes, it also reveals a conspicuous emphasis on family and community in a way which invokes traditional gender roles even as it ostensibly speaks to increased equality across society. Furthermore, the politics of gender also intersect with issues of disability, a theme which foreshadows the changes to the disability benefits system under the Coalition government,[7] and which become manifest as a source of anxiety in *The Mill*'s representation of gendered bodies that 'work', and those which do not. Cameron's championing of personal and community responsibility becomes especially acute in his subsequent policy of 'the Big Society', which I interpret as a development of Thatcher's celebration of the 'Victorian values' of philanthropy rather than state support. Yet, as we shall see, the concept of 'the Big Society' not only rests on an idealised view of Victorian society but also implicitly requires considerable support from the domestic sphere – the unpaid labour of women – to compensate for the shortfall in state funding.

The two series of *The Mill* can be understood as engaging with different facets of debates surrounding austerity and gender. My analysis of series one demonstrates how poverty is ostensibly combatted by the 'family values' of the Gregs who own Quarry Bank Mill. Initially, it seems that their paternalistic care towards their apprentices offers a productive alternative to the horrors of the workhouse; the latter is funded by Liverpool's 'ratepayers' (series one, episode two), and so to offer orphans not only employment but a family structure within the Mill seems to indicate that private, paternalistic enterprise can function as an antidote to inadequate public funding which is a drain on the income of working people. However, via depictions of sexual exploitation, failures of care and the unresolved problem of how to make disabled bodies 'productive', series one of *The Mill* exposes the intersection between gendered and economic power imbalances; the 'family' becomes a site of oppression rather than support, and in austere times it is the powerless who suffer most.

In series two, the neo-Victorian context is more acutely informed by themes of financial hardship; the first episode represents John Doherty, an Irish political activist, informing his followers that the current economic 'downturn' has been caused by 'a banking crisis in America' which has led to recession in Britain (series two, episode one). The recession means that the Greg family must make cuts to ensure continuing productivity; William Greg, now the patriarch of the business, informs his workers that all must take a 25 per cent reduction in wages to stave off redundancies, as 'we are all in this together' (series two, episode five). This direct invocation of Cameron's rhetoric should give us pause for thought, as series two of *The Mill* demonstrates the strain placed on a society where financial crisis necessitates a dependency on community support in the place of formal funding: family units must retreat to traditional gender roles, which in turn erupt in violence. Whilst series two seemingly does critique the ideal of Cameron's 'Big Society', however, it also struggles to allow women freedom from bearing the primary responsibility for care-giving in the family: the character of Esther Price is apparently punished for her attempts to balance her role of mother with her political conscience by the death of her son. Such a scenario indicates that despite *The Mill*'s investment in exposing the gendered power inequalities perpetuated by austere times, it cannot wholly depart from the notion that conservative 'family values' will act as a balm to fiscal instability.

Dependency, Responsibility and Gendering the Recession: David Cameron's Family Values

Cameron's 2009 Manchester conference speech has become somewhat infamous for its repeated refrain of 'we're all in this together'; a mantra of sharing the burden of the current hardships of the economic crisis, and a statement of solidarity in the face of the austerity measures that are to come in the form of cuts to government spending.[8] Unsurprisingly, ways in which such discourse belied evident class-related power differences between various sectors of society came under scrutiny in the media coverage of

Cameron's pronouncements.[9] In addition, as Claire O'Callaghan and I have identified elsewhere, this statement of equality rings hollow in the face of compelling evidence to suggest that austerity measures disproportionately affect women in both the work place and home.[10] Interestingly, however, Cameron's speech makes some allusions to improvements in gender equality in society; in a discussion of the situation of those in military service in Afghanistan, he makes reference to the 'brave men and women' working in the forces, indicating implicitly that women are now playing a significant role in traditionally male occupations (Cameron, 2009, n.p.). Furthermore, he draws attention to the increase in women candidates for parliament in the Conservative Party, thus suggesting that his party are actively contributing towards gender equality in the political sphere (Cameron, 2009, n.p.).[11]

Cameron also makes reference to his own domestic situation as a way in to explaining his personal investment in the importance of family: 'this is in my DNA: family, community, country' (Cameron, 2009, n.p.), but it is when the personal becomes political that his championing of the centrality of 'family' becomes more troubling. Reflecting on the social problems which have perpetuated the economic crisis, he explains:

> I know how lucky I've been to have the chances I've had. And I know there are children growing up in Britain today who will never know the love of a father. Who are born in homes that hold them back [...] Children who will never start a business, never raise a family [...] This is what I want to change.
> (Cameron, 2009, n.p.)

Although the speech makes much of the Labour government's 'breaking' of the economy and society via too much spending and interventions which have 'undermined responsibility', the above quotation also casts blame upon certain members of society as well. Signifiers of being a successful member of society – in other words, part of the solution to the recession – are a patriarchal, heteronormative family structure which should be replicated over generations and private entrepreneurship. Why an absent father should be invoked as more detrimental to a child's future, rather than an absent mother, remains unexplained, but such a formulation points towards a privileging of the patriarch as a guiding force in becoming a productive, financially viable adult. By inference, it is single mother families who are a burden on society; more specifically, a drain on the state coffers, presumably due to the benefits they may claim, but also in their supposed failure to produce suitably industrious children.

Cameron's example of how this sense of social 'responsibility' might be restored is conspicuously gendered. The plan to 'get Britain working' instead of relying upon state-funded support is justified as follows:

> It means the man who's lost his job and his confidence saying 'yes, I can set up on my own, I can take responsibility, there's nothing to stop me'. It means the people he takes on, who thought they were written off, thinking 'yes, I've got another chance and I can provide for my family again'.
>
> (Cameron, 2009, n.p.)

The reiteration of the traditional masculine role of breadwinner is overt here, but also the mode of setting up business which then leads to further employment opportunities for others invokes a paternalistic structure of work-place relations. Cameron manages to avoid gendering the workers who will benefit from such enterprises, but the image of the 'man' whose (presumably masculine?) confidence will be restored by imbuing his workers with financial and familial stability is a telling echo of the aforementioned remarks on children who might have been more financially and socially productive had they 'know[n] the love of a father' (Cameron, 2009, n.p.). Underpinning this vision of employer/worker relations is an implicit sense of hierarchy as well, for seemingly not everyone should have the drive to own their own business: apparently, some will just be content to be employed by more responsible, masculine types. As David Roberts explains, the Victorian ideology of paternalism rested upon a belief in the social need for hierarchical relations which might replicate a patriarchal family structure (Roberts, 1979, pp. 2–3). In summary, everyone needs to take responsibility for their economic and social worth, but those who lead the way will be men, in a macrocosm of the traditional power relations within the private space of the family.

In condemnation of the 'cycle of welfare dependency' which Cameron feels that the Labour government perpetuated, and which austerity measures will need to address, he offers the example of a 'guy' who had 'lost his job [...] and was desperate to get back into work' (Cameron, 2009, n.p.). Due to his financial commitments on his mortgage, the 'guy' needed to register for Job Seeker's Allowance:

> He'd twisted his ankle and walked in with a limp, so you know what they said? They told him he couldn't register for Job Seeker's Allowance because he wasn't fit to work so he'd have to go on incapacity benefit [...] This was a man who wanted to take responsibility for himself and his family and the system said no, you've got to depend on the state [...] The welfare system today sends out completely crazy signals [...] We're going to make it clear: if you really cannot work, we'll look after you. But if you can work, you should work and not live off the hard work of others.
>
> (Cameron, 2009, n.p.)

In this example, to be 'incapacitated' – put another way, disabled – is to be emasculated: prevented from fulfilling one's patriarchal obligation to support the family unit. Consequently, the need for state support, the dependency on benefits, becomes a feminised condition. An afflicted body, albeit only temporary, is an affront to masculinity. Furthermore, the division between bodies that 'work' and bodies that 'don't' instils an alarming conflation of corporeal and economic value. Troublingly, those who 'really cannot work' are still positioned as 'living off the hard work of others', despite this being couched as care – being 'look[ed] after' (Cameron, 2009, n.p.). Within this formulation, men who wish to fulfil the traditional expectations of being the patriarchal provider for their family unit should not be subjected to being the responsibility of someone else; seemingly, such dependency is the lot of the women and children.

It is important to recognise that Cameron's speech dwells upon another instance of attitudes towards disability in society, which is also underscored by questionable gendered ideologies. He recounts the case of Fiona Pilkington, a woman who killed herself and her disabled daughter, Francecca Hardwick, by setting fire to their car in October 2007 after 10 years of abuse and harassment from individuals in their local community. For Cameron, this tragedy was caused by failures in the police protection offered to Pilkington and her daughter, and a broader 'breakdown of responsibility' with regards to society more broadly:

> If no one would protect them then by ending their lives, she was keeping them safe […] A breakdown of morality in the minds of those thugs, a total absence of feeling or conscience. A breakdown in community where a neighbour is left to reach a pitch of utter misery. And a breakdown of our criminal justice system.
>
> (Cameron, 2009, n.p.)

Of course, Cameron is right to highlight the vulnerability of people with disabilities to hate crimes, which reflects deeply entrenched prejudices within society. And, as a subsequent inquest into this case has demonstrated, there were failings in the police force's dealings with Pilkington's persistent requests for help.[12] Clearly Cameron does not seek to overtly blame Pilkington for her act of appalling desperation, yet to deploy this story as a vehicle for his rhetoric on the failure of 'community' – as we shall see, a concept which becomes increasingly loaded when Cameron's Coalition government comes to power – does not quite mask the gendered contrast which is made between Pilkington and the 'guy' discussed above. The latter – a father – just wanted to look after his family and is being prevented by doing this by the 'crazy' welfare system (Cameron, 2009, n.p.). The former – a mother – must commit a terrible act because she has no further capacity to care for her daughter. The spectre of failure of maternal care haunts this example, thus offering a disturbing echo of the implicit blame being placed upon single mothers in Cameron's commentary on the social problems which have fed into the recession. In other words, mothers are positioned as necessarily dependent upon community and state assistance, and awful consequences might ensue if left to take control of their own destiny.

The policy changes which attended Cameron's government's leadership of the Coalition when elected in May 2010 are by now all too familiar; cuts would be made to the public spending budget with particular emphasis on the benefits system, which would affect the most vulnerable in society in a variety of ways. As a remedy for meeting the short-fall in financial support offered by the state as a result of these austerity measures, Cameron would revisit his 2009 celebration of 'community' in his concept of 'the Big Society', first touted in a speech delivered on 19 July 2010 in Liverpool. He describes this vision as follows:

> The Big Society is about a huge cultural change where people in their everyday lives, in their homes, in their neighbourhoods, in

their work places, don't always turn to officials, local authorities or central government for answers to the problems they face but instead feel both free and powerful enough to help themselves and their own communities.

(Cameron, 2010, n.p.)

Couched in terms of empowering 'everyday' people to exercise agency over their own lives, the material circumstances underpinning the 'Big Society' – 'a new culture of voluntarism, philanthropy, social action' (Cameron, 2010, n.p.) – are that there has been too much government spending on financial support for those who do not work which, in Cameron's formulation, 'has turned able, capable individuals into passive recipients of state help with little hope of a better future' (Cameron, 2010, n.p.). Again, the adjectives deployed here are gendered; to need state assistance from the benefit system is 'passive', thus coded as feminine, whereas being financially independent is about being 'able'; active, masculine. Ironically, however, this increased emphasis on personal, informal and privatised support mechanisms to compensate for cuts to government spending also places an increased responsibility upon domestic, familial networks to absorb this burden, and it is in this sense that such austerity measures reiterate the traditional care-giving role of women in the home. This correlation is crucial for the argument made by the Feminist Fightback Collective's article, 'Cuts are a Feminist Issue', in which they identify that 'evidence has shown repeatedly that in places where neoliberal projects of austerity have been rolled out, the bulk of the displaced responsibility fall to women' via unpaid domestic labour (Feminist Fightback, 2011, p. 76). More specifically, they critique the gendered assumptions which provide the foundation for Cameron's policy:

it is largely women who step in as the state retreats at high speed, leaving behind a gaping chasm of care. It is women's unwaged labour that constitute the mythical 'Big Society' – which is one reason why it is such a deeply gendered vision.

(Feminist Fightback, 2011, p. 82)

These are the 'family values' lurking behind Cameron's panacea for swinge-ing austerity measures: a retreat to a traditional, patriarchal organisation of the 'private' space of the home, which necessarily has an impact upon women's ability to participate in the public sphere of paid labour as well.

The way in which Cameron's 'Big Society' invokes Conservative Party rhetoric dating from several decades earlier has not gone unnoticed by critical commentators. As I mentioned in the Introduction to this chapter, Margaret Thatcher, who was in office as the prime minister of the UK Conservative government from 1979 to 1990, was notable for her investment in a certain, idealised view of 'Victorian values' which informed her attitude towards how society might be organised. In a television interview between Thatcher and Brian Walden which was screened on 16 January 1983, he quizzes her about the investment she reveals in 'Victorian values' and she responds with an affirmation of her support of nineteenth-century models of philanthropy: 'as people prospered themselves so they gave great voluntary things to the State [...] As our people prospered, so they used their independence and initiative to prosper others, not compulsion by the state' (Margaret Thatcher Foundation, 2005, n.p.). Evidently this nostalgic perception of a privatised method of financial support for a community or broader society conveniently glosses over issues of poverty and social deprivation which were not resolved by charity in the Victorian era (indeed, which are still pervasive today). Moreover, the similarities between Thatcher's vision of individual benevolence which lessens state obligation, and Cameron's 'Big Society' as a way of neutralising the austerity measures of the Coalition are plain to see. Alan Walker and Steve Corbett remark upon this connection – and also argue that both Thatcher's 'Victorianism' and Cameron's 'Big Society' ignore existing social power inequalities in terms of who has access to the time and income for philanthropy, who might be willing to share in this way, and who is actually likely to benefit. In their terms, the 'Big Society':

> chimes with nineteenth-century conservative communitarian opposition to state intervention, as well as the promotion of paternalism in the form of mutual aid, philanthropy and voluntary activity. But this view [...] is rose-tinted: exploitative conditions were rife in the nineteenth century and it took a much more active state to attain progress.
>
> (Walker and Corbett, 2013, n.p.)

Whilst Walker and Corbett do not pick up on the gendered power relations of this 'promotion of paternalism', their emphasis on the connection between nineteenth-century ideologies of social support which are separate from the state and the present Coalition's austerity measures offers an important context for the analysis of *The Mill* that follows. In what ways might a neo-Victorian television series – which, as evidenced by the reviews discussed above, is apparently committed to exploring the 'exploitative' aspects of nineteenth-century workplaces during the Industrial Revolution – expose the fallacy of Conservative Party idealisation of 'Victorian values'? More specifically, to what extent does the series' depiction of economic hardship and austere living based on class inequalities offer a critique of the gendered 'family values' espoused by Cameron as being a remedy to the twenty-first-century recession?

Paternal Problems: Gendering the Working Body in *The Mill*, Series One

The employees of Quarry Bank Mill as depicted in the first series of *The Mill* are never allowed to forget that they 'benefit' from a paternalistic mode of support from the Greg family. The Mill is largely staffed by girls and boys who have been taken from the workhouse and are employed as apprentices by the Gregs; under these terms they receive food and shelter, but are essentially indentured to the family until they come of age at 21[13] and might be kept on as adult workers living in the community village which surrounds the Mill. As Robert, the aspirational son of the patriarch and Mill owner Samuel Greg, opines: 'When there is no natural guardian, all of the privileges of a parent and all of the duties transfer to us. It's always been our philosophy here' (series one, episode one). Similarly, when Mr Timperley, the Apprentice House warden, is bringing Lucy Garner and her sister Catherine from the workhouse to be new apprentices, he explains: 'We're one big family here. Father, mother, and over 60 brothers and sisters. Work hard, be good, and you'll be orphans no more' (series one, episode two). The 'philosophy' being espoused is thus that a stable family structure will enable the young workers to be productive members of society; a formulation which chimes with Cameron's vision of the patriarchal family unit laying the foundations for renewed economic stability in contemporary British society. However, the unequal power relationships which accompany this idealised model of paternal employer/worker relations become brutally apparent in the behaviour of the lascivious factory manager Crout, who takes advantage of his position to sexually assault the young women of the Mill. When Esther Price, one of the more outspoken apprentices, insists that they should challenge this abuse, she is reminded by one of the other girls that 'They own us. They don't have to listen' (series one, episode one). Discussing the problem of familial metaphors in feminist discourse, Susan Ostrov Weisser and Jennifer Fleischner argue: 'families are often only the most private sites of warfare, of expressions of dominance and fields of hierarchical values, and never more so than when they masquerade as benevolent social extensions of natural relations, of benign patriarchal power' (Weisser and Fleischner, 1994, p. 3). The female apprentice's recognition that the girls of the 'family' are 'owned' forms a continuum between economic vulnerability, patriarchal and sexual possessiveness. In a paternalistic model of employment where the labour is exchanged for ostensibly benevolent protection, but also subordination, the young women's bodies themselves become the property of the extended patriarchal network of the Gregs, to use and abuse as seen fit.

This issue is made even more apparent when the younger Garner sister, Catherine, is returned to the workhouse due to perceived ill-health. Timperley is travelling with the young girl along a country lane, and suddenly stops the horse and cart to speak to her:

> I'm sorry, you were judged unfit for work which means that you were meant to go back to the workhouse and be a burden on the Liverpool rate player. They'll be vexed. Think you undeserving. But I know it's not your fault so I'm going to let you escape.
>
> (series one, episode two)

Timperley points her in the direction of the nearest town, explaining that she can rely on her own abilities to seek shelter and care. He enquires: 'How about a little kiss goodbye?', to which Catherine responds: 'If you allow me more than that, will you take me to the town?'. Timperley stares sternly at the child for several moments, eventually lifting her from the cart and responding with the statement: 'Goodbye Catherine' (series one, episode two). In this scene, Timperely's motive appears ambiguous. His actions have the potential to be understood as inspired by some benevolence; the workhouse is never represented as anything other than filthy and degrading throughout

29

both series. He might thus be invoking the privilege of paternalist work relations by taking control of her fate, granting her the agency to pursue her own way in the world and maybe even prosper. The possibility of private, philanthropic care from a local community is preferable to dependence on the formally funded 'benefits' of the workhouse supported by working people's wages. Of course, such a perspective provides a clear echo of Cameron's policy of 'the Big Society' which might organise their own networks of support and care based on volunteering and charity rather than state funds. It also exposes the underpinning value-judgement of the Coalition's cuts to benefits: some people apparently just are not as deserving of State support as others. Put another way, in releasing Catherine, Timperley enacts his own small contribution to austerity measures, risking the welfare of the vulnerable for the greater good of the already strained 'rate payer'. Nevertheless, the gendered and sexual power imbalances of their respective roles are overt; Catherine's bartering of her body for assistance reveals the sinister connotations of abuse behind Timperley's 'fatherly' request for 'a little kiss', and makes us wonder what else the child will have to exchange to gain care in the wider community. Despite her youth, she has already learned that her body is a commodity: economically disenfranchised, this is her only 'value' to society, and she has learned this under an ostensibly benevolent paternalistic structure of work.

In fact, Timperley's real motivation becomes apparent later in the episode, when we witness a montage of scenes: Catherine is huddled in her shawl, wandering the countryside; the apprentices tramp out of the workhouse, coughing from the cotton dust which permeates their working environment; Timperley enters a pub and requests 'the biggest steak you can cook, and have a drink yourself', placing a coin in the serving woman's palm (series one, episode two). Timperley's conspicuous consumption contrasts with the defencelessness of Catherine and the harsh conditions of the apprentices' life more broadly. The exchange coin has additional significance, as it is the apprentice fee which Timperley should have returned to the workhouse, but is now funding his greedy excess (for Timperley is a stout man, in contrast to the starved appearance of the apprentices). The message here is stark: austerity measures only serve to shore up the power of those who already have plenty. Furthermore, the fallacy of Timperley's vague hope that Catherine will receive community charity is abruptly evidenced by the episode's closing scene: the dead body of the female child lies in a field (series one, episode two). Whether her demise is due to starvation and exhaustion, or a more violent encounter, is never disclosed. But the death of the girl who would have sold herself in exchange for care is a symbol of the failure of the dream of a neo-Victorian 'Big Society'.

There is an additional importance in the reasons for Catherine's rejection from Quarry Bank Mill. Her sickly appearance leads Robert Greg to refuse her apprenticeship, announcing 'This is a manufactory, not a hospital' (series one, episode two). When chastised by his father, Robert justifies his decision: 'It's not like it was in your day! I have to compete, there's 600 mills in Lancashire alone' (series one, episode two). The world of capitalist enterprise has no place for the ailing or infirm; Catherine must become a burden upon the 'rate payer' again, in an echo of Cameron's implied condemnation of those who 'really cannot work' (Cameron, 2009, n.p.). The debates surrounding the economic value – or lack thereof – of people with disabilities in austere times is even more prominent in the series' sub-plot of Tommy, an apprentice who loses his hand in the first episode of series one due to an accident with one of the Mill's machines. He is cared for by Hannah Greg in the family home, and at the beginning of series one, episode two is seen standing awkwardly in the Greg's household kitchen, enquiring 'Are there any jobs I can do?' Mrs Timperley smirks disapprovingly at his question, responding 'I don't think so. Not with only one hand' (series one, episode two). The quandary of Tommy's continuing employment with the Gregs is repeatedly debated by the workers at the Mill. Daniel Bate, a skilled mechanic who has been taken on by the Gregs in spite of his involvement with political agitation for worker's rights, ominously remarks that Tommy will be 'back in the workhouse [...] he's as good as gone', whereas Susannah Catterall, an older apprentice with an optimistic faith in the extent of the Greg family's benevolence, insists that 'they'll find something for him here' (series one, episode two). Moved by Tommy's precarious fate, Daniel takes time to build the child a prosthetic hand. While this takes some practice in using, Tommy is soon installed as a domestic help under the supervision of Hannah Greg. In this formulation, the paternalistic ideology of the Greg's family business offers an alternative form of productive employment for a boy who would otherwise be a beneficiary of the 'rate payers' by returning to the workhouse.

Issues of gender intersect with this seeming advocacy of paternalism, however, as Tommy's disability means that he is placed in a role in the domestic realm which is more usually occupied by the female apprentices. Furthermore, a continuum is constructed between Tommy's maimed state and Susannah's pregnancy: carrying the illegitimate child of the other Greg son, William (another telling instance of the ways in which the paternal structure of employment at the Mill allows sexual access to working women by middle-class men), she begins to work closely with Daniel, who explains that Greg 'wants me to design and build a loom that turns a skilled man's job into something even a pregnant woman can do' (series one, episode two). Susannah defends her employer, explaining: 'He wanted me to be able to support myself and my child [...] The Gregs believe in looking after their employees', to which Daniel responds: 'Or maybe it's just cheaper paying a woman half a man's wage' (series one, episode two). As Maria Karamessini and Jill Rubery identify, there is evidence to suggest that women might initially experience slightly higher employment rates during times of broader financial crisis due to their susceptibility to being in lower paid jobs with part-time hours or temporary contracts (2014, pp. 324–325).[14] Daniel's cynical explanation for the apparent kindness of the Gregs operates in a similar way; gendered inequalities in pay ensure Susannah's 'cheapness' as a female employer, regardless of her pregnancy. But Daniel's ability to make mechanical adaptations to take account of Susannah's pregnancy and his construction of Tommy's prosthesis is telling. The disabled body becomes the equivalent of the pregnant body and this has dubious ideological messages for both sexes, for both conditions are figured as damaging the economic productivity of the workers. Tommy's missing hand becomes a form of symbolic castration, for he needs special allowances made in the same way as a pregnant woman; we are reminded of Cameron's anecdote about the 'guy' who is prevented from fulfilling his masculine duty to work and provide for his family due to an injury (Cameron, 2009, n.p.). On the other hand, Susannah's pregnancy is couched as an impairment to fully productive work, an association which denigrates both women and people with impairments.[15]

Ironically, Daniel's attempts to make Tommy's body 'work' again are futile; in the final episode of series one, Tommy disobeys Mrs Greg by telling Esther of the arrival of her sister, and he is summarily cast out from the quasi-familial care of Greg's home, after Mr Timperley has ceremoni-ally removed his prosthetic hand (series one, episode four). In the clos-ing scenes of that episode, we see that Tommy has indeed returned to the workhouse. Again, the failure of paternalist generosity is highlighted; children who are not sufficiently grateful for the assistance of their private benefactors to be appropriately subordinate do not deserve such care. Yet without a robust state benefit system, Tommy can have no role in society whatsoever, and must languish in the squalor of the poorly funded work-house. Deploying the lack of government support for people with disabili-ties in the nineteenth century as a neo-Victorian mirror for the Coalition's cuts to benefits, we see the potential impact of austerity measures on the most vulnerable of society. Nevertheless, there is a worrying restatement of one aspect of Cameron's 2009 speech, which relates to gendered care of people with disabilities: it is Hannah Greg, the family matriarch, who is responsible for the withdrawal of support for Tommy in her home. It is the failure of maternal care which is to blame for Tommy's fate, not an imposi-tion of patriarchal authority relating to the men of the family, and thus we are reminded of Cameron's example of the profound breakdown of Fiona Pilkington's care for her disabled daughter.

Significantly, Tommy does make a brief reappearance in series two of *The Mill*. In episode five, the Mill workers join a strike in protest against wage cuts and surge towards the workhouse, setting free the inhabitants. Tommy emerges, clearly further debilitated by the harsh conditions he has experienced, but comes under the care of Esther Price, who returns his prosthetic hand from the Mill's storage and houses him and several other young people in her home. The trouble is, she is in financial dire straits due to the strike: there is not enough food to go around in these austere times (series two, episode six). Even as talk amongst the strik-ers turns to the possibility of the union providing financial relief for the workers, Tommy is informed that now he has his prosthesis returned, he may return to the workhouse (series two, episode six). There are problematic echoes of the association of working bodies with mascu-linity – and the implicit feminisation of dependency – in Cameron's 2009 speech, and his subtle denigration of the ways in which people with disabilities might 'live off the hard work of others' (Cameron, 2009, n.p.). In times of economic hardship, the neo-Victorian 'Big Society' of charity and sharing of resources in the Mill's community cannot actually support a member of the group with a disability. Despite the prosthetic hand meaning that he might well be enabled to contribute, he is still deemed a burden and marginalised from the men and women whose bodies might 'work' better.

Austere Times for Feminism? *The Mill*, Series Two

If series one of *The Mill* demonstrated the ways in which paternalistic structures of employment leave workers vulnerable to abuse due to gender, class and disability, then series two focuses more specifically upon the strain placed upon the gender relations in an actual family unit during times of recession. As indicated by the above discussion of Daniel Bate, in series one he is firmly on the side of social justice, acutely aware of the susceptibility of women and children to exploitation under the auspices of the 'family values' of the Gregs. However, the ways in which his and Esther's stories entwine in series two demonstrates the limitations of his abilities to translate his political activism into the personal sphere when it comes to gendered power relationships.

The second series of *The Mill* sees Esther come of age and progress from indentured apprenticeship to employment as an independent woman who lives in the village and manages her own finances. In episode two, she jokingly suggests to Daniel that she should contribute a penny of her wages as payment for her membership of the worker's union he has established, to which he abruptly responds that 'the union is men only' (series two, episode two). When pushed by his wife, Susannah, to justify this exclusion, he explains: 'From a man's point of view, women workers undercut wages' (series two, episode two). This indicates a subtle change of emphasis from his comments to Susannah in series one, episode two, where his acknowledgement of gendered inequalities in wages instead critiques the capitalist greed of the Gregs; it seems that in times of recession, the onus of blame rests on women rather than employers. Nevertheless, inspired by Susannah's comment to Esther that she could 'get [the women] organised' in terms of a gender-specific union of workers, Daniel gives Esther a copy of Mary Wollstonecraft's *A Vindication of the Rights of Women* (1792) with the words: 'Read this and think about it. The thing is, together, in combination we're stronger than we are as individuals' (series two, episode two). The symbolism of this gift for a neo-Victorian audience is clear; Esther is marked as having feminist potential to bring change for the women of Quarry Bank Mill. As we shall see, the volume actually comes to operate as an ambivalent signifier of how feminist theory might translate into feminist practice in times of economic crisis. The next appearance of *Rights of Women* is under Esther's bed, being battered as she has sex with the son of a family of migrant workers, Will Whittaker. On this evening, Esther had previously arranged to meet with her friend Lucy Garner, who is still indentured to the Gregs and is beginning to suffer without Esther's protection in the apprentice house. However, Esther's desire for Will leads her to forget about the younger girl, and the close-up shot of the discarded book serves as a stark reminder of the ways in which individual desire can usurp the transformative potential of collective feminist action for women.

In episode four, the consequences of Esther's liaison with Will become manifest: although now estranged from him, she is pregnant with his child. Esther sits with Susannah discussing how she will cope as a single parent whilst maintaining her employment, and asks whether Susannah – who has recently had yet another child with Daniel – will act as a wet-nurse for 'a shilling a week?' (series two, episode four). Susannah is evasive, and in a subsequent exchange between her and Daniel we learn why this is the case: although Daniel suggests that his wife should nurse the child for no payment, as 'you're meant to be Esther's friend', Susannah responds: 'What, and then I can be Esther's skivvy as well as yours? [...] I'm going back to the Mill [...] you want me here cooking meals [...] I'm going back to the weaving shed' (series two, episode four). Daniel becomes aggressive, insisting that she should be grateful for having the economic security to stay at home instead of working and claiming 'The little 'uns need their mother' (series two, episode four). The argument reaches a climax in Daniel striking Susannah across the face and she flees to seek refuge with Esther. On Daniel arriving to reclaim his wife, Esther rebukes him by throwing her copy of *Rights of Women* to hit him in the face, exclaiming 'Here ... I finished it' (series two, episode four). This series of exchanges offers a pertinent microcosm of gendered and economic power relations, which are particularly relevant to austerity measures in the current recession. With no prospect of any state support as a working mother, Esther's financial survival is dependent upon Susannah remaining within the domestic sphere to nurse her child, and the latter is acutely aware of the ways in which this might be disempowering. A division is constructed between a woman who must labour in the work place and a woman who must labour in the home. As the Feminist Fightback Collective identifies, this opposition between '"working mothers" and the women they pay to look after their children' has become a 'tediously familiar motif' of twentieth-century media representations of class inequalities between women, which are only compounded in times of recession (2011, pp. 78–79). Moreover, this sense of inequality *between* women is compounded by Daniel's Cameron-esque appeal to his wife to offer her domestic labour for free. Put another way, Daniel's suggestion that Susannah should aid Esther's return to work at no cost devalues and privatises his wife's means of earning her own money, petitioning for an act of benevolence and charity worthy of a neo-Victorian 'Big Society' which leaves patriarchal social relations unchallenged. The extent of Daniel's exploitation of Susannah in the home is evidenced by the act of domestic violence, and the ironic echo of this blow by Esther's wielding of Wollstonecraft against Daniel seems a fitting reprimand to the patriarchal values he has espoused.

Yet the fact that this book remains apparently unopened by Esther is still concerning and might inadvertently act as a metaphor for *The Mill's* failure of feminist politics in other ways. In protest of the cuts to wages, the workers of Quarry Bank come together in a month-long strike. However, without any other source of income, the community's already limited means are stretched to breaking point, and the final episode of the series depicts a succession of shots of meagre rations being shared out amongst hungry families. Daniel is arrested for sedition and in his absence Esther must attend a rally in Manchester to hear news of other political actions taking place across the region. She thus realises her feminist potential as an activist, but must still rely on Susannah's help to care for her child. On returning from the rally, she discovers that her child, Billy, has died from starvation. Susannah desperately explains: 'I swear to you that Billy got no less than our Tony ... I know that Tony was bigger and stronger but I was feeding him solids too' (series two, episode six). When Esther visits Will's family who are housing the dead child's body, an argument breaks out concerning blame for the infant's death. Will's uncle, John Howett, cannot help but accuse Esther of neglect due to participating in strike action rather than meeting the needs of her son: 'She's a mother. She should know her own child was starving [...] In hard times, three-quarters of a wage is better than nothing' (series two, episode six). Although Will's aunt tries to defend Esther's actions, insisting that 'it isn't any one person's fault that Esther's baby has died', John's response is that 'We're all responsible for our own actions' (series two, episode six). This is *The Mill*'s final word on the tragedy. The single mother concerned with fighting austerity measures has her child perish, and the baby of a stay-at-home wife who was able to provide regular nourishment has survived. In 'hard times', women must fulfil traditional roles rather than agitate for change. In a conclusion with shades of Cameron's gendering of 'responsibility' in his 2009 speech, the series might expose the limitations of the Big Society as an answer to austere times, but it still cannot imagine a future for children whose mothers do not stay at home to provide privatised care.

The Mill can hardly be understood as an idealised version of Victorian values and offers some pointed criticisms of the dangers of the nostalgic undercurrents of Conservative discourse when it comes to offering solutions to the retraction of public funding to the Welfare State. In economic crisis, those who are already socially disenfranchised – women, the working classes, people with disabilities – will be particularly vulnerable to further marginalisation, unmasking the irony of 'we are all in this together' (Cameron, 2009, n.p.). Yet, to date, the series struggles to imagine a happy future for neo-Victorian women such as Esther Price who cannot or will not accept their domestic responsibilities. For *The Mill* – as for David Cameron – it is a traditional family structure that remains of value to the broader society.

Notes

1 This tension between conservative nostalgia and the ways in which neo-Victorianism might challenge the master narratives of the nineteenth century has been explored by critics such as Cora Kaplan (2007, p. 3), Ann Heilmann and Mark Llewellyn (2010, p. 6), and Christian Gutleben (2001, p. 167), amongst others.

2 See Helen Davies, 2012, pp. 34–35.

3 For example, see Louisa Hadley, 2010, pp. 8–10, and Elizabeth Ho, 2012, pp. 21–22.

4 Of course, as Claire O'Callaghan's chapter in this volume indicates, *Downton Abbey* can also be understood as engaging, albeit in ambivalent ways, with the recent economic downturn.

5 *Benefits Street* is a British documentary following the lives of a group of residents of James Turner Street, Winson Green, Birmingham, a high proportion of whom are unemployed and claiming a variety of benefits from the State. The series generated a political and media furore, with fierce debates surrounding whether this representation of life on benefits was a sympathetic portrayal, exposing the social problems created by economic inequalities and hardship, or a demonisation of the poor, fuelling resentment towards welfare 'scroungers' in the context of the recession. For a brief overview of some media reactions, see the article on the Channel 4 News website, '"Demonised" or "Humane"? Row Breaks on *Benefits Street*', published on 7 January 2014: <http://www.channel4.com/news/benefits-street-birmingham-channel-4-twitter-row>.

6 The Under-Occupancy Penalty (popularly known as the Bedroom Tax) was part of the Coalition government's austerity measures in the form of the Welfare Reform Act of 2012. Council and housing association tenants faced a reduction in housing benefits if they were judged as having 'spare' or unoccupied rooms in their accommodation. For a summary of the effects of the Bedroom Tax, see Shelter's guide: <http://england.shelter.org.uk/get_advice/housing_benefit_and_local_housing_allowance/changes_to_housing_benefit/bedroom_tax>.

7 In 2013, the Personal Independence Payments (PIPs) scheme replaced the Disability Living Allowance (DLA) in the UK under the swathe of welfare reforms made by the Coalition government. Disability charities were critical of the PIPs, arguing that the new system of assessment in which claimants had to undergo assessment had the potential to be intimidating and marginalising. Furthermore, disability groups also highlighted the money-saving aspects of the new scheme, pointing out that many people with disabilities would lose state support as a consequence. For further information, see BBC News, 'Disability Living Allowance Changes Begin', 10 June 2013, <http://www.bbc.co.uk/news/business-22804563>.

8 A transcript of David Cameron's full speech can be accessed here: <http://www.theguardian.com/politics/2009/oct/08/david-cameron-speech-in-full>.

9 See, for example, Patrick Butler's blog for the *Guardian*, 'Health, Housing, Poverty: The Coalition's Social Policy Record Audited', which offers some compelling evidence to suggest that it is the poorest in society who have carried the cost of austerity measures: <http://www.theguardian.com/society/patrick-butler-cuts-blog/2015/jan/27/health-housing-poverty-the-coalitions-social-policy-record-audited>.

10 See Helen Davies and Claire O'Callaghan, 2014, p. 227.

11 The number of women members of parliament elected in the most recent UK general election – May 2015 – is open to conflicting interpretations in terms

of progression towards gender equality. Although only 29 per cent of MPs are women, this represents a considerable rise (a third) from before the election, when the number of women in parliament stood at 23 per cent. There are notable differences between the number of women MPs between the two major political parties as of 2015: 68 for the Conservatives, compared with 99 for Labour. For further information, see <http://www.bbc.co.uk/news/uk-politics-32601280>.

12 For further details of this case and a report on the inquest which took place in 2009, see <http://www.independent.co.uk/news/uk/home-news/mother-killed-herself-and-daughter-in-car-fire-1789423.html>.

13 It is worth noting here that the age at which the workers in the television series are considered to have completed their apprenticeship – 21 – is different from the historical Mill, where apprentices were indentured until the age of 18 (Hanson, 2014, p. 22).

14 See the Introduction for a discussion of the 'man-cession'. Of course, such claims are belied by the compelling evidence provided in Karamessini and Rubery's edited collection, *Women and Austerity: The Economic Crisis and the Future for Gender Equality* (2014), which explores the multiple sites of women's disadvantage in the current age of austerity.

15 As Rosemarie Garland-Thomson has identified, some feminist critics have suggested that patriarchal discourse constructs femininity as a form of 'disability' and have sought to challenge the injustice of this association (Garland-Thomson, 1997, pp. 19–20). However, as Kim Q. Hall has argued, it is ironic that such critiques tend to implicitly leave the denigration of the disabled body intact (Hall, 2011, p. 4).

Bibliography

Anderson, Bill. [Dir.] (2014). 'Series Two, Episode Four', *The Mill*, Channel 4, 3 August.

—— (2014). 'Series Two, Episode Five', *The Mill*, Channel 4, 17 August.

—— (2014). 'Series Two, Episode Six', *The Mill*, Channel 4, 24 August.

BBC News. (2013). 'Disability Living Allowance Changes Begin'. 10 June. Available from: <http://www.bbc.co.uk/news/business-22804563> [Accessed: 30 April 2015].

Butler, Patrick. (2015). 'Health, Housing, Poverty: The Coalition's Social Policy Record Audited'. *Guardian*, 27 January. Available from: <http://www.theguardian.com/society/patrick-butler-cuts-blog/2015/jan/27/health-housing-poverty-the-coalitions-social-policy-record-audited> [Accessed: 13 March 2015].

Cameron, David. (2009). 'Conference Address: Conservative Party Conference 2009'. *Guardian*, 8 October. Available from: <http://www.theguardian.com/politics/2009/oct/08/david-cameron-speech-in-full> [Accessed: 13 March 2015].

—— (2010). 'Big Society Speech'. Gov.uk, 19 July. Available from <https://www.gov.uk/government/speeches/big-society-speech> [Accessed: 13 March 2015].

Channel 4 News. (2014).'"Demonised" or "Humane"? Row Breaks on *Benefits Street*'. Channel 4, 7 January. Available from: <http://www.channel4.com/news/benefits-street-birmingham-channel-4-twitter-row> [Accessed: 13 March 2015].

Davies, Helen. (2012). *Gender and Ventriloquism in Victorian and Neo-Victorian Fiction: Passionate Puppets*. Basingstoke: Palgrave Macmillan.

Davies, Helen, and O'Callaghan, Claire. (2014). 'All in this Together? Feminisms, Academia, Austerity'. *Journal of Gender Studies*, 23/3, pp. 227–232.

Feminist Fightback Collective. (2011). 'Cuts are a Feminist Issue'. *Soundings*, 49, pp. 73–83.

Garland-Thomson, Rosemarie. (1997). *Extraordinary Bodies: Figuring Physical Disability in American Culture and Literature*. New York: Columbia University Press.

Gutleben, Christian. (2001). *Nostalgic Postmodernism: The Victorian Tradition and the Contemporary British Novel*. Amsterdam: Rodopi.

Hadley, Louisa. (2010). *Neo-Victorian Fiction and Historical Narrative: The Victorians and Us*. Basingstoke: Palgrave Macmillan.

Hall, Kim Q. (2011). 'Reimagining Disability and Gender Through Feminist Studies: An Introduction'. In: Kim Q. Hall (ed.) *Feminist Disability Studies*. Bloomington and Indianapolis: Indiana University Press.

Hanson, David. (2014). *Children of The Mill: True Stories from Quarry Bank*. London: Headline.

Hawes, James. [Dir.] (2013). 'Series One, Episode One', *The Mill*, Channel 4, 28 July.

—— (2013). 'Series One, Episode Two', *The Mill*, Channel 4, 4 August.

—— (2013). 'Series One, Episode Four', *The Mill*, Channel 4, 18 August.

Heilmann, Ann and Llewellyn, Mark. (2010). *Neo-Victorianism: The Victorians in the Twenty-First Century, 1999–2009*. Basingstoke: Palgrave Macmillan.

Ho, Elizabeth. (2012). *Neo-Victorianism and the Memory of Empire*. London: Continuum.

Johnston, Judith and Waters, Catherine. (2008). 'Victorian Turns, Neo Victorian Returns'. In: Penny Gay, Judith Johnston and Catherine Waters (eds) *Victorian Turns, NeoVictorian Returns: Essays on Fiction and Culture*. Newcastle upon Tyne: Cambridge Scholars Publishing.

Kaplan, Cora. (2007). *Victoriana: Histories, Fictions, Criticism*. Edinburgh: Edinburgh University Press.

Karamessini, Maria, and Rubery, Jill. (2014). 'Economic Crisis and Austerity: Challenges to Gender Equality'. In: Maria Karamessini and Jill Rubery (eds) *Women and Austerity: The Economic Crisis and the Future for Gender Equality*. London: Routledge.

Lowther, Ed, and Thornton, Charlotte. (2015). 'Election 2015: Number of Women in Parliament Rises by a Third'. BBC News, 8 May. Available from: <http://www.bbc.co.uk/news/uk-politics-32601280> [Accessed: 1 September 2015].

Margaret Thatcher Foundation. (2005). 'TV Interview for London Weekend Television Weekend World ('Victorian Values')'. Available from: <http://www.margaretthatcher.org/document/105087> [Accessed: 13 March 2015].

Radford, Ceri. (2013). 'The Mill, Channel 4, Review'. Telegraph, 28 July. Available from: <http://www.telegraph.co.uk/culture/tvandradio/10205318/The-Mill-Channel-4-review.html> [Accessed: 13 March 2015].

Roberts, David. (1979). Paternalism in Early Victorian England. London: Crook Helm.

Runcie, Charlotte. (2014). 'The Mill, Series 2, Episode 1, Review: Like Dickens without the Wit or Humanity'. Telegraph, 20 July. Available from: <http://www.telegraph.co.uk/culture/tvandradio/tv-and-radio-reviews/10975899/The-Mill-series-2-episode-1-review-like-Dickens-without-the-wit-or-humanity.html> [Accessed: 13 March 2015].

Shelter. (2014). 'What is the Bedroom Tax?' Shelter: The Housing and Homelessness Charity, 4 September. Available from: <http://england.shelter.org.uk/get_advice/housing_benefit_and_local_housing_allowance/changes_to_housing_benefit/bedroom_tax> [Accessed: 13 March 2015].

Tully, Susan. [Dir.] (2014). 'Series Two, Episode One', The Mill, Channel 4, 20 July.

—— (2014). 'Series Two, Episode Two', The Mill, Channel 4, 27 July.

Walker, Alan, and Corbett, Steve. (2013). 'The "Big Society", Neoliberalism and the Rediscovery of the "Social" in Britain'. speri:comment: the political economy blog, 8 March. Available from: <http://speri.dept.shef.ac.uk/2013/03/08/big-society-neoliberalism-rediscovery-social-britain/> [Accessed: 13 March 2015].

Weisser, Susan Ostrov, and Fleischner, Jennifer. (1994). 'Introduction'. In: Susan Ostrov Weisser and Jennifer Fleischner (eds) Feminist Nightmares: Women at Odds. New York and London: New York University Press.

2

The Downturn at Downton: Money and Masculinity in *Downton Abbey*

Claire O'Callaghan

According to James Leggott and Julie Taddeo, *Downton Abbey* is a 'fortuitous tonic for audiences in "austerity" Britain, alive to prominent debates about economic difficulty, social disorder and stoicism in the face of adversity' (2015, p. xviii). Sadly, however, not even the aristocrats of *Downton Abbey* are immune to the effects of austerity. In series three of the popular and award-winning television series, which focuses on the trials and tribulations of the Crawley family and their domestic staff, it emerges that having placed the 'lion's share' of the Crawley fortune – comprising his wife's inheritance – into a Canadian railroad venture, the sixth of Earl of Grantham, Lord Robert Crawley, discovers that his financial investment has gone awry (Fellowes, 2014, p. 16). The Crawley financial crisis not only threatens the family's idyllic and privileged lifestyle but the future security of their country house estate and its sprawling service industries. In an uncomfortable exchange between man and wife, a sombre Lord Grantham (Hugh Bonneville) confesses to his wife, Cora (Elizabeth McGovern) that the 'bad' investment he made previously means that the family face financial ruin and must endure austere times. 'Has some of my fortune been lost?' the countess asks her husband, to which Lord Grantham sombrely replies, 'Some? All', before breaking down in tears in his wife's arms (Fellowes, 2014, p. 42). For the usually dignified patriarch of *Downton Abbey*, the expression of turmoil, anguish and emotional collapse denotes the severity of the situation. But, as this chapter will also demonstrate, this response provides an insight into the ways in which money and masculinity is perilously equated in the show.

Interestingly, according to Downton's writer and creator, Lord Julian Fellowes, the show's economic plotline is based on the real-life history of the Canadian Grand Trunk Line which, in the 1920s, was perceived as 'one of the most surprising failures of [its] generation' (2014, p. 15). The Grand Trunk Railway was a Canadian company financed largely by British capital that aimed to expand trans-continental travel across Canada to open up new areas of economic growth. However, the cost of construction, absentee management (since its head office and Board of Directors was based in London, England) and a failure to generate the necessary levels of traffic left the company debt ridden. As a result, in 1919, the Government entered into an agreement with the company for the acquisition of its entire stock, but those conducting the valuation rendered it worthless, thus losing the investment of numerous British stock holders. In the show, Robert is one such stockholder. Bewildered, he asks his lawyer, Murray, 'why did we invest so much?' (Fellowes, 2014, p. 15). But Murray is clear; it is Robert's fault: 'Lord Grantham, it was you who insisted we should. If you remember, we advised against it' (Fellowes, 2014, p. 15). In spite of Murray's plain recrimination, Robert is defiant in the face of his poor decision-making: 'It wasn't just me. Everyone said we couldn't lose. We knew hard times were coming for estates like Downton, and this investment would make it safe for the rest of time' (Fellowes, 2014, p. 15). Robert's rationale for his sizeable investment, then, is clear; the Canadian Railway had been a gamble financially, but one expected to pay off in order to secure Downton's future. The purpose of such historical context works to authenticate the drama's plotline, but of course, the tale of bad economic investment also bears an uncanny resemblance to that of the recent global financial crisis.

Considered the worst economic disaster since the 1930s, the near collapse of the global financial system in 2008 was caused (ultimately) by poor trading and investments *and* unsustainable financial decision-making that together challenged the security of financial spending. The outcome of the financial crisis triggered a ripple effect across the globe which threatened the collapse of numerous financial institutions (notoriously prevented by the bail out of banks by national governments) and the stock markets. The knock-on effect of global economic downturn led to recession and austerity both in the UK and abroad: prolonged unemployment and the failure and closure of numerous businesses, and a decline in consumer spending led to cuts across a plethora of governmental terrains.

Despite Fellowes's contention that *Downton Abbey*'s financial plotline is solely historical, the correlation between Downton's economy and the recent financial crisis is not coincidental. Like all historical texts, the show is mirroring contemporary culture albeit, in this case, channelled through the fortunes of one family and their country house estate, thus providing a specifically class-focused assessment of austerity. Notably, such is the show's parallel to recent world economics that numerous cultural commentators have begun to use the 'downturn' at Downton as the basis of prudent financial advice for consumers. In February 2013, for instance, *Forbes* magazine ran an article titled 'Downton Abbey Money Lessons' which suggested that risking one's investments on an apparently 'sure thing' is never a 'free lunch' (Kaplan, 2013, n.p.), while one month later, *the Wall Street Journal* offered a bullet point list to its users detailing 'What Downton Can Teach You about Your Money' (Green, 2013, n.p.).[1]

Reflecting the consequences of the post-2007 financial crisis, in the show, austerity also follows for the residents at the Abbey; the estate faces cuts in order to survive the dire economic situation in which it finds itself. As Lord Grantham reminds his soon-to-be son-in-law, Matthew (Dan Stevens), 'We're employers, Matthew. Providers of jobs. That is the point of us. For Downton to play its proper role in the area, we must provide jobs' (Fellowes, 2014, p. 202). As series three unfolds, the social and economic changes across each level of the household also (rather conveniently) echo the austerity measures instigated by governments around the globe in the wake of the economic crisis of 2008, a point I shall return to.

While there has been no easy panacea to the global financial crisis, luckily for Lord Grantham, Downton's financial misery is shortlived since Matthew – the rightful heir to the Abbey – emerges to saves the day. In parallel with the plotline concerning Lord Grantham's financial misery, the show sees Matthew inherit the estate of his deceased fiancé's (Lavinia) father, Reggie Swire; a timely intervention to balance the class difference between Robert's daughter, Lady Mary Crawley (Michelle Dockery) and Matthew, the middle-class lawyer from Manchester. After much soul-searching, Matthew agrees to invest his newly found fortune into the estate, thus saving Downton from closure (or at least substantial downsizing) which the family face with apprehension.

But while Downton's economic plotline is in dialogue with early twentieth-century history *and* twenty-first-century financial politics, what commentary does it offer on gender, economics and austerity in the new millennium? Women are *the* source of money at Downton: Cora and her inheritance are the basis for Robert's investment[2] and Lavinia's death provides Matthew with his own financial (and therefore, class) stature.[3] Male prosperity at Downton, it seems, is dependent on women's finances, and yet, *Downton Abbey* is largely androcentric in its consideration of the relationship between money and gender, something which reflects, perhaps, the way in which historically men have played the role of breadwinner and held responsibility for familial financial management.

If, however, in a change to the famous proverb, money makes the man, the affluence of the Crawley women and the penniless quandary that Lord Grantham finds himself in suggest that through *Downton Abbey* Fellowes critiques the entwined politics of capitalism and patriarchy. But this is far from the case. To the contrary, as this chapter considers, the show ultimately endorses capitalism and economics as the preserve of men and reinforces the problematic idea that masculinity is often constituted by money. As Robert Gould indicates, money not only 'equals success' but 'men are often judged and measured by their money, what they are "worth" ' (1991, p. 61). Reflecting this, this chapter critiques the show's portrayal of gender, money and financial crisis. I argue that not only does *Downton Abbey* endorse the dubious idea that money does indeed make the man, but it also suggests that financial insecurity is 'unmanly' and thus viewed negatively and as reflecting masculinity in crisis. Although women are affected significantly by the Abbey's financial woes – particularly, as I will demonstrate, in the effects of austerity measures – and they play a role in securing Downton's future, women are ultimately rendered as passive, tokenistic mechanisms by which patriarchy prevails and a narrative apparatus by which the crisis in masculinity can be resolved. *Downton Abbey*'s storyline may well reflect the economic contexts of twenty-first-century society, but the show's exploration of gender is problematic and distinctly outdated.

The Ruin of Robert Crawley

The relationship between economic sustainability and men has always been at the heart of *Downton Abbey*. Since the first series the show has gravitated around the anxiety-inducing implications of the absence of primogeniture, that is, the right, by law, of the firstborn male child to inherit the family estate. Series three takes this anxiety one step further. 'The ruin of Robert Crawley'– as Fellowes puts it in the notes to the script – reflects the now well-documented notion that masculinity in contemporary society is in crisis (2014, p. 15).[4] According to numerous critical commentators, with the destabilisation of the white, heterosexual family unit, the previously unwavering figure of the masculine patriarch is now under threat.[5] For the critic Roger Horrocks, the crisis in masculine identity and power derives not just from the disintegration of 'old forms' of life in Western culture (by which he means traditional and conservative family structures in which a patriarch is both the breadwinner *and* authoritative head of the household) but also from the fact that men are 'struggl[ing] to establish *new* relations with women and [with] each other' (1994, p. 1). Accordingly, for Horrocks, men's inability to reconceive of themselves beyond conservative gender roles in a culture in which masculine 'normality' is no longer stable makes them vulnerable and fragile. For the feminist scholar Rosalind Coward, however, the crisis in masculinity is also attributed to broader changes in society and culture. Coward notes the specificity of 'globalisation and recessions' that, she says, 'have dealt men a number of blows' (1999, n.p.), as reasons why masculinity – or conceptions of masculine gender – are undergoing change. Indeed, for her, revisions to the economic and global context in the late twentieth century coupled with men's 'changed status in the family[,] has made [men] especially vulnerable' to what we might describe as gender trouble (Coward, 1999, n.p.).

Coward's insight came long before the recent economic downturn and yet her view is, perhaps, provided with fresh impetus in the wake of the post-2007 crisis since the recent economic downturn *has* been conceived of in gendered terms. Indeed, the 'credit crunch' as it has been colloquially termed has also been designated as both a 'man-cession' and a 'he-cession' because, it is argued, men have not only been the primary victims of recession in terms of jobs and men are the dominant workforce in industries that have been worst affected by austerity.[6] One critic keen to make this argument is Hanna Rosin. Although her argument extends beyond the domain of economics, Rosin argues that following the feminist revolution, society is now living under matriarchy such that the decline of modern man and the rise of woman is apparent across numerous domains, not least money and power, employment and education. As a result, Rosin suggests that men have been the major victims of the recent financial crisis because they have experienced recession the hardest in social and economic terms. In a suitably sceptical feminist response, the historian Mary Beard proposes that if Rosin is to be believed:

> vast numbers of the male American working class have been transformed from proud breadwinners to unemployable couch potatoes. Their womenfolk, on the other hand, have seized the opportunities offered by the economic changes of the last few years; they have retrained, requalified and taken the driving seat.
>
> (Beard, 2012, n.p.)

For Beard, and many feminist organisations, such arguments are nonsensical and unfounded.[7] Moreover, reflecting Beard's disbelief, Diane Negra and Yvonne Tasker have also dismantled such views by arguing persuasively that the so-called 'man-cession' is a rhetorical exercise emerging from news media outlets through to Hollywood purely to give 'priority' to male suffering not because men *are* necessarily suffering but because 'women and young people who are impacted significantly by economic events do not have the media or cultural visibility that their situation warrants' (2013, p. 4). The notion of a 'he-cession', then, is, for many, a myth that simply reflects gendered inequalities in contemporary culture.

Nonetheless, as Hamilton Carroll indicates, in 'man-cession' narratives, tales of masculine failure are a pervasive trope, for 'it is by admitting defeat, by narrating lives of missed opportunities [and] poor financial decisions, and failures of commitment, that the [male] protagonist [is] able to [go on and] develop a tenuous form of success' (2014, p. 204). In other words, a crisis in masculinity and a focus on male failure is not merely an important aspect of gendered narratives concerning recession and austerity but an essential component in re-stabilising masculine authority and power.

Significantly in Downton Abbey, Fellowes brings these issues together through his portrayal of Lord Grantham. Although Robert initially questions Murray's assessment of the dire financial situation – exclaiming, 'But it can't be as bad …' (Fellowes, 2014, p. 7) – he nonetheless perilously equates financial crisis *and* failure in relation to his role as the patriarch at the Abbey: 'I won't give in, Murray. I've sacrificed too much to Downton to give in now. I refuse to be the failure, the Earl who dropped the torch and let the flame go out' (Fellowes, 2014, p. 16). The fracture of Downton's financial security signals a failure in Lord Grantham's role as the head of the household which is – as he indicates implicitly – reliant on the successful combination of his class stature, his family, *and* the family's home security. Together, these are the factors that have worked to construct Lord Grantham's masculinity, but they are now called into question precisely because of his newfound financial instability.

Interestingly, in the scenes that follow, Lord Grantham is shown as disempowered and out of the control of Downton's estate and associated economic decision-making. Having returned from London to hear Murray's news, Robert 'catches up with Cora on the stairs' (Fellowes, 2014, p. 20):

ROBERT: Did you know about the new footman?

CORA: Of course. He's already here.

ROBERT: Why did no one tell me?

CORA: What do you mean? We talked all about it last night. In my room …

ROBERT: Well … Nobody else must be taken on. Absolutely no one. Until things are settled.

CORA: What things?

(Fellowes, 2014, p. 20)

Here, Robert chooses to ignore Cora's question, denying his wife the knowledge that *her* fortune is lost and that the Abbey is in imminent dire straits. His response to the news of domestic expenditure is, in light of his newfound financial difficulties, one of shock, but more importantly, that he questions the decision – 'Why did no one tell me?'– validates the sense that Robert has lost control of the estate. He is bemused as to why he has been excluded from the decision-making in *his* household and on whose authority the financial/domestic decision has been made. That, as Cora indicates, he *was* informed about the new footman and, despite his recollection, he approved the decision, reinforces the idea that Lord Grantham is in crisis. Robert's momentary amnesia and subsequent singular response – 'Well ...'– indicates embarrassment at this self-realisation but, of course, it also serves to placate his wife who has just endured the brunt of her husband's agitation (Fellowes, 2014, p. 20). Unsurprisingly, though, because Robert views himself as the Earl who 'dropped the torch' in Downton's financial management, he addresses the situation by re-asserting his patriarchal authority to his wife and across the household more broadly, and his instruction is clear (Fellowes, 2014, p. 16). As the repetition of words indicates, Downton cannot hire any more staff. The effect of that decision means that the Abbey, therefore, must endure austerity.

Austerity at the Abbey

Austerity, which has now become shorthand for a focus on frugality, self-sufficiency and fiscal prudence in economic and political life, is portrayed in different ways in *Downton Abbey* dependent on factors of class *and* gender. For the Crawley family, the effects of austerity are articulated most acutely in relation to the perceived loss of their family home, the Abbey itself. With Cora's money gone, the family face the prospect of downsizing, but they greet this challenge in fairly stoic terms.[8] Fellowes only offers one or two exchanges between Robert and Cora on the matter. The couple 'joke' about how the sale of the Abbey might be advertised: 'Desirable nobleman's mansion with surrounding estate and properties' (Fellowes, 2014, p. 146) and they also speculate on moving from Yorkshire to 'some land further north, at Eryholme on the border with Durham' where they hold another property that they could 'make something of' and even rename as 'Downton Place' (Fellowes, 2014, p. 144).

Importantly, Robert's decision not to 'tell the staff that the end is nigh', that is, that Downton must be sold, provides insight into the way in which his masculine authority is constructed and maintained (Fellowes, 2014, p. 146). He opts to delay any announcement of Downton's imminent closure until after his daughter's nuptials to the incoming heir, Matthew (Fellowes, 2014, p. 146). The wedding enables Robert to maintain the façade of 'normality' at Downton as well as conceal his financial troubles which, as noted, he connects directly to his failed masculinity. In his own words, 'without the wedding to hide behind, there's no reason not to get on with it and astonish the world with the extent of my wretched failure' (Fellowes, 2014, p. 185). Admitting defeat to his wife and crying before her may be one thing, but appearing 'unmanly' to his children and staff is a step too far for Downton's patriarch, thus endorsing the idea that his masculinity must be maintained in order for his authority to be upheld.

Interestingly, Fellowes refuses us the opportunity to witness Lord Grantham's 'public' humiliation. We see Robert about to tell Mary of the situation, but we only have Cora's account of the discussion and even this is brief. As she tells her mother-in-law, Violet (Maggie Smith), Robert told Mary 'what may happen' and 'He felt sick for a week' (Fellowes, 2014, p. 84).[9] By denying further insight into the emotional effects of the financial crisis on the estate's patriarch, Fellowes preserves and maintains a sense of upper-class British stoicism towards austerity. Downton is embroiled in the glamorisation of austerity (or 'austerity chic' as it has been termed) and this is as much to do with Fellowes's fetishisation of, and nostalgia towards, British aristocratic lifestyles of the past as it is to do with locating gender within the context of class.[10] That the effects of austerity on the Crawley family are reserved and kept to a minimum suggests that austerity affects only the middle and lower-classes. Put another way, the residents of Downton are not, as the former British Prime Minister David Cameron would have it, then, 'all in it together' (2009, n.p), a political austerity rhetoric which Helen Davies critiques at length in chapter one.

Indeed, for the household staff employed 'downstairs' at the Abbey, the effects of austerity are rendered more overtly and materialistically than for their 'upstairs' counterparts, and are conveyed specifically in class *and* gendered terms. As Downton's long-standing and reliable Butler, Mr Carson, tells Lord Grantham, 'Mrs Hughes [the Housekeeper] is short of a new housemaid, Mrs Patmore [the cook] wants a kitchen maid and I need a new footman' (Fellowes, 2014, p. 201). The strain of staff shortage takes its toll on morale and staff inter-relations as their ability to 'get things done properly' (to borrow Carson's words) is tested. Mrs Hughes is the most vocal in her criticism of the austerity measures being imposed upon the staff by Lord Grantham: 'Oh, for heaven's sake, we can't do things properly until […] his lordship allows us the staff we need' (Fellows, 2014, p. 110). Her comment critiques the imposition of austerity measures on the serving staff at the Abbey, suggesting that in the short term, cuts never allow institutions to run effectively.

More specifically, however, the portrayal of austerity 'downstairs' at the Abbey echoes the broader effects of the UK economy post-2007 that have become significant in discussions of gender and austerity. As much evidence now shows, despite fears of a 'man-cession', austerity has – in *real* terms – had more of an impact on women than men.[11] Returning to Carson's assessment, Downton echoes this on a micro level through its own ratio of a 2:1 disproportionate effect of austerity on female and male staff; for every male role affected at the Abbey, two women bear the brunt of the cuts. Nowhere are these effects more apparent than in Downton's busy kitchen. Here, it is Daisy, the scullery maid, who feels the effects of austerity most acutely. In an exchange with her boss, Mrs Patmore, Daisy observes:

DAISY: I'd like to know where the new kitchen maid is. That's what you promised. They've got a new footman. Where's the kitchen maid?

MRS PATMORE: I know, and I'm sorry. But I spoke to Mr Carson tonight and they won't be taking anyone new on.

DAISY: Except a footman.

MRS PATMORE: I don't know how Mr Carson managed it because his lordship's put his foot down. But you're called my assistant now, and you've seven shillings extra every month.

DAISY: You've still kept me here with a dishonest reputation.

MRS PATMORE: Oh, dear. Have you swallowed a dictionary?

(Fellowes, 2014, p. 37)

Daisy's disgruntled observation that despite the obvious need for a new kitchen maid and Lord Grantham's apparent refusal of new staff, a footman *has* still been taken on (to service the family's needs rather than address the gaps in domestic provision) highlight the varied inequalities at play in the effects of austerity. In his notes to the script, Fellowes recognises that historically, the doubling up of roles due to gaps in service often meant that serving staff were doing 'a hell of a lot more work' than the additional pay they were given recognised in material terms (2014, p. 37). But in relation to austerity, Daisy's position reflects the concern that 'women are at once shouldering the responsibility for the crisis by assuming the work of austerity, and those most likely to be negatively affected by its impacts' (Bramall, 2013, p. 112). Daisy's workload has doubled and she has been given seven shillings more a month in payment for this work, but she recognises that strategic decisions have been made that have not taken into account other gaps and prevailing inequalities in domestic services. Despite the financial recompense for her work, Daisy is disempowered both by Mrs Patmore (and her sarcastic riposte to her new kitchen maid which, in Downton's terms, is nothing new), the fact that she is told – rather than asked – to take on more work without the opportunity to make an informed choice for herself, *and* the fact of her age, class and gender. As the youngest female of the lowest serving rank in Downton's service machinery, saccharine Daisy goes unnoticed and unacknowledged in her articulation of the effects of austerity. She must just 'make do' (to borrow a well-known World War II austerity phrase) with the situation and be grateful that the Butler has got her any additional wages at all. In this way, *Downton Abbey* not only highlights the nexus of class and gender with regards to the effects of austerity but also suggests that age, social rank and stature within class dynamics play a further role in this complex socio-economic policy.

The Post-Recessional Fool

In his discussion of post-recession narratives concerning masculine failure, Carroll asks:

> What effect has financial crisis […] had on dominant narratives of white male privilege? How does white masculinity account for its own current (mis)fortune? How, in specific instances […] are men understood to have failed? What forms does failure take? Who does it effect? How [is] it overcome? How, moreover, does failure become not only constitutive but recuperative?
>
> (2014, p. 205)

With respect to Lord Grantham, Downton offers two responses to these questions. The first is evident via Robert's coalition with Matthew (itself a nod towards the governmental Coalition arrangement in place in the UK during the period in which the series was produced). Although Robert welcomes Matthew's suggestion to 'give him Reggie's money' which will rescue Downton from financial ruin, he rejects the offer as a donation and presents a counter-proposal to Matthew to construct the exchange as an investment: 'If we stay, you'll share the ownership. It'll be your house, your estate, as much as mine. We'll be joint Masters' (Fellowes, 2014, p. 186). Matthew is effectively bailing out Lord Grantham and saving the Abbey from sale. Although Robert articulates the business partnership as a joint arrangement (and in gendered terms since the men will be 'joint Masters' of the estate), the bailout fails to address Robert's ongoing feelings of masculine inadequacy (Fellowes, 2014, p. 186). As he tells Mary, ' "A fool and his money are soon parted." And I have been parted from my money, so I suppose I am a fool.' (Fellowes, 2014, p. 348). In response to Carroll's assertion, then, a sense of foolishness is how Fellowes constructs Robert's patriarchal masculine failure, a somewhat generous way to conceive of a man who gambled and lost his wife's entire fortune.

However, Robert's awareness of his own masculine disempowerment is, interestingly, coupled with the growth of Matthew's social and economic authority. That Matthew's influence is based purely on his own rise in financial value demonstrates how, once again, Downton affirms the notion that money and masculinity are not only entwined but that money enables and facilitates patriarchal power. Matthew's growing masculine authority and Robert's diminished sense of self paves the way for an egotistical clash between the men, a survival of the fittest dynamic, so to speak. Having invited Matthew to 'look through the books and meet our accountants' since he might 'have some good ideas' about how to run the estate, Matthew uncovers grave concerns in Downton's financial management: 'Well, as far as I can tell, there's been no proper management for years. Rents are unpaid, or far too low. There's no real maintenance scheme. And the assets are underused or else ignored entirely' (Fellowes, 2014, p. 239). For Matthew, Downton is 'being mismanaged' and Robert's refusal to discuss it directly creates conflict between the men (Fellowes, 2014, p. 251). If, as Fellowes says in an interview with *Vanity Fair*, 'Robert's entire existence is predicated on managing this estate. His DNA is in the very bricks', then Matthew's discovery of Robert's mismanagement serves only to reinforce Lord Grantham's failings (Kamp, 2012, n.p.). This can only mean one thing: as seen previously, Robert can only address his inadequacy by reasserting his patriarchal authority, which he does again now, but with tragic consequences this time with regards to his daughter's life.

The death of Lord Grantham's pregnant daughter, Sybil (Jessica Brown-Findlay), then, becomes the secondary mechanism by which Robert's masculine crisis is played out. In episodes four and five of series three, Fellowes entwines the plotlines concerning Matthew's vocal expression of Downton's management (Lord Grantham's 'mismanagement') with the storyline concerning Sybil's death. Sybil experiences pre-eclampsia, a fatal disorder in pregnancy characterised by extreme hypertension. Although this condition is one that can happen to any woman during pregnancy, Fellowes places Robert at the centre of a debate surrounding Sybil's fate. In other words, she becomes the mechanism for Fellowes to reinforce Lord Grantham's loss of patriarchal control as well as his urgent need to reclaim authority. More troublingly, as I will show, Sybil's death becomes the mechanism for Robert's restitution.

In episode five, Sybil's pre-eclampsia is detected by the family's local GP, Dr Clarkson (David Robb) but rejected by Sir Philip Tapsell (Tim Pigott-Smith), a senior clinician from London who has been invited by Robert to Downton to oversee the delivery of his grandchild.[12] The clash between the medics divide the family over what's best for Sybil: Dr Clarkson advocates Sybil's immediate removal from the house to a local hospital for an emergency caesarean, whereas Sir Philip rejects the diagnosis of pre-eclampsia entirely and views Dr Clarkson's 'interference' as 'unprofessional and verging on insolent' (Fellowes, 2014, p. 283). Although Robert perceives himself as a fool, the domestic dispute provides the mechanism by which he *can* regain control, and so he does, opting to side with Sir Philip: 'I think we must support Sir Philip in this' (Fellowes, 2014, p. 284). Robert's authoritative comment suggests that he has the 'casting vote' on the matter, but as Mary quickly reminds her father, 'it's not [y]our decision. What does Tom say?' (Fellowes, 2014, p. 284). Tom Branson (Allen Leech), Sybil's husband, is a lesser man in Robert's eyes because he is a Catholic, an Irish Republican, a socialist and, more problematically, he is also the Crawleys' former chauffeur. Irrespective of these issues, though, Tom is Sybil's husband. Yet this does not matter to Lord Grantham, for Robert greets the challenge to his authority by reasserting his power and, significantly, he embroils his monetary power into the matter: 'Tom has not hired Sir Philip. He is not master here' (Fellowes, 2014, p. 284). In other words, Lord Grantham has authority because he is master of the house and he is paying for Sybil's medical care, something which, in his view, gives him the privilege and power to determine what is in her best interests even when it overrides the view of her husband. Once again, then, *Downton Abbey* dangerously equates masculinity and patriarchal authority with financial privilege and class stature.

Importantly, this moment of authoritative assertion on Robert's part, is one that places him in conflict with the rest of the family. They are concerned with Sybil's well-being rather than the financial basis of the matter or the status of those involved, and it is Cora and Violet who vocalise this most acutely:

> CORA: You're being ridiculous. Obviously, we have to talk to Tom. [Robert is shocked. He looks at his mother.]
>
> VIOLET: Don't look at me. Cora is right. The decision lies with the chauffeur.
>
> (Fellowes, 2014, p. 284)

The scene concludes at this point. On a textual level, the women have the final say, but in the scene that follows, Tom is placed in the midst of the predicament, quite literally. On screen, Tom is situated in the middle of the Abbey's grand foyer: on one side stands Robert with Sir Philip and on the other stands Cora and the other members of the family beside Doctor Clarkson. Symbolically, at least, Tom is in the centre and thus in command, but not in Lord Grantham's eyes. Still, he is asked to make the decision regarding his wife's health, but Sir Philip intervenes and appeals to Robert to seize control of the situation: 'Lord Grantham, can *you* please take command' (p. 285), which he does. Robert puts the options to Tom, but he does so with a clear bias that favours Sir Philip: 'Tom, Doctor Clarkson is not sure he can save her. Sir Philip is certain he can bring her through it with a living child. Isn't a certainty stronger than a doubt?' (p. 285).

In the scenes that follow, Sybil gives birth to a baby girl, but she dies shortly afterwards. The viewer is shown in graphic detail the seizures brought on as a result of the pre-eclampsia she experiences and we witness her death in bed with her husband and mother around her pleading with her not to die. The other members of the family – including her father – stand beyond, shocked and helpless at the situation. The script reads:

> The fight and struggle is over and [Sybil] is at peace. Clarkson checks for her pulse. Robert is in a complete daze.
>
> ROBERT: But this can't be […] This cannot be.
>
> (Fellowes, 2014, p. 293)

In the midst of Sybil's death, then, the script is clear that the focus is as much on Robert as it is Sybil, and Robert's dumbfounded response implicates him in her death. In a moment that recalls his earlier confusion regarding the hiring of a new footman, Robert is confused about the situation and once again, his gamble – as his words to Tom implied – has not paid off. It is left to Cora, Robert's wife, to articulate the gravity of the situation:

> if we'd listened to him [Dr Clarkson] Sybil might still be alive. But Sir Philip and your father knew better, and now she's dead […] You [Robert] believed Tapsell because he's knighted and fashionable and has a practice in Harley Street. … You let all that nonsense weigh against saving our daughter's life which is what I find so very hard to forgive.
>
> (Fellowes, 2014, pp. 301, 312)

Here, Cora reinforces the effects of Robert's poor decision-making. Recalling the investment in the Canadian Grand Trunk Line which Murray indicated was at Robert's insistence, the decision to support Sir Philip was also because of Robert's stubborn persistence, and the result, this time, is a tragic loss of another kind. Robert's 'bad' decision, then, has led directly to his daughter's death. On face value this might appear to be a critique of a misguided masculine patriarch, but this is not the case. Rather, it is a morbid, nostalgic snapshot of the gender politics of the past and 'an unhealthy obsession with class, and a peculiarly dusty form of conservatism' (Groskop, 2014, n.p.). Class snobbery is perhaps the only thing being challenged here as the effect of the plotline uncomfortably equates 'bad management' with the death of a young, pregnant woman. Here, Sybil is very much the victim of an egotistical, class and gendered imperative that equates money with masculinity and masculinity with authority. It is Robert's need to reclaim and re-assert his authority that has been diminished because of his financial crisis that he effectively bullies the family into supporting Tapsell. Problematically, then, Sybil's death constitutes a punishment for Robert's crisis of masculinity. But why should the form of Robert's failure be most pointedly visualised in the death of his daughter?

Fellowes pursues the political complexity of this moral quandary, but I suggest that his critique of Lord Grantham and the way in which his 'foolishness' is resolved remains unsatisfactory and problematic. Although Cora is clear that Robert is to blame for his part in the events that led to her daughter's death, Violet tells her son: 'my dear, when tragedies strike we try to find someone to blame, and in the absence of a suitable candidate we usually blame ourselves. You are not to blame. No one is to blame' (Fellowes, 2014, p. 301). Robert rejects this, acknowledging that 'there is truth in it' (in what Cora has said) (p. 302), but he does not admit he was wrong in supporting Tapsell. Nor does he acknowledge the possibility that had he not done so, Sybil may have survived. In other words, Robert is not made to address his guilt and to make matters worse Fellowes creates a plot that undermines his responsibility in Sybil's demise. Here, Violet asks Doctor Clarkson to rectify the fact that he has 'caused a division between my son and his wife, when the only way they can conceivably bear their grief is if they face it together' (Fellowes, 2014, p. 335). She requests the Doctor 'review[s] the evidence [of Sybil's death], honestly and without bias'; in other words, tell them *he* was wrong and that Tapsell and thus Robert was right (Fellowes, 2014, p. 335). Clarkson, however, rejects this, stating that he that cannot 'tell an outright lie' (Fellowes, 2014, p. 335), but due to the pressure placed on him by the Dowager Countess, he reneges on this and goes on to do just that. Clarkson tells Robert and Cora that 'When everything is weighed in the balance, I believe Lady Sybil was going to die' (Fellowes, 2014, p. 358). This lie is masked, couched in terms of probability, but it works effectively to exonerate Robert's culpability. Lord Grantham may be responsible for the decision that undermined his daughter's chance of survival, but he is not made to face the reality of that responsibility. Clarkson's lie thus enables the mourning couple to reunite and in the final image of the scene Robert puts his arms around his weeping wife. Not only are man and wife (re)united in their grief visually but the implication is that domestic 'normality' at the Abbey is restored.

In the note to the script, Fellowes asks:

> Is it right to conceal the uncomfortable truth? This, for me, is
> the issue, because Clarkson is really letting Robert off the moral
> hook that he ought to have faced, that he was wrong to trust
> the London expert, rather than the man who knew Sybil. And
> I think Violet's motives in seeking the Doctor's support are
> defensible but flawed [...] I don't criticise her for that, but it
> doesn't mean she's necessarily right in making Clarkson falsify
> the truth.
>
> (Fellowes, 2014, p. 335)

Fellowes, it seems, then, has had his cake and eaten it. He has 'ruined' Robert
Crawley, shown him to be a failure and made him morally culpable in his
daughter's death, but he has then restored him via a storyline that invites the
audience's sympathy towards him *because* he is a grieving parent. So why
make Clarkson tell this lie? The answer is simple: for patriarchal 'normality' to be resumed, domestic harmony must be restored. Fellowes, it seems,
views patriarchal authority nostalgically and because of this Robert's crisis
of masculinity cannot go on any longer.

Conclusion: Lessons from the Abbey

Downton Abbey may offer a twenty-first-century commentary on austerity
and economic policy, but its gender politics are distinctly historic, questionable and, I suggest, less than in keeping with those of the new millennium. The recycling of the idea that masculinity is in crisis only serves the
purpose of valorising the figure of the white, aristocratic male patriarch.
More problematically, the particular crisis in masculinity that is played out
in *Downton Abbey* positions women as the passive victims of such a male
gender crisis. After all, while Daisy bears the brunt of austerity, Sybil pays
the price of Robert's need to reassert his flagging ego.

Carroll suggests that recession discourses of masculine failure are usually characterised by the protagonist's admission of 'defeat' which, crucially,
allows them to go on 'to experience a tenuous form of success':

> Unable and crucially unwilling to rely on outmoded forms of mas-
> culine self-empowerment[,] men [in post-recessional narratives]

are able to secure potential futures, for both themselves and their families, by admitting that traditional gender roles were both pernicious to both women and men.

(Carroll, 2014, pp. 204–205)

Downton Abbey resists this approach as Robert neglects to admit his failings. Not only does he refuse 'to be the Earl who dropped the torch' (despite the calamities on his 'watch') but he neglects to apologise for his part in his daughter's death; the nearest he gets to acknowledging his culpability is his reference to the 'truth' in his wife's criticism (Fellowes, 2014, p. 16). As such, *Downton Abbey* clings nostalgically to outdated ideas of gender and economics in which money makes masculinity *and* fuels masculine ego and power. Sadly, it also glorifies (and restores) the white, aristocratic patriarchal male subject even when that figure is 'guilty' of 'bad management'.

Notes

1 These are just two examples of the many media pieces that can be found on the topic, and the show has not just been used as the basis for consumer guidance but to provide lessons in economics and the specificities of the economy, something seen in the *Washington Post* article 'Eight Things Downton Abbey Can Teach Us about the Modern Economy' (Mufson, 2014, n.p). Indeed, 'popular economics' is a new trend in economic writing, with *Downton Abbey* finding prominence in John Tamny's work *Popular Economics: What the Rolling Stones, Downton Abbey, and LeBron James Can Teach You about Economics* (2015).

2 Since the first series, Robert has been open about the fact that he initially married Cora purely for economic reasons, but their marriage has been a happy one and he has fallen in love with her along the way.

3 Despite being the rightful heir to the Earldom of Grantham, Matthew is a middle-class man by birth and profession (a lawyer).

4 In UK politics, not only did the former British Minister of Education, David Blunkett, announce measures to boost the performance of boys in schools following the publication of A-level examination results in 2000, the year in which, for the first time, females performed better than males, but more recently, in 2013, the shadow Minister for Public Health, Diane Abbott, gave a speech entitled 'Britain's Crisis of Masculinity', in which she suggested that young British men were 'isolated and misdirected by a boundless consumer outlook, economic instability and whirlwind social change' (Abbott, 2013, p. 2).

5 In addition to Roger Horrocks's and Rosalind Coward's discussion of a perceived crisis in masculinity discussed here, further explorations of the topic can be found in Susan Faludi's *Stiffed: The Betrayal of the American Man* (1999) and Anthony Clare's *On Men: Masculinity in Crisis* (2000).

6 For a discussion of the so-called 'he-cession' and the recent financial crisis, see Hanna Rosin's 2010 article 'The End of Men' and the accompanying book, *The End of Men: And the Rise of Women* (2012).

7 See, for example, the Feminist Fightback Collective's powerful paper, 'Cuts are a Feminist Issue' (2011).

8 Cora's response to the loss of her money is a rather bizarre absence in the script. In the exchange between her and Robert – described in the Introduction to this chapter – Cora anticipates the news of financial loss when she asks her husband, 'Has some of my fortune been lost?' (Fellowes, 2014, p. 42). And yet his response – 'Some? All.' – produces little response. She is only concerned for her husband: 'Oh, my dear. How terrible for you', to which Robert has to tell her, 'It's not so good for you, either' (Fellowes, 2014, p. 42). Even then, Cora's response placates the situation: 'Don't worry about me. I'm an American. Have gun, will travel' (Fellowes, 2014, p. 42). Fellowes suggests that:

> the point of this scene [...] is to make it clear that this marriage has long passed the point where Cora's money is a principal factor [...] She is not an English toff, and the fact that they're going to sell the house and move to another house is not the end of the world for her. She's mainly sorry for him.
>
> (Fellowes, 2014, p. 42)

For me, however, this glosses over the gender politics at stake. Cora may well be past the point where her inheritance matters to her, but by giving her a somewhat simplistic response to her husband's plight endorses an outdated stereotype of the angel in the house; the dutiful, passive and supportive wife who puts her husband's needs above her own. Clearly, later in the series, as this chapter will discuss, Cora does challenge her husband's behaviour, but her inability to do so over economic matters problematically reinforces an archaic notion that money is the business of men.

9 Instead, Fellowes portrays Mary as scrambling around to save the Abbey from financial ruin. This may suggest women are empowered, but in fact Mary is shown to be naive and unrealistic in her approach to financial restitution. For instance, Mary speaks with her mother and grandmother, Martha (Shirley McLaine) about further financial investment from the American side of the family to which she receives Martha's refusal to invest: 'Oh, I'm so sorry [...] I cannot rescue Downton. It's a shame if it has to go, but I can't[.] The world is changed. These houses were built for another age' (Fellowes, 2014, p. 130). Likewise, the tension between man and wife over the Abbey's economic fortunes

are displaced from Robert and Cora and onto Mary and Matthew; they are the couple who fight about money and the future of the Abbey, as Mary's snide remark to Matthew indicates, 'After all, darling, you're the one who's pushing us out' (Fellowes, 2014, p. 96). Moreover, it is Mary who pursues evidence that Reggie Squire's will was genuine in order to convince Matthew he does deserve the money, and she argues continuously with Matthew over his seeming moral indecision in the face of the financial dire straits that Downton faces. In other words, quite bizarrely, Fellowes shows Mary – a woman – to be more proactive than the male breadwinner – her father – in her desperation to save the Abbey. This may appear to be a feminist plotline, but it serves only to undermine Lord Grantham further since he is unaware of Mary's actions.

10 For a more in-depth discussion of 'austerity chic', see chapter two of Rebecca Bramall's *The Cultural Politics of Austerity* (2013).

11 See the numerous policy reports and charity guidance cited in the Introduction to the collection, most notably the material published by The Women's Lobby and The Fawcettt Society.

12 In the script to the show, Fellowes's critique of Tapsell is clear: 'he is a snob doctor[,] his manner is emollient' (p. 266), but his attitude to Lord Grantham is less than clear.

Bibliography

Abbott, Diane. (2013). 'Britain's Crisis of Masculinity'. *Demos*, 16 May. Available from: <http://www.demos.co.uk/files/DianeAbbottspeech16May2013.pdf> [Accessed: 30 April 2015].

Beard, Mary. (2012). 'The End of Men: And the Rise of Women by Hanna Rosin – Review'. *Guardian*, 3 October. Available from: <http://www.theguardian.com/books/2012/oct/03/end-of-men-hanna-rosin-review> [Accessed: 2 February 2015].

Bramall, Rebecca. (2013). *The Cultural Politics of Austerity*. Basingstoke: Palgrave Macmillan.

Cameron, David. (2009). 'Conference Address: Conservative Party Conference'. *Guardian*, 8 October. Available from: <http://www.theguardian.com/politics/2009/oct/08/david-cameron-speech-in-full>[Accessed:10 December 2014].

Carroll, Hamilton. (2014). '"Stuck between Meanings": Recession-Era Print Fictions of Crisis Masculinity'. In: Diane Negra and Yvonne Tasker (eds) *Gendering the Recession: Media and Culture in An Age of Austerity*. Durham, NC and London: Duke University Press.

Clare, Antony. (2000). *On Men: Masculinity in Crisis.* London: Arrow Books.

Coward, Rosalind. (1999). 'Women are the New Men'. *Guardian,* 1 July. Available from: <http://www.theguardian.com/world/1999/jul/01/gender.uk3> [Accessed: 3 January 2014].

Faludi, Susan. (1999). *Stiffed: The Betrayal of the American Man.* New York: Harper Collins.

Fellowes, Julian. (2014). *Downton Abbey: The Complete Scripts Season Three.* London: Harper Collins.

Feminist Fightback Collective. (2011). 'Cuts are a Feminist Issue' *Soundings,* 49, pp. 73–83.

Gould, Robert. E. (1991). 'Men, Money and Masculinity'. In: Sheila Klebanow and Eugene L. Lowenkopt (eds) *Money and Mind.* New York: Plenum Press.

Greene, Kelly. (2013). 'Money Lessons from Downton Abbey', *Wall Street Journal,* 1 March. Available from: <http://www.wsj.com/articles/SB100014241278873232 93704578330243703304194> [Accessed: 3 February 2015].

Groskop, Viv. (2014). 'Downton Abbey's Class Nostalgia is Another Toxic British Export', *Guardian,* 17 September. Available from: <http://www.theguardian.com/commentisfree/2014/sep/17/downton-abbey-nostalgia-british-export-stereotypes> [Accessed: 17 December 2014].

Horrocks, Roger. (1994). *Masculinity in Crisis: Myths, Fantasies and Realities.* Basingstoke: Palgrave Macmillan.

Kamp, David. (2012). 'The Most Happy Fellowes'. *Vanity Fair,* December. Available from: <http://www.vanityfair.com/culture/2012/12/julian-fellowes-downton-abbey> [Accessed: 3 February 2015].

Kaplan, Eve. (2013). 'Downton Abbey Money Lessons'. *Forbes,* 21 February. Available from: <http://www.forbes.com/sites/feeonlyplanner/2013/02/21/downton-abbey-money-lessons/> [Accessed: 19 August 2013].

Leggott, James and Taddeo, Julie (eds). (2015). *Upstairs and Downstairs: British Costume Drama Television from the Forsyte Saga to Downton Abbey.* London: Rowman and Littlefield.

Mufson, Steven. (2014). 'Eight Things Downton Abbey Can Teach Us about the Modern Economy'. *Washington Post,* 10 February. Available from: <http://www.washingtonpost.com/blogs/wonkblog/wp/2014/02/10/eight-things-downton-abbey-can-teach-us-about-economics/> [Accessed: 29 January 2015].

Negra, Diane and Tasker, Yvonne. (2013). 'Neoliberal Frames and Genres of Inequality: Recession-era Chick Flicks and Male-centred Corporate Melodrama'. *European Journal of Cultural Studies* 16:3 (2013), pp. 344–361.

—— (2014). *Gendering the Recession: Media and Culture in An Age of Austerity.* Durham, NC and London: Duke University Press.

Rosin, Hanna. (2010). 'The End of Men'. *The Atlantic*, July–August. Available from: <http://www.theatlantic.com/magazine/archive/2010/07/the-end-of-men/308135/> [Accessed: 20 March 2015].

—— (2012). *The End of Men: And the Rise of Women*. New York: Riverhead.

Tamny, John. (2015). *Popular Economics: What the Rolling Stones, Downton Abbey, and LeBron James Can Teach You about Economics*. New York: Regnery Publishing.

3

Wartime Housewives and Vintage Women: A. S. Byatt's *Ragnarok: The End of the Gods* and Reframing Popular Nostalgia

Leanne Bibby

British novelist and critic A. S. Byatt's most recent book *Ragnarok: The End of the Gods* (2011) is in certain ways more experimental than her better-known novels and stories, although it has one strategy in common with many of them: the texts use the language of myth to test the limitations of patriarchal, historical narratives of the mid-twentieth century. This chapter contends that *Ragnarok*, with its timely depiction of a young girl and her mother living through World War II and the postwar years, can be read productively alongside relevant forms of nostalgia in popular culture (evoking 'vintage' images of wartime- and 1950s-set, domesticated femininity), intensely fashionable by 2011 and remaining so to the present time. Rebecca Bramall has delineated the links between different meanings of 'austerity' in the United Kingdom cogently. She defines austerity as an 'unstable discourse' (2013b, p. 10): variously as a set of coalition government policies and political narratives, as an 'other' that defines left-wing struggle against it, and as an 'object of desire' in popular culture exemplified partly by the craze for 'austerity chic' in fashion, crafts, television and stylishly 'thrifty' behaviour (2013a, pp. 3–7; 2013b, p. 24).[1] Byatt's book was published in March 2011, weeks before the wedding of Prince William to Catherine Middleton, and at a time when 'tradition' itself became the height of fashion in the United Kingdom and beyond. At the book's moment of publication, British design trends centred on the Union Jack, bakery businesses flourished as the meal of afternoon tea enjoyed a revival, and street parties – simulacra of community-based celebrations of the end of the Second World War – were celebrated again against the background of a new 'age of austerity' heralded by politicians. Many consumers, it seemed, wanted to celebrate in commodified 'retro' style, in defiance of economic adversity following the 2008 global financial crisis, while also gesturing towards another past time of such adversity as though from a 'safe' distance.

In the words of novelist Jessica Mann, 'Distance has lent enchantment to the popular view of the life most girls and women led in the 1950s' (2013, location 51–57), and this enchantment (applicable also to modern evocations of the 1940s) is a powerful driver of this aspect of popular culture.[2] 'Retromania' has become an appealing, eye-catching and lasting trend in popular culture, not least in the self-expression of vintage enthusiasts themselves, some of whose blogs on fashion, cookery and lifestyle have made them into popular and respected voices on their chosen subjects. 'Being well dressed is a form of politeness',[3] proclaims The Glamorous Housewife on her website of the same name, populated with tips on vintage clothing, 'domestic design', recipes for 'the family' and guests, and advice on marriage, relationships and good manners – all inflected with pretty imagery and 'inspiration' from the middle decades of the twentieth century. This Housewife shares details and pictures of nostalgic hairstyles, jewellery and decor, alongside a popular post defending her feminist politics: 'I believe that a feminist believes men and women are equal. Period. [...] If I choose to be a CEO of a fortune 500 [sic], I could make that choice'.[4] In a similar embrace of this paradox – celebrating the notion of choice in order to replicate a time of little choice for women – The Retro Housewife testifies on her blog that 'I was born in the wrong generation, there is no doubt about that. I absolutely idolize the retro housewives. The way they truly loved and embraced their role as a homemaker is so inspiring'. This blogger is then quick to stress that she also supports 'women in the workplace and women being successful' – 'Please don't misunderstand'.[5]

Several blogs titled 'The Vintage Housewife', originating in the USA, follow a similar pattern, often produced by self-identified housewives and showcasing products, recipes and objects of nostalgia for the 1940s and 50s.

One 'Vintage Housewife', a prolific blogger since 2008, sports extravagantly curled, peroxide-blonde hair, bright makeup and replica 1940s and 50s clothing, as well as driving a pink-and-white camper van; she writes in 'rockabilly'[6] slang about her family and the nostalgic locations and events she frequently attends. Like that of The Glamorous Housewife, these blogs also explore problems linked to parenting, relationships and, not infrequently, the outwardly uncertain politics of their lifestyle choices. Another, newer blog titled The Vintage Housewife includes an 'Intro to this Project' section, in which the author writes in response to the stereotypical 'angry feminists' she imagines condemning her for her identification with housewives of the past:

> Pipe down, Bra Burners. […] [Feminism] means that I have the freedom to choose to do whatever I want to do, including studying up on how to be a fifties housewife and then blogging about it. Who knows? Maybe after a few months of following these rules I'll decide that being a fifties woman is completely ridiculous and I'll become an empowered feminist like you.[7]

Here, once more, the blogger emphasises the fluidity of her choice of role and that is also a narrative. In the UK, vintage trends have become prominent consumer choices in popular advertising and fashion imagery: the familiar 1940s or 1950s 'vintage' woman or housewife, in petticoats or with elaborate 'victory roll' curls and headscarf, has made nostalgia visible and material, particularly in the primarily feminine domains of clothing, cosmetics and homeware. With these objects, evidently marketable and desirable to many, come narratives of women's lives in wartime and the postwar years. Meanwhile, a social and political culture of austerity shapes social life, indeed giving nostalgic design and products a sense of 'appropriateness' for both those old and these new times, as Bramall observes (2013b, p. 24). Since I began researching this chapter, the number of vintage websites run by companies and individuals has increased noticeably. A large number of personal websites, even when their authors describe themselves as favourable to feminist politics, nonetheless seem to testify to a certain, popular disenchantment with feminism, with some women eager to forsake the insecurity of working life (and juggling that life with family responsibilities) and take refuge instead in the seemingly historical notion of proud, resilient and glamorous housewifery.

Vintage trends are consequently troubling for some commentators. Feminist writer Laura Brightwell, blogging in the aftermath of Elizabeth II's Diamond Jubilee celebrations in 2012, raised doubts about popular nostalgia's political and class implications:

> This glamorisation of domestic work is potentially troublesome at a time when British women have the most economic freedom we have ever had. That we are, once again, expected to labour over our baking (spotted dicks all round, please!) and to love it, is a bit problematic.
>
> (2012, n.p.)

Similarly, journalist Tonya Davidson describes the nostalgia growing up alongside popular culture images of the mid-twentieth-century decades as potentially 'retrosexist' because 'dressing in excessively girlish fashions and uncritically embodying the styles of a sexist bygone era are not politically neutral practices' (2014, pp. 26–27). However, in common with Bramall (2013b), Davidson then rightly describes the 'camp femininities' that characterise certain vintage performances of gender, and their subversive potential; this is indeed lost when the 'irony of domestic nostalgia' is lost, for instance when women yearn earnestly to be a character in the glamorised 1960s world of the US TV drama *Mad Men* (2007–2015), here termed 'nothing more than a fashion shoot' (2014, pp. 26–27).

In her timely memoir *The Fifties Mystique* (2012) – whose title deliberately echoes that of Betty Friedan's 1963 book *The Feminine Mystique*, a founding text in second wave feminism which critiques of the 1950s mythic 'happy housewife heroine' – Mann is correct in stating that 'distance has led enchantment to the popular view' of the 1950s and thereabouts (2013, location 51–57). Still, however, that idea of enchantment is important to many women in ways that demand further, respectful consideration. There is a need to look again, critically, at the precise images of women's lives reproduced by 'vintage women': usually imaginative, colourful and treated as having questionable political authority by the women who assert their choice to be housewives – and maybe, also, to do other things in the future. They draw on an adaptable mythology both of women's pasts and their still, in austere times, uncertain futures, exercising often critical and creative readings of the historical evidence supplied by vintage clothing, recipes and, as referenced by one Vintage Housewife blogger, 1940s and 50s home economics textbooks (2014).[8]

The war, its aftermath and related fears and privations are distant from the vintage housewives' narratives, replaced with imaginative 'enchantments' of women's realities; this kind of popular nostalgia is for lifestyles more new than old, and reconstituted of selected, older, memorable and 'appropriate' forms, to borrow Bramall's term (2013a, 2013b), rather than straight 'reproductions' of anything original. The vintage bloggers described here make conscious decisions to adopt a style that amplifies their desired femininity, without determining their personal politics or their futures. This style is usually much more brightly coloured, blowsy and exaggerated than the sombre eye on glamorous but static, melancholy lives portrayed in *Mad Men*. Bramall and Davidson, then, are right to compare popular vintage in its performative, 'ironic' forms to camp, and drag, as nostalgic styles do bring strongly to mind Judith Butler's description of the features and meanings of female impersonation:

> *In imitating gender, drag implicitly reveals the imitative structure of gender itself – as well as its contingency.* Indeed, part of the pleasure, the giddiness of the performance is in the recognition of a radical contingency in the relation between sex and gender in the face of cultural configurations of causal unities that are regularly assumed to be natural and necessary.
>
> (1990, p. 187, emphasis in original)

Elsewhere, Butler contends that 'there is no original or primary gender that drag imitates, but *gender is a kind of imitation for which there is no original*' (2004, p. 127, emphasis in original); as is well known, drag thus unsettles notions of essential, natural or ideal gender characteristics. Tellingly, vintage bloggers describe explicitly the *roles* they choose to inhabit and celebrate, acknowledging tacitly that those roles are not consequences of given gender, but are best 'put on' and 'played' with escapist joy and creativity (after being bought by way of cosmetics and clothing, a notably un-thrifty aspect of the performance), as any other role they might choose. There is an intense, playful pleasure apparent in vintage bloggers' performances of exaggerated femininity and housewifery, which appear in many cases to have been drawn directly from 1950s advertisements, likely bearing little relation to 'real' lives, past or present. This femininity is indeed a mediation between past and present standards of behaviour (Bramall, 2013b, p. 76), and is reconcilable with contemporary feminist politics because it is non-essential, loud, cartoonish, chosen, changeable and disconnected from 'history' itself.

I say these performances are disconnected from history, but they remain linked to it in important ways, a point highlighted by vintage's affinity with historical austerity narratives of the British context in particular, and also its resistance to austerity-driven privations following the financial crisis and multiple recessions of recent years. As Helen Davies discusses at length in her chapter in this collection, in David Cameron's infamous 2009 'age of austerity' speech, the Conservative Party leader gave an influential but inadequate account of the British past and future.[9] He combined apocalyptic images of the 'deep, dark clouds over our economy, our society, and our whole political system' with condemnation of 'The highest borrowing in peacetime history' and 'The deepest recession since the war', aligning the contemporary moment, seemingly, with historical times of hardship (Cameron, 2009, n.p.). Cameron defended austerity as necessary using a narrative of how 'we' had been here before and had survived, exhorting 'us' personally to 'stick together and tackle this crisis' so that 'our children and grandchildren [would] thank us for what we did for them and for our country' (2009, n.p.), thus constructing a future as theoretical and mythological as the past.

Cameron's myth-spinning, however, inadvertently gestured towards more progressive, effective ways of re-reading the past. In light of the frightening economic realities of recessions and austerity, popular, vintage culture's nostalgia is easily criticised as a naive and politically questionable retreat from challenging times, especially when retromania appears to be primarily a feminine, white and middle-class trend emblematised by not-inexpensive Cath Kidston knitting bags[10] and time-consuming, decorative baking. But crucially, the colourful retromania of the few years since Cameron's speech is conceptually, critically and imaginatively engaged with austerity culture in a way his rhetoric was not. Vintage imagery translates historical narratives selectively and inventively into bright, pleasurable and malleable objects of a politically changed and changing present day, and symbols of hoped-for futures. Using vintage websites such as those described earlier, for example, families facing smaller incomes and higher prices can access plentiful information on saving money with ease, while cupcakes and 'upcycling' of vintage clothing[11] represent affordable luxuries (for some).

As well as inhabiting roles, adherents of vintage demonstrate an awareness of how they can and do re-narrate selected histories in the present day, in order to alter futures for the better. In their consciousness of their own narratives and creative potential, they become agents of mythopoeia, defined as myth-production or myth-expansion (Baldick, 2008, n. p.). A. S. Byatt's *Ragnarok* intervenes in a cultural moment of intense popular nostalgia to contribute to a reframing of thinking about gender and wartime/postwar nostalgia, because the book explores directly the role of myth narratives in remembering and re-narrating gendered histories. Conventionally, but tellingly, the *Oxford English Dictionary* defines a 'myth' as a story seeking to explain aspects of a society's past, often an imaginative or fanciful version of that past (2015, n.p.). In addition to this definition, Byatt's writing theorises myth partly as a feminist mode of representing pasts as well as desired futures, in relation to, but not limited by, dominant historical narratives. Her writing conceptualises 'nostalgia' not as a backward-looking belief in supposedly better, bygone times, but as an inventive impulse. Mediated usually by critically-minded, creative, female protagonists, Byatt's nostalgias and myths are thus not straightforward carriers of patriarchal tradition; instead her texts incorporate a sense of the power of narrative to do their feminist work.

In the following extract, from Byatt's 1978 novel *The Virgin in the Garden*, young intellectual Frederica Potter becomes aware of the postwar narratives of her recent life and its historical contexts – notably, its feminine, pleasurable aspects – as readable, changeable phenomena; moreover, her readings enhance those narratives' significance:

> The haberdashery had always been a favourite haunt. They had come here in their early days for lace collars for party dresses, ribbons for hair, tape, elastic, buttons and press-studs. Frederica in 1953 was disposed to see these visits as tedious rituals, although she saw that it might be possible to see them otherwise, with a kind of Dickensian nostalgia for the details of a vanished life, which was, in fact, how in 1973 she came to see them.
>
> (Byatt, 1978, p. 251)

Several of Byatt's other fictions utilise the language of myths and folktales explicitly to represent women's narrative power over their culture and its 'enchantments'. In 'The Story of the Eldest Princess', a short tale included in the volume *The Djinn in the Nightingale's Eye* (1994), the 'eldest princess' of the title embarks on a quest that leads her to 'outwit' the story of a princess's traditional, sexual destiny: ' "You are a born storyteller," said the old lady. "You had the sense to see you were caught in a story, and the sense to see that you could change it to another one" ' (Byatt, 1994, p. 66). These protagonists discover a gift for mythopoeia, as a response to the unfixed narratives they inhabit and that have been officially organised patriarchally.

Byatt's *Ragnarok* depicts a young, female reader of Norse myths, 'the thin child', who uses the mythopoeic potential of reading, thought, memory and speculation to disintegrate the narrative of her own narrow, uncertain life in the 1940s, as well as a looming, domestic future mirroring that of her frustrated, Cambridge-educated mother (Byatt, 2011, p. 3). The text 'looks back' on the many dangers of women's lives at this time not normally confronted by nostalgic forms of popular culture, not with bleak realism but with methods of inventive 'enchantment' vintage women might find familiar. *Ragnarok* quickly announces its concern with the mythic, narrative forms of history: 'There was a thin child, who was three years old when the war began. She could remember, though barely, the time before wartime when, as her mother frequently told her, there was honey and cream and eggs in plenty' (Byatt, 2011, p. 3). Byatt was born in 1936 and, like her protagonist 'the thin child', inherited a book of Norse myths by Wilhelm Wägner titled *Asgard and the Gods* from her university-educated mother; *Ragnarok* is thus a multimodal experiment in rewriting 'real' pasts. Formally, it is far removed from Byatt's long, historical bestsellers *Possession: A Romance* (1990) and *The Children's Book* (2009), being composed in three sections: the story of 'the thin child' told in the spare, precise language of folktales, a central retelling of the Norse myth of the end of the world and of the gods, and finally a critical reflection on that retelling by the author herself. The text challenges conventional narratives of the past using multiple, mythic narratives both interrupted and complemented by a myth of apocalypse – a destruction of old ways, relished by the 'thin child' herself.

Ragnarok's feminist mythopoeia and focus on women of the generation idolised in vintage culture reveal the often complex feminist functions
of women's relationship to historical narrative and nostalgia, illuminating
why they might rewrite 'memory' itself. In common with some of the vintage bloggers I have mentioned, Byatt has publicly disassociated herself
from overt feminist agendas, while defending her work's feminist politics.
She has contended that *Possession*, with its narratives of women artists
and intellectuals thinking and writing their way toward autonomy, is an
example of a 'very, very feminist book', while on the other hand, she has
expressed her wish not 'to be ghettoized by modern feminists into writing about women's problems': 'I think in metaphors, not in propaganda'
(Tredell, 1994, pp. 60–61). Byatt's work prioritises feminist narrative functions above declared agendas, an idea that proves to be equally liberating
for modern vintage women who celebrate interchangeable narratives. For
Byatt's own critically-minded women characters, 'traditional values' are
myths to be negotiated among multiple versions of feminine life. I would
argue that this is part of popular culture's current, potentially 'progressive
politics of austerity', suggested by Bramall (2013b, p. 30). In *Ragnarok's* final
section, 'Thoughts on Myths', Byatt isolates myth as a concept, explaining
that the word 'myth' 'comes from "muthos" in Greek, something said as
opposed to something done' (2011, p. 157). 'Saying', telling, producing and
reproducing culture, are key. *Ragnarok's* thin child understands her world
through mythic narratives passed on primarily by her reader-mother; the
child learns, then, to understand such narratives subjectively in order to
improve her experience of World War II.

The most significant of these narratives concern the genders and the
spheres the child and her mother inhabit: her mother's life is 'paradoxi-
cal. Because there was a war on, it was legally possible for her to live
in the mind, to teach bright boys, which before the war had been for-
bidden to married women' (Byatt, 2011, p. 4). The thin child narrates
disheartening realities into bearable stories: 'Her mother was more real,
and kinder, when it was a question of grouped letters on the page' and
her fighter pilot father 'was in the air, in the war, in Africa, in Greece,
in Rome, in a world that only existed in books' (2011, p. 4). This dis-
missal of the 'real' is more than simple, 'looking-back' nostalgia for
childhood coping mechanisms; Byatt also mobilises a variety of myths,

from apocalyptic notions of the war ('They faced the end of the world they knew', 2011, p. 4) to altered versions of the real world, suggesting vital alternatives to the cultural myths of 'tradition' that, for example, formerly confined the thin child's educated mother to her home. More than a subject of history, and of the dominant culture and its mindsets, the thin child is now an agent of them.

Laurence Coupe's descriptions of mythopoeic language and forms (1997) can here contextualise the thin child's imaginings of her life and family. Coupe theorises myths similarly to Byatt's texts, as stories featuring archetypes or recurring figures and themes, some laying claim to paradigmatic status, for instance, images of the home front housewife and the hero soldier. Individual myths gain their apparent power and authority from their inclusion of recognisable paradigms, but also, as Coupe stresses, from their reworking of those paradigms. Myths comprise no truly 'pure' paradigms because 'Exceptions to, and contradictions of, any particular paradigm are endless' (1997, pp. 5–6). Whatever impression the myth might give, there are endless potential variations on its figures. Thus, the conservative, nostalgic ideal of the housewife is not actually an ideal, but a very specific myth to be read in those terms. This provides vital background to the early twenty-first century impulse to recall the past imaginatively.

Coupe cites the philosopher Paul Ricoeur in emphasising mythic narrative's 'exploratory significance', hugely important within a feminist reading of the cultural histories which Byatt negotiates. Archetypes and paradigms within mythology signal an apparent hierarchy, for example in placing the wartime housewife within the home (or the home front) and away from the public sphere; however, this is a specific, not universal, scenario:

> myth may imply a hierarchy, but it also implies a horizon: it is 'a disclosure of unprecedented worlds, an opening on to other *possible* worlds which transcend the established limits of our *actual* world' (Ricoeur 1991: 490). In other words, while myth may be paradigmatic, and while it may imply a social and cosmic order, or perfection, it also carries with it a promise of another mode of existence entirely, to be realised just beyond the present time and place.
>
> (Coupe, 1997, pp. 8–9)

The thin child's wartime narratives are explicitly mythopoeic, in Coupe's sense: she escapes dangers by looking for the 'horizons' at the edge of myths and testing paradigms' limitations. She fears her housewife mother's domestic, feminine fate, but this reality is a problem with potential, narrative solutions. Sensing alternatives, she reads the chaotic myths in *Asgard* and tells complementary stories to answer her realities and to feel secure – as indeed might any modern, critically-minded woman uncertain of her fate. Byatt's possible nostalgia for her childhood reading is part of this creative, progressive mythopoeia. Roberta Rubenstein writes that nostalgia 'encompasses something more than a yearning for literal places or actual individuals. While homesickness refers to a spatial/geographical separation, nostalgia more accurately refers to a temporal one' (2001, p. 4). In the thin child's narrative, as in the outputs of nostalgic writers and businesspeople today, 'time' fills with desired spaces and objects. *Ragnarok* instructs that nostalgia is not only imaginative by definition, but also empoweringly so. The text requires and exploits memory's personal-historical paradigms – home, mother, father, past and future – to demonstrate that these are meaningful, but no longer entirely literal.

Byatt's language is dreamlike, surreal and sensuous, suggesting nostalgia whilst indicating nostalgia's powers in the mind of a critical reader:

> The picture [a scene from *Asgard*] gave the child an intense, uncanny pleasure. She knew, but could not have said, that it was the precise degree of formlessness in the nevertheless scrupulously depicted rocks that was so satisfactory. The reading eye must do the work to make them live, and so it did, again and again, never the same life twice, as the artist had intended. She had noticed that a bush, or a log, seen from a distance on her meadow-walk, could briefly be a crouching, snarling dog, or a trailing branch could be a snake, complete with shining eyes and flickering forked tongue.
>
> (2011, p. 10)

The 'ordinary paradise of the English countryside' (2011, p. 3) becomes a flat and deceptive paradigm next to the vividly drawn, Norse scene, revealing the frightening, but exciting, possibilities at reality's mythic horizons. Myth makes her world larger than her home or her geographical area, threatened by war: 'That book was an account of a mystery, of how a world came together, was filled with magical and powerful beings, and then came to an end. A real End. The end' (2011, p. 9). Endings mean that traditions, dependent on concepts of time's progress and a future benefiting from the ways of the past, lose some of their authority. The thin child recalls that her mother was 'gallant and resourceful in wartime' (sincere praise, but also a pointed reference to the historical *and* modern cliché of heroic home front women), and that she also 'did inhabit the countryside and its stories' (Byatt, 2011, pp. 150–151). The parameters of the mother's feminine 'story' shift with her work as a teacher, which in her daughter's telling brings her into the messy nature of the countryside with its 'hedgehog dripping fleas' and 'vast slimy clumps of frogspawn' (2011, pp. 151–152), instead of the classroom.

The patriarchal mythology underpinning and restricting their lives is changeable because of wartime uncertainties, but that war limits their freedom: the thin child's mother teaches 'bright *boys*' (my emphasis) only, and temporarily. This is another haunting form of 'the end of the world.' Despite the 'despair [the thin child] did not know she felt' (2011, p. 4), imaginatively, she then finds vital possibilities within disorder:

> This way of looking was where the gods and giants came from.
> The stone giants made her want to write.
> They filled the world with alarming energy and power.
>
> (2011, p. 10)

This 'way of looking' may reject provisional ideas of the past and the future (2011, p. 10). Traditions and 'pure' paradigms, linked to the sense of linear history disrupted by war, operate according to conventions. In *Ragnarok*, mythopoeia is paradoxically, challengingly, both a part of and a mode of resistance against patriarchal traditions – it writes myths of 'appropriate' life trajectories, while showing their limits. The thin child considers the Norse tales' mysteriousness in *Asgard and the Gods* in terms of the conventions of stories. Exhilaratingly, she 'knew enough fairy stories to know that a prohibition in a story is there to be broken' (2011, p. 22); the tales' images 'were coiled like smoke in her skull, humming like dark bees in a hive' (2011, p. 31). These last metaphors suggest the darkness and destruction attracting the thin child, even while she looks for refuge from her 'despair'. Stories allow her to contemplate wartime destruction safely, as 'they didn't live in her, and she didn't live in them' (2011, p. 31). Destruction here means both physical death and loss (symbolised in the thin child's fear for her father, and her damage to unopened flower buds) and the desirable destruction of patriarchal narratives as ideas, only. The thin child watches soldiers pass through her small town in convoys and imagines her airman father as part of the Norse god Odin's Wild Hunt: this is 'a good story' because 'meaning, fear and danger were in it, and things out of control' (2011, p. 41). If things are indeed out of control, then the heroic, patriarchal logic of her father going away and not returning – deemed a noble sacrifice, officially – can be subverted.

Ragnarok's sections are named emblematically, as the thin child navigates uncertain historical narratives alongside myth's liberating inordinateness: between 'A Thin Child in Wartime' and 'The End of the World', and 'Ragnarök' and 'The Thin Child in Peacetime', there is a single-paragraph section titled 'The Thin Child in Time'. The thin child's imaginative dependence on myth has often removed her from any sense of time: 'Imagining the end of things, when you are a child, is perhaps impossible' (Byatt, 2011, p. 127). Also, her almost ahistorical inner life is a rejection of other temporal endings. Her own narrative escapes her control: she has nightmares of deaths by hanging, now a part of the history she has partly ignored and partly reimagined, but she does not acknowledge that she understands death as a 'fact' (2011, p. 127). Her other, crucial fear asserts itself here, of a future of 'dailiness' as a housewife, or the boredom of domestic repetition, before the book's retelling of 'Ragnarök' itself. In this final, Norse tale of apocalypse, time and order are suspended, the earth freezes and at first the 'men' of the earth are 'excited' because this 'was a test of strength. A test of manhood' (2011, p. 132). Gendered narratives of strength are then nevertheless destroyed, with everything else. The narrative itself breaks into fragmentary sentences and ideas: 'Wind Time, Wolf Time, before the World breaks up. / That was the time they were in' (2011, p. 135).

'The Thin Child in Peacetime' requires this apocalypse narrative as 'a form of knowledge itself', to know that the world's discourses are fragile, uncertain, specific and changeable; she reads *Asgard* selectively because she 'needed the original end, the dark water over everything', unchanged by later Christian 'contamination' with the return of gods and men to inhabit the world (2011, p. 147). She needs this myth because her story's positive 'ending', her father's return and her family's return home, is no ending at all and is tinged with sadness owing to her fear of a future of boredom. She treasures a set of books, more feminine than *Asgard*, 'of Flower Fairies with well-written verses and elegant pictures. Dogrose, Lords and Ladies, Deadly Nightshade, violets, snowdrops and primroses' (2011, p. 152). In these lines as in the Norse myths, beauty and poison coexist, and order with unbound, unpredictable danger. Furthermore, the return to peace and 'order' slowly devastates the thin child's mother and provides a specific fate for her daughter to resist:

> The long-awaited return took the life out of the thin child's mother, the thin child decided many years later. Dailiness defeated her. She made herself lonely and slept in the after-noons, saying she was suffering from neuralgia and sick head-aches. The thin child came to identify the word 'housewife' with the word 'prisoner'.
>
> (2011, p. 152)

This insight into her mother's pain is perhaps the book's central vindication of mythopoeia as a mode of survival. The child's mother is a 'prisoner' of a pre-set narrative of feminine life, but importantly, the 'housewife' is a para-digm that has never been made 'pure' or 'perfect'. The thin child's mother is set alongside the unpredictable, androgynous god Loki, whom no struc-ture – physical, biological or cultural – could contain. For all her earlier education, her responsibilities to home and family are totalising and she unfortunately has no mythopoeia at her disposal. Nonetheless, crucially, she has handed her books down to her daughter, whose future is a narrative the thin child is equipped to rewrite.

Ragnarok does not end with the end of the war, because such an end-ing would belong to the grand narrative – Jean-François Lyotard's term for overarching, explanatory theories of the world (1984) – of war victories as good triumphing over evil, within a framework of masculine heroism and patriarchal glory. For the thin child and her mother, Jessica Mann's phrase is acerbically appropriate: in 1945, 'peace broke out' (2013, location 66) and the patriarchal order of the world seemed set to be restored. Byatt does not finish the story with a drive towards the 'perfection' of a 'finished' myth. The thin child's mythopoeic reading of her world contests the threat of the 'dailiness' apparently destroying her reading, thinking mother, and she continues her active, imaginative reading of *Asgard*. Unlike the mythographers who would 'perfect' myths and assign them authority, however, the thin child cherishes the idea of the possibilities on the other side of dailiness:

> A gate closed in her head. She must learn to live in dailiness, she told herself, in a house, in a garden, at home, where there was butter again, and cream, and honey, good to taste. She must savour peacetime.
>
> But on the other side of the closed gate was the bright black world into which she had walked at the time of her evacuation. The World-Ash and the rainbow bridge, seeming everlasting, destroyed in a twinkling of an eye. The wolf with his hackles and bloody teeth, the snake with her crown of fleshy fronds, smiling Loki with fishnet and flames, the horny ship made of dead men's nails, the Fimbulwinter and Surtr's conflagration, the black undifferentiated surface, under a black undifferentiated sky, at the end of things.
>
> (Byatt, 2011, p. 154)

This is the frightening, barely knowable and exhilarating narrative that the thin child has 'made' out of the myths in *Asgard* and the war. She cannot 'savour peace-time' and its promised economic plenty because it signifies a return to other kinds of 'order' beside peace in Europe, that would define and trap her female mind and body (2011, p. 154). The above images of the Ragnarök apocalypse respect no grand narratives of order, instead switching fluidly between colours and darkness, mythical trees, gods and animals, and contrasting with the softer sentences and sounds depicting mythical English gardens and un-rationed luxuries. There, the thin child's story reaches a stop, not an ending, without submission of the girl or the narrative to a fixed future or set of values.

Conclusions: Feminist Mythopoeia and Horizons

The thin child fears the 'dailiness' of housewifery as a danger of postwar life, but Byatt leaves her with the imaginative power to resist it – a very similar imaginative potential deployed within the early twenty-first century's popular nostalgia for the same historical era. In *Ragnarok*, Byatt's feminist mythopoeia replaces the same patriarchal notion of cultural, 'shared' memory that delineates conventional nostalgia as a simplistic construction of an idealised past, rather than a creative path towards other possibilities exemplified by many modern vintage and wartime housewives' embrace of identities 'between' the historical housewife and modern feminist (Hollows, in Bramall, 2013b, p. 112). Recognition of a similarly creative mythopoeia at work in fashionable nostalgia or vintage culture reveals this culture to be a multiplicitous set of resisting readings of the past, whose functions would be undermined by any drive towards 'perfect', finished myths. Conventional nostalgia's wish for unity (and belief in certain 'lost' standards and values) is exactly that: a wish that historical discourses, multiple accounts of the past, cannot fulfil. Byatt's fictions expose nostalgia's inventive, discursive work, so that Frederica Potter's memories of the 1950s haberdashery are replete with new, charming significance because she is a powerfully critical reader of histories. *Ragnarok* scrutinises how contemporary culture's nostalgic narratives simultaneously connect with and critique modern, political discourses of the present age of austerity: both appeal to wartime and postwar narratives' paradigmatic images and to their limitations, especially those with antifeminist implications of oppressive 'tradition'.

Coupe, referencing literary critic Kenneth Burke's theories, advises readers of any myth to 'consider what it is "doing" as well as what it is "saying"': that is, to bear in mind the pragmatic impulse which would have occasioned it in the first place' (Coupe, 1997, p. 7). To privilege a certain myth or interpretation of that myth is to project 'a certain idea of perfection onto material that may have more practical functions' (Coupe, 1997, p. 7). Byatt's fiction demonstrates this with her repeated motif of dailiness, feared by her women protagonists who resist it, as readers may, by recognising its specificity among other narratives. Vintage culture, then, asserts its own critical 'imperfection' and its 'practical functions' by omitting images of housewifery's dailiness in favour of fantastical alternatives. Today's fashionable 'vintage women' need not contemplate wartime's physical or ideological dangers, and thus may not need to reference Norse mythology, but they are no less concerned than the thin child with finding the horizons of mythic narratives – of history, femininity, work, family – in order to project new futures. The nostalgias promulgated by these writers, entrepreneurs, public figures and followers of the trend, including the bloggers I referred to earlier, are part of the creation of pragmatic mythologies of the past's relationship to the present, a process similar to the one isolated strikingly in *Ragnarok*.

Reading vintage culture as mythopoeic reveals its unfixed political allegiances, for instance in its depictions of housewives and domesticity. The thin child fears mindless, feminine dailiness, as Byatt has said she did herself:

> this was to do with the fate of women in my generation. I was terrified of being shut in a kitchen with a washing tub and, later, a washing machine. I was terrified of the repetitiveness of ordinary things, which can be made to seem glamorous in a novel.
>
> (Byatt and Frosh, 2004, p. 148)

The 'eldest princess' of Byatt's short tale, too, avoids marriage to a handsome woodcutter when she realises that a form of dailiness has killed his previous wives (1994, p. 60). Dailiness is not housewifery itself but rather a fixed, repetitive version of it, one of patriarchy's historical victories. Modern vintage culture does not really depict dailiness, and instead of merely omitting or disavowing women's historical problems, vintage culture relies on the multiple, narrative nature of the historical imagery and myths underpinning it. Again, vintage's proponents fill their pasts, presents and futures with desired objects. *Ragnarok* dramatises an analogous process by way of its 'internal', imaginative critique, examining and utilising myth in the ways I have described, and by exposing the deceptive historical paradigms on which a narrow, prescriptive form of nostalgia (this is the proper, 'traditional' way to do things) would depend.

The numerous 'vintage' websites and personal blogs now online, and books published, of the type that might fuel fears of growing antifeminism, actually reveal promisingly multiplicitous adaptations of the paradigms of the wartime and postwar housewife and the dailiness they obscure. These websites' owners may or may not be declared housewives, but are usually educated, articulate, artistic and of course, highly web-literate; they are agents of mythopoeia, whether feminists in stated agenda or 'in practice', via the transforming discourses their images suggest. Furthermore, beside their glamorous (re)constructions and explorations of feminine identity, useful narratives of resisting austerity itself remain prominent. On her website wartimehousewife.com, under the heading 'Old Values in Modern Times', the 'Wartime Housewife' herself, Biff Raven-Hill, sets out her mission statement of keeping certain 'traditional values' alive for the benefit of economically difficult modern times; values centred on the home, frugality, avoiding waste and buying second hand. The website and its construction of the Housewife's 'wisdom' and authority in these matters (that are, after all, based on much laudable economic advice) depend on our acceptance of the virtue of 'past' wisdom and of certain narratives of World War II's heroic, home front women. However, the site's substantial archive of advice on saving money, parenting and home cooking is presented not in terms of straightforward nostalgia for the past, but in terms of ideas of taking responsibility for the present that do not depend on any real idealisation of an essential, traditional femininity. This and other 'neo-traditional' (Miller, 2013) narratives work within modern myths of the past and also the future, turning historical narratives into suggestions of other modes of existence, 'to be realised just beyond the present time and place' (Coupe, 1997, pp. 8–9). They adapt 'traditional values' by looking to the hardships of the past (including the time before the modern women's movement) while re-using its glamorous, although helpfully dislocated, stereotypes.

In common with A. S. Byatt's mythopoeic fictions, proponents of contemporary vintage culture use mythopoeic forms of historical narrative to constitute what Byatt's thin child regarded as 'a form of knowledge' (2011, p. 147) with which to process a troubling reality: new ways of appearing, living and coping in an era of austerity. Many women agents of nostalgia and mythopoeia today, whether novelists, journalists or bloggers, supply colourful, optimistic and creative myths of femininity, resourcefulness, work and politics, which should not be dismissed as simply retrograde and backward-looking. Rather, they often locate the horizons at the edge of patriarchal historical paradigms by making their vintage images purposefully as excessive, ironic and inventive as 'new' vintage products like billowing Vivien of Holloway[12] dresses. These discourses do not constitute a serious resistance to feminist politics in times of austerity, but instead are a proliferation of knowledges located outside the 'lines' posited by 'traditional values', and prizing historical mythopoeia: the hopeful narrative that we have indeed been here before, have survived and will survive again, in *different* ways. Where this mythopoeia is feminist in aim or function (or both), it constructs a feminist literacy that is especially necessary in times of austerity: one that looks backwards in time to find or create ways of living, working and thinking that sustained previous generations, but which can combine comfortably with the gains of modern women's movements. Byatt's *Ragnarok* proposes ways of reading nostalgias that allow its adherents to place themselves imaginatively in versions of the past while utilising feminism's critical modes; there, moreover, they are never completely outside the present moment in which feminist politics are available to them in every aspect of life.

Notes

1 My work in this chapter follows Bramall's thorough examinations of the relationships between 'austerity' and popular culture in her article 'Popular Culture and Anti-Austerity Protest' (2013a) and her book *The Cultural Politics of Austerity: Past and Present in Austere Times* (2013b). Several chapter headings in Bramall's book indicate our shared concerns and consideration of similar phenomena (such as vintage culture and its adherents), for instance 'The Past in the Present: History, Memory, Ideology, and Discourse' and 'Turning Back Time: Feminism, Domesticity, and Austere Femininities'. Bramall analyses current meanings of the historical 'austerity Britain' and the appeal of the 'material and affective attributes' of discourses of austerity (2013a, p. 8), such as consumer culture, whereas I pursue the narrative aspects of this relationship of the past to the present through A. S. Byatt's appropriation of historical accounts' mythic qualities. Bramall's book is especially useful for its very detailed and illuminating review in Chapter 6 of feminist perspectives on the 'housewife' figure (2013b, pp. 111–136).

2 The edition of *The Fifties Mystique* referenced here is the 2013 electronic version, read on a Kindle device.

3 See The Glamorous Housewife's 'About' section: <http://theglamoroushousewife.com/about/>.

4 See the post titled 'Can You be Feminine and a Feminist?', 10 December 2012, at The Glamorous Housewife: <http://theglamoroushousewife.com/2012/12/can-you-be-feminine-and-a-feminist/>.

5 See The Retro Housewife's 'About The Retro Housewife' section: <http://theretrohousewifelife.com/about/>.

6 'Rockabilly' refers to 'early American pop music that originated in the American South in the 1950s; it combined elements of country music with rock and roll' and was 'typified by Elvis Presley's recordings in 1954–1955 for Sun Records' (Gloag, 2015, n.p.). Currently, the term is more likely to refer to the 1950s-style,

nostalgic aesthetic in dress, cosmetics and décor which draws on American imagery.

7 See The Vintage Housewife (2013): <http://myquestfordomesticity.blogspot.co.uk/p/intro-to-this-project.html>.

8 See the post titled 'New Year, New Project' at The Vintage Housewife: <http://myquestfordomesticity.blogspot.co.uk/2013/01/new-year-new-project.html>.

9 A transcript of David Cameron's full speech can be accessed here: <http://www.theguardian.com/politics/2009/oct/08/david-cameron-speech-in-full>

10 See the website of the successful clothing and homeware retailer Cath Kidston, for examples of how popular nostalgia can inform design, if not politics: <http://www.cathkidston.com>.

11 'Upcycling' is used here in the context of second-hand clothing, particularly previous decades' fashions, which shoppers purchase in vintage shops and in-corporate into new 'looks' (sometimes altering them by hand). British television presenter Dawn O'Porter nurtured this trend in her 2014 Channel 4 pro-gramme *This Old Thing: The Vintage Clothes Show*, in which she advised guests and viewers on choosing vintage clothes, and also on sewing and alterations. O'Porter published a tie-in book on the subject, *This Old Thing: Fall in Love with Vintage Clothes* (2014). O'Porter's series and book, combining a thrifty ethos with an injunction to spend (money and time) but spend wisely, engaged with an established trend exemplified by public figures such as Kirstie Allsopp, the author and presenter of a number of vintage and 'handmade'-themed books and programmes of recent years.

12 The British nostalgic clothing retailer, Vivien of Holloway, offers creative 1940s and 1950s facsimiles: <http://www.vivienofholloway.com>.

Bibliography

Baldick, Chris. (2008). *The Oxford Dictionary of Literary Terms*. Oxford: Oxford University Press. Available from: <http://www.oxfordreference.com> [Accessed: 16 December 2014].

Bramall, Rebecca. (2013a) 'Popular Culture and Anti-austerity Protest.' *Journal of European Popular Culture*, 3 (1), pp. 9–22.

—— (2013b) *The Cultural Politics of Austerity: Past and Present in Austere Times*. Palgrave Macmillan Memory Studies. Basingstoke: Palgrave Macmillan.

Brightwell, Laura. (2012). 'Is "Cupcake Feminism" all Empty Calories?' *The F Word: Contemporary UK Feminism*, 10 August. Available from: <http://www.thefword.org.uk/features/2012/08/cupcake_feminis> [Accessed: 12 February 2015].

Butler, Judith. (1990). *Gender Trouble*. 2nd edition. Abingdon, UK: Routledge.

—— (2004). 'Imitation and Gender Insubordination'. In: S. Salih and J. Butler (eds) *The Judith Butler Reader*. Malden, MA: Blackwell Publishing.

Byatt, A. S. (1978). *The Virgin in the Garden*. 3rd edition. London: Vintage.

—— (1990). *Possession: A Romance*. 2nd edition. London: Vintage.

—— (1994). 'The Story of the Eldest Princess'. In: A. S. Byatt, *The Djinn in the Nightingale's Eye*. 2nd edition. London: Vintage.

—— (2009). *The Children's Book*. London: Chatto and Windus.

—— (2011). *Ragnarok: The End of the Gods*. Edinburgh: Canongate.

Byatt, A. S., and Frosh, Stephen. (2004). 'Conversation between A. S. Byatt and Stephen Frosh'. *Psychology and Psychotherapy: Theory, Research and Practice*, 77 (2), pp. 145–159.

Cameron, David. (2009). 'Tory Spring Conference Speeches in Full'. Politics.co.uk. Available from: <http://www.politics.co.uk/comment-analysis/2009/04/27/tory-spring-conference-speeches-in-full> [Accessed: 12 February 2015].

Coupe, Laurence. (1997). *Myth*. London: Routledge.

Davidson, Tonya. (2014). 'Dishing Out Domestic Nostalgia'. *Herizons*, Fall, pp. 24–27.

Friedan, Betty. (1963). *The Feminine Mystique*. New edition, 2010. London: Penguin.

The Glamorous Housewife. Available from: <http://www.theglamoroushousewife.com> [Accessed: 12 February 2015].

Gloag, K. 'Rockabilly'. In: Alison Latham (ed.) *The Oxford Companion to Music*. Oxford Music Online. Available from: <http://www.oxfordmusiconline.com> [Accessed: 12 February 2015].

Lyotard, Jean-François. (1984). *The Postmodern Condition: A Report on Knowledge*. Translated by G. Bennington and B. Massumi. Manchester: Manchester University Press.

Mann, Jessica. (2012). *The Fifties Mystique*. Digital edition, 2013. St Clement, Cornwall: Summaries and Plain Digits. Available from: <http://www.amazon.co.uk/The-Fifties-Mystique-Jessica-Mann-ebook/dp/B00CKCC27U/ref=sr_1_1?s=digitaltext&ie=UTF8&qid=1386752168&sr=1-1&keywords=the+fifties+mystique> [Accessed: 12 February 2015].

Miller, Lisa. (2013). 'The Retro Wife: Feminists Who Say They're Having It All – by Choosing to Stay at Home'. *New York Magazine*. Available from: <http://nymag.com/news/features/retro-wife-2013-3/index2.html> [Accessed: 12 February 2015].

O'Porter, Dawn. (2014). *This Old Thing: Fall in Love with Vintage Clothes*. London: Hot Key Books.

—— (2014). *This Old Thing: The Vintage Clothes Show*. Channel 4.

Oxford English Dictionary, 3rd edition. 2015. 'Myth'. Available from: <http://www.oed.com/> [Accessed 12 February 2015].

The Retro Housewife Life. Available from: <http://theretrohousewifelife.com/> [Accessed: 12 February 2015].

Rubenstein, Roberta. (2001). *Home Matters: Longing and Belonging, Nostalgia and Mourning in Women's Fiction*. Basingstoke: Palgrave Macmillan.

Tredell, Nicholas. (1994). 'A. S. Byatt'. In: *Conversations with Critics*. Manchester: Carcanet Press.

The Vintage Housewife. (2008). Available from: <http://thevintagehousewife. blogspot.co.uk> [Accessed: 12 February 2015].

The Vintage Housewife. (2013). Available from: <http://myquestfordomesticity. blogspot.co.uk/> [Accessed: 12 February 2015].

Vivien of Holloway. Available from: <http://www.vivienofholloway.com> [Accessed: 12 February 2015].

The Wartime Housewife. Available from: <http://www.wartimehousewife.com> [Accessed: 12 February 2015].

4

'Thatcher's Bloody Britain!': Unemployment and Gender in Neoliberal Britain in *The Young Ones* and *Men Behaving Badly*

Lauren Pikó and Evan Smith

Even as the goal of full employment was reluctantly conceded by 1970s Labour governments, it was only in the 1980s – under Margaret Thatcher's Conservative government – that unemployment was reconfigured as an inevitable – even, ironically, a desirable – aspect of a thriving, post-industrial British economy. This radical change in government policy was not merely a shift in political direction but was accompanied by a transformation in cultural values around the role of work and unemployment. Through an examination of the ways that popular English television programmes from the 1980s and 1990s reflected and constructed ideas of unemployment as inevitable (and almost desirable), this chapter will explore the evolving acceptance and normalisation of unemployment on British television between 1979 and 1997, the Thatcher to John Major years.

Focusing on two specific popular British comedy programmes, *The Young Ones* (1982–1984) and *Men Behaving Badly* (1992–1998), we trace how attitudes towards work and unemployment shifted from the early years of Thatcherism to the Major years, moving from something undesirable and controversial with the electorate to something unavoidable and necessary in order to keep other parts of the economy afloat, such as inflation rates. In *The Young Ones*, the high unemployment of Britain in the 1980s is portrayed as a political disaster and a symptom of a country on the brink of collapse. For the students of Scumbag College, the future looks bleak, with the only jobs available for Rick (Rik Mayall), Vyvyan (Adrian Edmondson), Neil (Nigel Planer) and Mike the Cool Person (Christopher Ryan) being in the police or the army. Similarly, *Men Behaving Badly* is situated in the era when the students of the 1980s have become adults. Now in their mid-thirties, they are stuck at the lower end of the social mobility ladder supposedly offered by Thatcher's 'popular capitalism'. Under John Major's Conservative government (November 1990–May 1997) which succeeded Thatcher's reign, the socio-economic situation stagnated after the 80s, with the limited economic 'choices' on offer being only dead-end middle management desk jobs as occupied by Gary (Martin Clunes), or unemployment, shown to be a sheltered yet pleasant experience for Tony (Neil Morrissey), but depressing and threatening for Deborah (Leslie Ash).

By tracing representations of young male unemployment from Thatcher's election in 1979 through to the 1990s, we see the depiction of unemployment increasing as a cultural norm on British television to become a newly acceptable feature of the economic and social landscape. Yet in *Men Behaving Badly*, the neutralised and carefree male experience of unemployment is haunted by Deborah's darker, more threatening experience. Through the portrayal of gender and unemployment in these British comedy programmes, we see a retreat from outright political resistance to the individualism of the lounge room; in other words, the depoliticisation and neutralisation of unemployment. Via this longer historical lens and emphasis on cultural construction, these programmes reveal the normative anchors that underpin the gradual political acceptance of radical policy changes instigated by the Thatcher government.

Work under Thatcher

One of the lasting legacies of the Thatcher governments was a fundamental shift in how Britons work. Government policy from 1945 to 1979 was marked by bipartisan support for 'full' employment and an assumption that this was a viable economic target which would ensure utmost productivity and international competitiveness. In practice, this meant that governments regulated in favour of supporting existing economic patterns such as majority full-time employment provision, a national economic emphasis on manufacturing and heavy industries, and ensuring stable and continuous patterns of job provision. The Thatcher government was elected in 1979 on a policy platform which constructed the economic crises of that year as a 'Winter of Discontent', wherein the failings of the existing economic order had enabled over-powerful trades unions to hold the Callaghan government to ransom on wage claims (Tomlinson, 2000, p. 49). Throughout the subsequent Thatcher governments, this almost apocalyptic narrative of state crisis was repeatedly deployed to justify drastic changes to state economic policy in favour of neoliberal and monetarist ideologies. Cuts to state welfare provision and increasingly confrontational industrial relations policies were central to this process. Part of the intended effect of these changes was to alter cultural expectations and practices around employment, with unemployment now presented in monetarist terms as a necessary condition of a competitive marketplace, and with casual, part-time and insecure work becoming more widespread.

Under this new economic regime, the ideal of full employment was dismissed as a form of interventionist socialism, while substantial policy deregulation opened up the British economy to an especially drastic transition to post-industrialism. This process was not only celebrated by Thatcher governments but was specifically leveraged to weaken organised labour while creating conditions more favourable to globalise financial capitalism. While Harold Wilson's Labour government (1964–1970) had championed the idea of a post-industrial Britain, this had been part of a wider technocratic enthusiasm for the 'scientific revolution' (Wilson, 1964, p. 14), and was in tension with the party's avowed support for domestic heavy industry. Under the Conservatives from 1979, however, post-industrialism helped facilitate an already ideologically desirable shift away from a heavy-industrial economic base, while framing the resistant remnants of that base as 'the enemy within' (Haviland, 1984, p. 1). This divide-and-rule approach exacerbated wider global economic shifts and effectively devastated the local economies of Britain's industrial regions in a short space of time (Evans, 2013, p. 33).

The human cost of these policies was compounded further by the use of monetarism to cut inflation during the government's first term. This contributed to a sharp rise in unemployment, which peaked at 3.2 million in 1985 (Evans, 2013, p. 47). The introduction of policies which exacerbated unemployment levels at the same time as deregulating the private sector and decreasing state support for individuals contributed to a situation where millions became unemployed, wages for those in work stagnated in comparison with corporate profits, and formerly unionised heavy industries went into terminal decline, from which parts of the country have never recovered.

Into this climate *The Young Ones* was broadcast; it first appeared on BBC television in late 1982. At this time, Britain had experienced two monetarist budgets by the Chancellor Geoffrey Howe and the ramifications of the Medium Term Financial Strategy (MTFS) which had been unveiled in the 1980 budget. This economic and industrial agenda resulted in a far-reaching steel strike in January 1980, riots across Britain in the summer of 1981, the launch of the 'People's March for Jobs' campaign and a revolt of 'the wets' (those who opposed Thatcher's monetarist policies) within the Conservative Party. However, the greatest material, social and cultural effect that Thatcher's early monetarist policies had on Britain was the rapid rise in unemployment.

'Unemployment haunted British culture in the early 1980s', wrote Richard Vinen (2010, p. 125), something which is evident in *The Young Ones*. The Conservatives had campaigned successfully in 1979 on the high level of unemployment under Labour (1,299,300 in May 1979), but the figures increased significantly under Thatcher during her first term in office, so that by January 1982, it had reached 3 million (Levitas, 2005, p. 44). Remaining high until 1986, an elevated level of unemployment was seen as a necessary evil and the price to be paid for curbing inflation by the Thatcher government. In her autobiography, Thatcher herself wrote about this:

> Other ministers [...] believed that unemployment over three million – the figure now predicted – was politically unacceptable [...]. My own analysis was entirely different: the way to achieve recovery was to ensure that a smaller proportion of the nation's income went to government, freeing resources for the private sector where the majority of people worked.
>
> (Thatcher, 1993, p. 148)

While unemployment reached high levels nationwide, it was especially damaging for ethnic minorities, women and young people, with unemployment for those under the age of 24 rising to 1.2 million in 1981 (Stewart, 2013, pp. 85–86). *The Young Ones* was very much aimed at this demographic and it portrayed the limited choices facing British youths in the early 1980s, with unemployment referred to continuously throughout.

The Young Ones and Unemployment in the Early 1980s

Janine Utell has written that *The Young Ones* 'challenge[d] the hegemony of Thatcherism', using laughter to highlight the 'profound ruptures and transformations in society' under Margaret Thatcher's Prime Ministership (Utell, 2009, pp. 152–53). *The Young Ones* debuted on the BBC in November 1982, but it developed from the evolution of the 'alternative comedy' scene that emerged in the late 1970s and gained momentum in the early 1980s.[1] The 'alternative comedy' scene emerged as a reaction to the leading styles of comedy that existed in Britain in the 1970s largely characterised by racist and sexist comedians who had toured the country's working men's clubs, as well as the Oxbridge-educated and middle-class sitcoms that dominated British broadcasting at the time. The idea for *The Young Ones* came from Rik Mayall – a graduate of Manchester University, alongside Edmondson and co-writer Ben Elton – who imagined a traditional sitcom scenario (four students sharing a flat) injected with political edge, slapstick violence and surrealism. Within this dynamic, *The Young Ones* offered insights into how the seismic shifts already discussed were popularly perceived while parodied from the 'margins of society'.

In *The Young Ones*, the issue of unemployment is referred to in several episodes. In the episode 'Demolition', the 'yoof' TV programme *Nozin' Around* includes a segment on unemployment. The female presenter Maggie explains it this way:

> more young adults are becoming unemployed on account of they can't find work! Basically, the problem is this: if you haven't got a job, then you outta work! And that means only one thing – unemployment.

> ('Demolition', series one, episode one)

This simplistic reduction of unemployment to being 'outta work' resembles the cynical thinking of the Conservatives that viewed it as unrelated to underlying structural issues, such as the shrinking economy or the effect of monetarist policies. Rather, it was depicted as a naturally occurring phenomenon, which chiefly afflicted the unmotivated, while those who looked for work would be rewarded for their efforts. This sentiment drove Norman Tebbit's comment at the 1981 Conservative Party conference that during the Depression his father had not rioted due to unemployment, but rather '[h]e got on his bike and looked for work' (Haviland, 1981, p. 1). Both Jones (2012) and Tyler (2013) have shown how under Thatcher employment was transformed into a measure of a person's worthiness and moral standing, and that those who were unemployed were seen as abject entities readily discarded by the state.

Unemployment and the search for work is the main focus of the episode 'Cash', when the group decide unilaterally that Neil must get a job. After looking through the 'situations vacant' section of the newspaper, it emerges that the *only* job advert is for the Army. The advert says:

> JOIN THE PROFESHIONELS, IT'S GREAT! YOU CAN HAVE
> A GUN IF YOU WANT! AND THERE'S MONEY IN IT (NOT
> THE GUN). H.M. ARMED FORCES.
>
> ('Cash', series two, episode two)

This (deliberately misspelled) advert is a parody of the advertising campaign of 'Join the Professionals' by the UK armed forces in the late 1970s–early 1980s, which sought to attract significantly more recruits to the Army. In reality, the campaign attempted to emphasise 'more of the distinctive professional volunteer ethos in a similar way to the pre-First World War Army' (Lamonte, 2010, p. 33), but when depicted in *The Young Ones*, the campaign reduces it to the seemingly important things for young unemployed men in the 1980s – money and the chance to fulfil a typical boyhood fantasy of using a weaponised gun. The parody advert in the show satirises the appeal to this fantasy, but the actual campaign was also criticised by the UK armed forces for its 'Hollywood' approach (Chappell, 2005, p. 9).

'Cash' emphasises the dire economic situation of the time and the lack of suitable employment for many youth. The Army and the police were state institutions that did not experience the same spending decreases as other government agencies under Thatcher.[2] Traditionally these professions were avenues for jobseekers with few qualifications and/or limited experience, so were seen as an option for the young within the unemployed population.

Importantly, employment in the Army and the police were also considered masculine and socially acceptable expressions of state power within the new neoliberal landscape. As deindustrialisation and unemployment swept through the north of England (and Scotland and Wales), the notion that unemployment was causing a 'crisis of masculinity' was widespread with the effect that the traditional identity of the British working class man was being eroded (Bruegel, 2000, p. 79). Since the end of the World War II, manufacturing (and similar industrial jobs) were seen to offer 'viable if restricted options for working-class males' and, as Nayak indicates, '[h]owever arduous these jobs were, they were seen to provide stability, lifelong labour, masculine camaraderie, and a pride in either "craft" or "graft"' (2003, p. 7). In the 1980s (*and* throughout the 1990s), deindustrialisation removed the economic importance of many men who had been employed in a skilled, manual labour capacity and, for many, deindustrialisation also removed a sense of identity and notions of 'manhood'. As Gibson-Graham says of the similar depiction of unemployed steelworkers in the award-winning film *The Full Monty* (1997), 'Not merely unemployed, the men are impotent and politically immobilized' (1999, p. 63).

Although the students in *The Young Ones* and the older unemployed men in *The Full Monty* represent just two sections of British society considered marginal within the new neoliberal political/economic framework, the students of Scumbag College *resisted* the status quo by avoiding submission to the dominant gender paradigms of the time. While employment in the police and the armed forces *were* refuges for men whose traditional employment options were cut off by the changing economic landscape, entrance into these hyper-masculine vocations required conformity to their practices; deviation was generally not tolerated. This notion is explicitly satirised in 'Cash' when Neil is pushed into trying to join the armed forces. After getting his long hippy-ish hair (half) cut by Vyvyan and donning an ill-fitting suit grudgingly rented from Mike, Neil – on his way to enlist – is told by Vyvyan's hamster, Special Patrol Group, 'Don't tell them you're a pacifist' ('Cash', series two, episode two). After being pushed through the doors of the Army Careers Information Office by the other three, Neil is then forcibly thrown out and onto the pavement (and into a line of 'normal' young men looking to enter the office), remarking, 'I only said I was a pacifist!' ('Cash', series two, episode two). Following rejection by the Army, Rick then spots a recruitment poster at the front of a local Metropolitan Police station that says 'We take absolutely everyone', and so the group pushes Neil into the building. Here, Neil is welcomed by the comedian Alexei Sayle who is dressed as Benito Mussolini (parodying the left-wing concept of the police as 'fascist' [Smith 2014]). Despite informing him that he did not think he was 'correctly job motivated' to join the police, Neil is told that the only thing you need to know how to do to become a police officer is go 'CCCCHHHH' (the sound of static over a police radio) ('Cash', series two, episode two).

With a lack of new manual labour roles being created across the 1980s and 1990s and a large number of job losses in manufacturing in the 1980s, academic qualifications were seen as a path to more stable employment (Bruegel, 2000, p. 88). But even if you had a qualification, finding a job in the 1980s remained difficult, something demonstrated in the episode 'Summer Holiday', also the final episode of the series. Here, Rick, Vyvyan, Mike and Neil find themselves homeless, living on the streets, and Rick blames Thatcher directly for this:

> Thatcher's Britain. Thatcher's bloody Britain! Look at me. I'm young, I'm pretty. I've got 5 O Levels. Bloomin' good grades as well, considering I didn't do a sod of work cause I'm so hard. And look at me now! Homeless, cold, and prostitute.
>
> ('Summer Holiday', series two, episode six)[3]

Rick's words highlight the precarious position that young people started to find themselves in under Thatcher's government, particularly as the high level of unemployment increased in conjunction with a squeeze on available and affordable housing, the effect of which was a sharp rise in the number of youth on the streets of British cities, especially London. In 1980, the Thatcher government introduced the Housing Act, which allowed councils across the country to sell off much of their existing housing under the so-called 'right to buy' scheme,[4] but as Richard Vinen has noted, while more than a million council homes were sold in the 1980s, only around a sixth were bought by their tenants, with most being bought as investments (Vinen, 2010, pp. 202–203). This policy exposed many lower-class Britons, especially young people, to crooked landlordism and exploitative rent increases, and combined with high youth unemployment, a greater number of British youth were made homeless in the early 1980s as a result.

The Young Ones ends with the four young men attempting to escape their current destitute situation through crime. After successfully robbing a bank and escaping on a double-decker bus, Rick is more optimistic about the future and looks to throw off the shackles of Thatcherism:

> Who needs qualifications? Who cares about Thatcher and unemployment?! We can do just exactly whatever we want to do! And you know why? Because we're Young Ones. Bachelor boys! Crazy, mad, wild-eyed, big-bottomed anarchists!
>
> ('Summer Holiday', series two, episode six)

The four of them sing Cliff Richard's popular hit 'Summer Holiday' (a song that celebrates taking time off work), even though they are all homeless, unemployed and, effectively, on the run. In the concluding scene – also the last of the series – Rick's optimism turns out to be short-lived as Neil drives the bus through a billboard plastered with a Cliff Richard poster and then off an actual cliff a few seconds later. This final symbolic moment, which marks the death of the young ones, functions as a heavy-handed message which suggests that the only way out of the miseries of Thatcherism and unemployment were crime or death.

Portrayals of Women in *The Young Ones*

Considering gendered experiences of unemployment in 1980s Britain, Beatrix Campbell asserted that 'women are the poorest of all' (Campbell, 1984, p. 57). Although the period follows the momentous gains of the 1970s and the second wave of feminism, women largely remained victims in both the private and public spheres – facing exploitation or unemployment in the workplace while still being the major contributor to uncompensated domestic work in the household. Yet, for all its radical critique, *The Young Ones* was male focused in its treatment of gender and unemployment, and hardly considered how Thatcherism affected women. This not only reflects the masculine focus of the alternative comedy subculture at the time, but also a wider shift in how progressive movements in Britain viewed women and women's liberation. By the 1980s, the women's liberation movement of the 1960s and 1970s had splintered into many different guises. Some forms of feminism in the 1980s were derided in otherwise progressive or radical circles as 'middle class', 'bourgeois' or 'identity politics', and thus feminism was, in many instances, effectively ignored as a side issue (Weir and Wilson, 1984, pp. 74–103; Bruley, 2014, pp. 155–172).

Such attitudes towards women by ostensibly 'progressive' men are evident in *The Young Ones*, particularly in the show's narratives and the limited number of characters played by women in the series. The lip-service paid to feminism is also apparent in the micro politics of numerous scenes and particularly when Rick the student lefty 'right on' stereotype, tries to emphasise his anti-sexist credentials in front of the group. In the episode 'Bambi' (series one, episode one), for example, when Rick, Vyvyan and Mike are discussing why a woman named Mary does not go to parties and Vyvyan describes her as 'the one with the enormous tits', Rick tells him off for 'being so sexist'. On the surface this seems like a feminist critique of sexism, but Rick's calling out of Vyvyan is undermined by the facetiousness of the following exchange:

RICK: They're called breasts, and everybody has them.
VYVYAN: Well, I don't.
RICK: Yes, and nor did Adolf Hitler!

('Bambi', series one, episode one)

Vyvyan then describes Mary as 'Ol' Yellow Pages',[5] and Rick, in his usual sanctimonious 'right on' manner, says 'I believe some of the more politically unsound members of the University call her that'. But, once Vyvyan explains to Mike how Mary gained her nickname, Rick relishes gossiping about her anyway, snivelling 'Anyway, Mary decided not to go to the party, for the obvious reason' ('Bambi', series one, episode one). Here, Rick admonishes Vyvyan for his use of sexist language, but then contradicts his 'feminist' perspective by indulging in gossip about women's sexual activities. This highlights that while many 'progressive men' made an effort to publicly make pro-feminist statements and pay lip-service to the notion of treating men and women equally, the same men often fell back into traditional sexist habits and judged women on their sexual behaviour, a double standard they rarely applied to (other) men.

The difference in attitudes towards the sexual behaviour of men and women can also be seen in the episode 'Time' (1984), when Rick pretends that he has slept with a woman who he finds in his bed one morning. Even though he brags about this non-existent conquest, he tries to balance male bravado with a superficial non-sexist attitude:

NEIL: You mean, you, like, scored with a chick?

RICK: Well, of course, I wouldn't put it in such sexist terms, Neil, but yes
[...]
Even when I'm unconscious, I can pick up the birds. I mean, forge meaningful relationships with birds ... chicks ... tarts ... women. Women!

('Time', series two, episode four)

Here, Rick tries to resist lapsing into sexist language, but it is only with the last lines of the exchange that his anti-sexist attitudes are foregrounded as a façade, reverting back to traditional sexist language of the young male under peer pressure.

'Time' further shows that even for 'progressive' men, sexual conquest has often been seen as a testament to their masculinity. After the woman, Helen Mucus, reveals that Rick did not, in fact, sleep with her, Vyvyan describes Rick as a 'girly virgin' and proceeds to violently berate Rick for this ('Time', series two, episode four). Indeed, throughout the series, the term 'girly' is used frequently as an insult between the male students. However, the episode 'Nasty' (series two, episode three) also features a scene where sexual conquest is seen as *the* defining quality of manliness. Fearing being bitten by a South African vampire (actually an enterprising electronics salesperson played by Sayle), Vyvyan announces that vampires only attack virgins and that if anyone does get bitten, then everyone will know that they are a 'sissy virgin'.[6] Each of the group, even when facing death, seeks to maintain their 'manly' façade by declaring that they are not virgins. Mike, who passes himself as a 'ladies' man' throughout the series, is put under pressure here; he is shown to be *as* scared as the rest of his housemates about their virginity being revealed, but he confronts the issue directly saying 'OK, guys! There's only one way out! We've all got to lose our virginity!' ('Nasty', series two, episode three). However, the young men are ultimately saved from revealing their seeming emasculation as virgins as well as from having to lose their virginity to each other when the sun comes up and the vampire is killed.

For the most part, women were alien to the male world that the group occupied. This is obvious in 'Time' when the presence of a strange woman in the student house causes the students to act manically as they each try to impress her in their own strange ways: Rick dances to monks chanting on the radio, Vyvyan does push-ups, Neil loses the ability to speak properly, and Mike jokes about Helen taking off her clothes. But another example of the 'foreignness' of women to the group can be seen in the episode 'Interesting' (series one, episode five) when Rick goes through a party guest's handbag and thinks that a tampon is a toy mouse, which he proceeds to dip in the woman's drink, while the rest of the party look on disgusted. Significantly, then, the presence of women further infantilises the men, whose experiences of unemployment and economic precarity have already placed them outside traditional male adult economically functional roles.

Although many famous female comedians and actresses appear in *The Young Ones* – including Jennifer Saunders, Dawn French, Helen Atkinson-Wood and Emma Thompson –the roles they play within the show are small. *The Young Ones* was, effectively, a male-orientated show and reflected the concerns of young men as Britain underwent significant economic, political and social change. It shows that even for men who viewed themselves as 'progressive', women continued to be objectified as sexual 'things' and as something to measure one's status and masculinity by, particularly when other factors, such as employment, were no longer available. Through keeping this primary focus on men's experiences, *The Young Ones* satirises the emotional immaturity of its characters while implicitly linking this to their regressive leisured experience of unemployment. The main characters are both satirised and celebrated for existing outside traditional economic roles, and for the way in which this experience confuses their relationship to conventional masculinity.

Men Behaving Badly, Work and Unemployment

By the time of the Major and Blair governments in the 1990s, the abandonment of full employment policy was complete and substantial unemployment rates were now accepted as a feature of the political landscape. As Hugo Young writes, 'How to stop worrying and live with unemployment was one of the principal lessons Thatcherism administered to the country, and it achieved a permanent social shift in the process' (1990, p. 534). By 1987, the Thatcher government's economic policies were more widely accepted and it was that year in which the government returned its largest electoral mandate, as well as a stock market crash following a brief inflationary boom. The ensuing recession officially lasted until 1992 and not only fed the increasing precariousness of a neoliberalised workforce, but destabilised the increasing numbers of lower- and middle-income mortgagees who had purchased homes under the Chancellor Nigel Lawson's drive to increase home-ownership.

In October 1990, the month before Thatcher's resignation, unemployment rose to 10.9 per cent from its November 1989 level of 7.7 per cent, rivalling the levels of the early 1980s (Campbell, 2009, p. 453). Unemployment reached another peak of 10.6 per cent (3 million) in the first quarter of 1993 (Jenkins, 2010, p. 35). While these figures slowly declined by 2004, and were far from celebrated, the political and media response to such fluctuations was distinctly more muted than had been the case when unemployment figures approached one million in the early 1970s (Turner, 2008, p. 103). It was into this environment that the BBC sitcom *Men Behaving Badly* rose to prominence. Based on his 1989 novel of the same name, Simon Nye's first television series premiered on ITV's London franchise Thames Television in 1992. The programme followed housemates Dermot (Harry Enfield) and Gary (Martin Clunes) as they negotiated contemporary sexual politics. Following Enfield's departure at the end of the first series, Neil Morrissey's character Tony was introduced as a more bohemian, carefree foil to Gary's reluctant embrace of traditional economic responsibilities. When the programme moved to BBC1 in 1994, it was given a post-watershed timeslot, allowing it greater scope to cover adult content. This pushed the programme to greater success and increased audience numbers.

As the programme become more popular from 1994 onwards, it began to engage substantively more with the binary gender dynamics with which it had experimented in series one. Despite Clunes' protestations that '[the show's] not about anything', plotlines repeatedly debated specific topics covering differing gender attitudes to pornography, monogamy, fitness, sex and financial responsibility (Abbott, 2013, n.p.). Through explicitly debating contemporary masculinity and femininity, *Men Behaving Badly* became understood in British media as typifying the rise of 'lad culture'. Peaking in popularity as a concept in the mid-1990s, 'laddism' was loosely understood as a juvenile, hyper-consumerist form of masculinity reacting against women's increased presence in public life, and usually attributed to working-class or newly affluent young males (Gill, 2003, p. 47).

Lads at Play? *Men Behaving Badly* and Unemployment

Despite its association with 'laddism', *Men Behaving Badly*'s central male characters are in their thirties and they locate themselves explicitly as outside mainstream youth culture. Emphasising 'laddism' as a descriptor for the show has tended to limit focus on its other main preoccupation: the relationship between employment and leisure, both forced and unforced. Within the limitations of its overtly cisgendered and heteronormative binary logic, *Men Behaving Badly* sets up the experience of work and unemployment as fundamentally informed by gender roles and expectations, but also as a space of real and pervasive anxieties and uncertainty.

During its most popular series, running story arcs focused on the differing experiences of unemployment experienced by Deborah and Tony, and the tensions between the tedium of enforced leisure and the unfulfilling nature of secure work. Tony's past work life is itinerant; in 'Rich and Fat' (series five, episode six), he announces that he has had 72 jobs since leaving school. When Tony's character is first introduced in series two, he runs a used record stand at a local market; by series three this business has 'collapsed', not due to the recession, as Deb suspects, but rather due to being quite literally knocked over by a strong gust of wind ('Bed', series three, episode two). Tony eventually gets a job as bartender at the local pub, but then he loses it only to successfully reapply, thus creating a pattern of recurring unemployment interspersed with spells of underemployment.

Tony makes a rare political comment about this experience during a brief stint volunteering with elderly people, suggesting they are 'both regarded by an uncaring world as an underclass' ('Infidelity', series four, episode two). He also attempts briefly to embrace a 'new age' money-free lifestyle before being laughed out of that choice by Dorothy. Yet further critiques of capitalism or of the precarious job market is precluded by Tony's generally enjoyable experience of unemployment as an extension of his leisure time. His time is spent mainly watching children's television and drinking on Gary's sofa (for example, 'Lovers', series three, episode one). His enjoyment of idly 'having a sit' during the day is thus ridiculed but nonetheless presented as luxurious and enjoyable ('Stag Night', series six, episode one). Tony's unemployment is portrayed as a perpetual state of child-like abandon, where his 'laddish' alcohol consumption and refusal of emotional adult responsibility are compounded by his gleeful enjoyment of lacking an adult economic social role.

Tony's emotional regression is a major target of satire in *Men Behaving Badly* yet this experience of unemployment is consistently presented as safe and even luxurious. Tony nominally pays rent for living in Gary's flat, however it is implied (heavily) that this rent is never paid. Indeed, Tony goes backpacking around Europe while unemployed, with no suggestion of how this trip is subsidised ('Hair', series five, episode one). It is constantly assumed that Gary will support Tony financially, meaning his unemployment never carries any implied risk to his future prosperity or relationships. This depiction of unemployment as essentially benign indicates men's unemployment could be represented as an apolitical concern of the private sphere, where the relinquishing of adult responsibility is both harmless and pleasurable. Significantly, Tony and Gary's supportive financial relationship is never feminised, but serves only to reinforce the masculine associations of their favoured forms of leisure: drinking, talking about women's bodies and watching television.

Despite this depiction of Tony's working life, *Men Behaving Badly* presented an alternative depiction of unemployment which hinted at the precariousness of Britain's post-recession recovery and its potential to damage individual lives. This was explored through Deborah (Deb), Tony's neighbour and love interest. After she loses her job as a restaurant manager in series three, Deb experiences a deep and lasting depression. She loses interest in her appearance, becomes anxious and withdrawn, and is wracked with uncertainty about her future, both financial and personal ('Bed'; 'Hair'). Deb is a homeowner, wondering how to pay her bills and her mortgage; she describes herself sitting endlessly on the couch worrying about finances and how to survive. These divergent experiences are frequently juxtaposed for comic effect:

> DEBORAH: I haven't worked for ages, I don't do anything all day, if it wasn't for worrying about bedsores I probably wouldn't get out of bed at all.
> TONY: Me too. Brilliant.
>
> ('Casualties', series three, episode three)

Deb's unemployment is a recurring theme from this point onwards and it is suggested that her bouts of depression, escapist obsessions with astrology and pursuit of unsuitable men are driven by these circumstances. The storyline is resolved through Deb's decision to start an undergraduate degree, though whether her psychology degree is intended as a career change is unclear ('Your Mate v Your Bird', series five, episode four). As Bruegel (2000, pp. 88–89) has described, increased access to university education helped drive women's increased participation in the workforce during the 1990s, though graduate female unemployment rates remained higher than those of men. *Men Behaving Badly* ended while Deb was still a student, and therefore never resolved the issue of how Deb returns to work. However, the silence on the issue of how Deb plans to use her degree – if at all – indicates that the tension surrounding Deb's employment status is not easily resolved.

Deb's position as a single female homeowner also exposes her to macroeconomic forces that Tony avoids. The notion of a 'property own-ing democracy' was central to numerous Conservative policies in the late 1980s in particular, with the effect of greatly increasing consumer debt through mortgage lending (Evans, 2013, p. 164). Deb's mortgage opens her up to increased financial instability, yet is presented as part of her more 'responsible' character. When Deb and Tony finally *do* form a relationship, she is consistently frustrated by his domestic irresponsibility which has been facilitated by Gary's ongoing subsidy.

While Tony's situation is uniquely insulated from economic instability and financial responsibility, Deb's experience indicates that far from being completely celebrated, unemployment can only be presented as 'true' leisure when it is privately subsidised. Unemployment in *Men Behaving Badly* is therefore incompletely normalised, with Tony's benign enjoyment haunted and offset by Deb's experience of loss, instability and genuine risk. The gendered dimensions of this experience of risk are profound; Tony's leisured, safe and irresponsible joblessness is contrasted explicitly with Deb's precarious and threatening experience of unemployment as a psychological as well as an economic burden. This problematises the depiction of unemployment to a much greater extent than in *The Young Ones*; alongside the pure satire of irresponsibility, *Men Behaving Badly* uses women's experience as a foil and contrast to more accurately depict the realities of Britain's increasingly precarious economy.

Lads at Work: Private Welfare, Silent State

Stable employment and financial security, however, are not presented as unproblematically desirable. While the leisure of both Tony and Gary is contingent on Gary's job security, his stable employment is not presented as fulfilling or inherently desirable. Gary's experience of a job-for-life is unique in the programme; he took an office junior position straight from school and has consistently been employed by the same security firm ever since, hoarding the majority of his pay, with his only significant expenditures being a home purchase and his excessive beer consumption. His employees, George and Anthea, are caricatures of harmless but tedious middle-aged people; they function as a constant reminder that Gary awaits their fate later in life. He endures his work life by offsetting the tedium of employment with beer and TV at the day's end; career climbing or career change are not options available to him, since work exists only to pay for his leisure. The stasis of this daily cycle is presented as inescapable and sedating, obscuring Gary's frustration while precluding any alternative to it.

Gary's unfulfilling work not only provides the capital which facilitates the main characters' leisure, but also Tony's 'privatised' welfare. Throughout the show, in both Deb and Tony's experiences of unemployment, the idea of state support of any kind is not mentioned or even hinted at for either

103

character. The only potential recipient of state support is the affluent, stably employed homeowner Gary, who sarcastically comments that his subsidy of Tony's unemployment makes him 'eligible for a grant from the council' ('Rich and Fat', series five, episode six). Not only is there no expectation of state assistance for the unemployed, Gary's private bankrolling of Tony's lifestyle is suggested as more deserving of reward, hinting at the 1990s growth of middle-class state support at the expense of traditional welfare.

The only other hint of state service provision in the show is through another female figure, Dorothy, and her job in nursing. While it is not confirmed that she works at a public hospital, Dorothy's interest in documentaries on the NHS and workplace fundraising hint at her possible employment by the state. In the episode 'Rich and Fat', Dorothy fundraises for operating tables. But rather than questioning why a hospital could not afford such basic equipment or why private subsidy by individuals is the appropriate response to this financial support, the episode uses this incident purely to represent Gary as miserly. As such, through Dorothy's work the state's under-resourcing of welfare provision becomes an acceptable given and responsibility for welfare is wholly individualised. In this context, then, it is unsurprising that Deb's experience of unemployment is so fundamentally distressing; without the safety net of a well-paid friend, she has nowhere to turn.

From the Alternative to 'No Alternative'

The portrayal of the silencing of the state and the redefinition of state involvement in welfare provision was central to the redefinition of political narratives through and after the 'crisis' of 1979 (Hay, 2010, p. 452). The significance of this for the 1990s is that despite Labour's unexpected political loss in the 1992 election, the Conservatives' ongoing electoral dominance was broken only when Labour reconfigured its policy base towards that of the Tories (Turner, 2013, p. 272). This rightward shift into 'New Labour' involved embracing market-friendly 'flexibility' by eroding workers' entitlements, the devolution of government responsibilities to the private sector, and acceptance of unemployment as a driver of economic growth (Hall, 2011, p. 717). It was from 1992 to 1997 in particular, then, that the process of the reconfiguration of the British state begun in 1979 was completed, with the final silencing of mainstream party opposition to the new configuration of state power. *Men Behaving Badly*'s explicit engagement with work and leisure as well as binary gendered relationships not only reflects but also replicates this process of redefinition by hiding the state's involvement and by privileging escapism, which the show presents as chiefly accessible to men, while women experience the brunt of the withdrawal of state support.

Unlike in the youthful homosocial world of *The Young Ones*, which explicitly opposed a new 'status quo', *Men Behaving Badly* positioned itself as reflecting the realities of 1990s life for men and women in their thirties. While *The Young Ones* wrote its characters out of society and culture by throwing them off a cliff, *Men Behaving Badly* leaves its male characters in perpetual stasis on the couch. At the same time, it posits an unhappy alternative in female characters that resist that deadening; they are no happier for seeking responsibilities and securities which are not available to them, and they too gravitate back to Gary's couch (more and more) as the series roll on. *The Young Ones* had grown from the prospects of an 'alternative' comedy scene; by the time of that *Men Behaving Badly* was broadcast, however, there seems to be no alternative. The show suggests that the best that can be achieved in life is temporary oblivion in front of the TV with a can of lager.

In this sense, the domestic framework of *Men Behaving Badly* demonstrates most fully the retreat from satirical structural critique which *The Young Ones* had modelled so consistently. During the period between the two programmes, unemployment moved from being understood as a political and collective structural problem, to a purely individual struggle. This individualism remained deeply gendered, with women shown to be more vulnerable and more deeply threatened by unemployment than men for whom unemployment can become a privately subsidised extension of leisure. Ultimately, however, for all, the rebellion and anger of *The Young Ones* was supplanted by sedentary consumerist escapism, and by an uneasy acceptance of the new precariousness of British economic life.

Notes

1 For more on this see Wilmut and Rosengard (1989), MacDonald (2002), and Peters (2013).
2 Between 1978/1979 and 1989/1990 there was a 62 per cent increase in public spending on police services in the UK, which paid for a 16 per cent increase in

police manpower and a 22 per cent increase in civilian personnel (Loveday, 1992, pp. 297–298).

3　It is interesting to note that Rick mixes up the words 'destitute' and 'prostitute' in this line, which is a throwaway joke for his male character, but it may also refer to the precariousness of homeless women at the same time, whereby prostitution is often a means of survival for many young destitute women.

4　The 'right to buy' scheme was introduced by the Housing Act 1980 which allowed tenants after three years to buy their house or flat from the local council, with a discounted sliding scale depending on the length of tenancy. Although if sold within five years, the owners would have to share their capital gains with the council, many of these houses fell into the hands of property developers and landlords rather than the aspirational working class.

5　The business telephone directory in the UK was called the Yellow Pages and in the 1980s had the slogan, 'let your fingers do the walking'.

6　It is also worth noting that homophobia was common in left politics at this time (see Robinson 2011) and terms like 'sissy' and 'poof' were used as insults in *The Young Ones*, revealing that progressiveness only went so far in the alternative comedy scene of the early 1980s.

Bibliography

Abbott, Kate. (2013). 'How We Made Men Behaving Badly'. *Guardian*, 19 March. Available from: <http://www.theguardian.com/tv-and-radio/2013/mar/18/how-we-made-men-behaving-badly> [Accessed: 3 December 2014].

Bruegel, Irene. (2000). 'No More Jobs for the Boys? Gender and Class in the Restructuring of the British Economy'. *Capital & Class*, 24/2, pp. 79–102.

Bruley, Sue. (2014). 'Jam Tomorrow? Socialist Women and Women's Liberation, 1968–1982: An Oral History Approach'. In: Evan Smith and Matthew Worley (eds) *Against the Grain: The British Far Left from 1956*. Manchester: Manchester University Press.

Campbell, Beatrix. (1984). *Wigan Pier Revisited: Poverty and Politics in the 80s*. London: Virago Books.

Campbell, John. (2009). *The Iron Lady: Margaret Thatcher, from Grocer's Daughter to Prime Minister*. London and New York: Penguin Books.

Chappell, Mike. (2005). *The British Army in the 1980s*. Oxford: Osprey Publishing.

Dennis, M. [Dir.] (1994). 'Lovers', *Men Behaving Badly*, series three, episode one, BBC1, 1 July.

—— (1994). 'Casualties', *Men Behaving Badly*, series three, episode three, BBC1, 15 July.

—— (1995). 'Infidelity', *Men Behaving Badly*, series four, episode two, BBC1, 1 June.

—— (1996). 'Hair', *Men Behaving Badly*, series five, episode one, BBC1, 20 June.

—— (1996). 'Your Mate v Your Bird', *Men Behaving Badly*, series five, episode four, BBC1, 11 April.

—— (1996). 'Rich and Fat', *Men Behaving Badly*, series five, episode six, BBC1, 25 July.

—— (1997). 'Stag Night', *Men Behaving Badly*, series six, episode one, BBC1, 6 November.

Evans, Eric J. (2013). *Thatcher and Thatcherism*. London: Routledge.

Gibson-Graham, J. (1999). 'Capitalism Goes the "Full Monty"'. *Rethinking Marxism* 11/2, pp. 62–66.

Gill, Rosalind. (2003). 'Power and the Production of Subjects: A Genealogy of the New Man and the New Lad'. *Sociological Review Monograph* 51, pp. 34–56.

Hall, Stuart. (2011). 'The Neoliberal Revolution'. *Cultural Studies*, 25/6, pp. 705–728.

Haviland, J. (1981). 'Thatcher Faces Growing Rift in Cabinet'. *The Times*, 16 October.

—— (1984) 'Thatcher Makes Falklands Link'. *The Times*, 20 July.

Hay, Colin. (2010). 'Chronicles of a Death Foretold: The Winter of Discontent and Construction of the Crisis of British Keynesianism'. *Parliamentary Affairs*, 63/3, pp. 446–470.

Jackson, P. [Dir.] (1982). 'Demolition', *The Young Ones*, series one, episode one, BBC2, 9 November.

—— (1982). 'Interesting', *The Young Ones*, series one, episode five, BBC2, 7 December.

—— (1984). 'Bambi', *The Young Ones*, series two, episode one, BBC2, 8 May.

—— (1984). 'Cash', *The Young Ones*, series two, episode two, BBC2, 15 May.

—— (1984). 'Nasty', *The Young Ones*, series two, episode three, BBC2, 29 May.

—— (1984). 'Time', *The Young Ones*, series two, episode four, BBC2, 5 June.

—— (1984). 'Summer Holiday', *The Young Ones*, series two, episode six, BBC2, 19 June.

Jenkins, Jamie. (2010). 'The Labour Market in the 1980s, 1990s and 2008/09 Recessions'. *Economic & Labour Market Review*, 4/8, pp. 29–36.

Jones, Owen. (2012). *Chavs: The Demonization of the Working Class*. London: Verso.

Lamonte, Jon. (2010). 'Attitudes in Britain Towards its Armed Forces and War 1960–2000'. Unpublished PhD thesis, University of Birmingham.

Levitas, Ruth. (2005). 'Fiddling while Britain Burns? The "Measurement" of Unemployment'. In: Ruth Levitas and Will Guy (eds) *Interpreting Official Statistics*. London and New York: Routledge.

Loveday, B. (1992). 'Right Agendas: Law and Order in England and Wales'. *International Journal of the Sociology of Law*, 20, pp. 297–319.

MacDonald, Charles. (2002). *That's Anarchy! The Story of a Revolution in the World of TV Comedy*. Hartwell, Vic: Temple House.

Nayak, Anoop. (2003). 'Last of the "Real Geordies"? White Masculinities and the Subcultural Response to Deindustrialisation'. *Environment and Planning D: Society and Space*, 21, pp. 7–25.

Peters, Lloyd. (2013). 'The Roots of Alternative Comedy? The Alternative Story of 20th Century Coyote and Eighties Comedy'. *Comedy Studies*, 4/1, pp. 5–21.

Robinson, Lucy. (2011). *Gay Men and the Left in Post-War Britain: How the Personal Got Political*. Manchester: Manchester University Press.

Singer, Peter. (1981). 'My First Principle is to Be Funny', *International*, 6/4, November, pp. 16–17.

Smith, Evan. (2014) ' "I Hope You're Satisfied Thatcher!": Capturing the Zeitgeist of 1980s Britain in *The Young Ones*', *Agora*, 49/4, pp. 14–22.

Stewart, Graham. (2013). *Bang! A History of Britain in the 1980s*. London: Atlantic Books.

Thatcher, Margaret. (1993). *The Downing Street Years, 1979–1990*. New York: Harper Perennial.

Tomlinson, Jim. (2000). *The Politics of Decline: Understanding Post-war Britain*. Harlow; New York: Longman.

Turner, Alwyn. (2008). *Crisis? What Crisis? Britain in the 1970s*. London: Aurum Press.

—— (2013). *A Classless Society: Britain in the 1990s*. London: Aurum Press.

Tyler, Imogen. (2013). *Revolting Subjects: Social Abjection and Resistance in Neoliberal Britain*. London: Zed Books.

Utell, Janine. (2009). 'Negotiating Dissent: The Adrian Mole Diaries and *The Young Ones*'. In: Ray B. Browne and Lawrence A. Kreiser, Jr (eds) *Popular Culture Values and the Arts: Essays on Elitisim Versus Democratization*. Jefferson, NC: McFarland & Company.

Vinen, Richard. (2010). *Thatcher's Britain: The Politics and Social Upheaval of the 1980s*. London: Pocket Books.

Weir, Angela, and Wilson, Elizabeth. (1984). 'The British Women's Movement'. *New Left Review*, 1/148, November–December, pp. 74–103.

Wilmut, Roger, and Rosengard, Peter. (1989). *Didn't You Kill My Mother-in-Law? The Story of Alternative Comedy in Britain from the Comedy Store to Saturday Live*. London: Methuen.

Wilson, Harold. (1964). *Purpose in Politics: Selected Speeches*. London: Weidenfeld & Nicolson.

Young, Hugo. (1990). *One of Us: A Biography of Margaret Thatcher*. London: Pan Books.

5

From Homebuyer Advisor to Angel of the Hearth: The Development of Kirstie Allsopp as the Female Face of Channel 4 'Squeezed Middle' Austerity Programming

Diane Charlesworth

This chapter looks at the space which has been opened up by austerity debates and discourse for the female voice as one of authority in British television. What has been written on the female television personality of UK broadcasting is both 'limited and sporadic' (Holmes, 2011, p. 33) (with the notable exceptions of Bennett, 2008 and 2010; Holmes, 2011; Woods, 2013).[1] As Bennett (2010) contended, in his historical analysis of UK televisual fame, television had the potential to provide considerable space for female performers, given its development as a domestic technology and the possibilities it has to address women as audiences. In reality, the longevity required front-of-camera for audience resonance and professional authority, in the case of factual forms (more than fictional), has been problematic for women working in the industry across the years, in comparison to their male counterparts, and hotly debated in recent times (Jermyn, 2013). Nevertheless, as Bramall notes:

> In the current conjuncture, the 'work' of austerity – of making, saving, digging, mending, and being resourceful and 'thrifty' – can be regarded as useful and appropriate. Significantly, these

> are activities that are understood to be located in the home, in the sphere of domesticity. Through [...] the reiterated association of these practices with qualities conventionally associated with femininity (such as patience, care, altruism and the ability to be organized and to multitask), this work gets coded as work for women.
>
> (Bramall, 2013, p. 112)

From the down-to-earth, back-to-basics business sense of Mary Portas and her attempts to revive the fortunes of small businesses and the local high street in *Mary, Queen of the High Street* (Channel 4, 2013) to domestic financial advice and household management in the form of the Women's Institute matronly persona of Mrs Moneypenny for Channel 4's *Superscrimpers* (Channel 4, 2011–present), female voices and performances have been marshalled during the recession to organise local and domestic space on the television screen. In particular, the UK broadcaster Channel 4 has played a key role in this process, driven by its need to develop its presence as a commercial public service broadcaster in a shifting television ecology in the digital age. Its austerity programming fits into a longer tradition of re-negotiating the concept of 'public service'. This re-negotiation, across the stewardships of four different Chief Executives (CEs), arguably started as far back as the beginning of the millennium, as competition for television advertising and funding sharpened. Until the end of Andy Duncan's tenure in November 2009, an argument was being made for the contestability of the licence fee as part of the channel's future funding.[2] This saw the development of a strand of 'state-of-the-nation' programming appearing in the early 2000s schedules, establishing a stable of cultural intermediaries (Philips, 2005) offering advice on developing better selves for a better society: the neo-liberal citizen (Ouellette and Hay, 2008). This included, notably, the transformation of Jamie Oliver from 'mockney'-lad chef into paternal moral entrepreneur with his campaign documentaries from *Jamie's Kitchen* (2002) through to *Jamie's Dream School* (2011).[3] Criticism of industrial food production and debates about sustainability were articulated through a repertoire of masculinities personified by Oliver, Heston Blumenthal, Gordon Ramsay and Hugh Fearnley-Whittingstall in a season of documentaries broadcast in 2008 and 2009 under the title *The British Food Fight*. Again, at the end of 2011 and into 2012, a set of programmes under the title *The Great British Property Scandal* was broadcast. These involved a different cast of male presenters, architect George Clark presenting two documentaries, one highlighting the housing shortage crisis in Britain and calling for a National Low Cost Loan fund and the second discussing the amount of unoccupied housing stock. A further two-part documentary/challenge programme with presenter-designer Kevin McCloud called *Kevin's Grand Design* aimed to disprove the building industry's claims that affordable and sustainable housing is not profitable.

This chapter, however, looks at one of Channel 4's key female television personalities, Kirstie Allsopp, visible to audiences since 2000 as part of the UK reality television boom. Given her family background, as the daughter of the 6th Baron of Hindlip (a consistent feature of, and more or less first 'fact' mentioned in any biographical piece written about her),[4] she is not the most obvious choice for presenting reality television programming in a recession period. Yet, between 2009 and 2013, Allsopp fronted a series of recycling and upcycling home improvement and domestic crafts programmes, including *Kirstie's Homemade Home* (Channel 4, 2009 series 1 and 2010 series 2), *Kirstie's Handmade Britain* (Channel 4, 2011), *Kirstie's Vintage Home* (Channel 4, 2012) and *Kirstie's Fill Your Home for Free* (Channel 4, 2013). The discourses of heritage, self-endeavour and industry, feminism and celebration of femininity and a particular form of domesticity are here unpacked in relation to the first two series in the above list – *Kirstie's Homemade Home* (series 1) and *Kirstie's Handmade Britain* – and the mediated personality of Allsopp.

Arguably Allsopp, by the time of the recession, had become an asset to Channel 4 as an onscreen presence for a number of reasons. Some commentators questioned whether, with the economic downturn, the mode of address of property programmes like *Location, Location, Location* (Channel 4, 2000–present) and *Relocation, Relocation, Relocation* (Channel 4, 2004–2011), which Allsopp with her co-presenter and business partner, Phil Spencer had fronted, would be deemed inappropriate for the times (Hamad, 2013). This was a sentiment underscored by journalists such as Lucy Mangan from the *Guardian*, who wrote that Allsopp: 'belongs in a time of plenty' and that 'under current conditions, she sits in the national landscape like a second Empire sofa in a student flat' (Mangan, 2011, n.p.). However, this underestimated the shift in discourse in these two particular property programmes and others like them over the period. As mapped by Nunn (2011), in many examples of this reality television sub-genre there had been a change in narrative and presenting register, with a gradual move away from a focus on property as investment to its value as a home signifying security and stability. This was particularly evident in a programme like *Relocation* which focused on couples moving away from urban centres out to the countryside or the coast, to develop a better work–life balance, often to provide a less stressful environment for the starting of a family. Whether re-assessing one's mid-point priorities or celebrating the start of retirement options the narrative structure and the oft-repeated phrase became that of 'finding the forever home'.[5]

What was – and is – Allsopp's function in *Location* and *Relocation*? Given the longevity and popularity of the two series, the audience has seen her develop from a slim twenty-something in a business suit, through maternity, to matronly glamour. This maps her move from homebuyer advisor and entrepreneur[6] to 'angel of the hearth'. More importantly for Channel 4's branding purposes, in Bennett's terms, she has moved from television-personality-as-vocational-expert, to a television-personality-as-personality, defined by an 'intimate, spontaneous, immediate performance style' (Bennett, 2010, p. 119). As Bennett argues:

> Two important consequences follow from an understanding that 'being oneself' is a performance that has to be worked at. First, that television personalities' on-screen personas – their televisual images – are a form of labour, which goes towards both the creation and maintenance of the personality's own fame and its attendant awards, as well as a form of labour that is part of the political economy of the industry itself. Second, that this performance can therefore be evaluated in terms of the pleasures it offers and the successes (or failures) it achieves.
>
> (Bennett, 2010, p. 119)

As they have continued on-screen in the two property shows, Allsopp and Spencer have developed an on-screen and voiceover repartee which resembles that of an old married couple. Spencer jokingly refers to her as his 'TV wife' and in various interviews recounts the surprise large numbers of the television-watching public express on learning that they, in fact, have different partners off-screen (see, for example: Glennie, 2014, n.p.). On-screen, he ribs Allsopp about her class, although, as a 'quarantined discourse' (Bonner, 2003, pp. 137–70), this is not openly articulated. Instead, it is implied in his comments about her clothing (over-glamourous or old-fashioned) and her obvious lack of understanding or even awareness of lower-brow culture and sport. The shows make a feature of the duo, having taken the case of a client couple each, at various points joining forces. This is generally for Allsopp to come in and do some 'straight talking', and only occasionally, with the roles reversed, for Spencer to smooth over troubled waters and to stop her losing patience with a particularly difficult participant. She scolds him for being too diplomatic with picky or over-expectant clients and for not laying down the realities of a situation. In this way, Allsopp presents herself as knowing her own mind, pragmatic and to be relied upon to tell it as she sees it. She depicts herself and the woman, in the case of heterosexual couples on the show, as being the ones with the say and in control. Where this is occasionally not the case and the male partner is represented as steering the decision-making, much is made, in Allsopp's performance and presentation, of her fighting the female client's corner to be sure that she is happy in the domestic space. In the early years of the programmes, this was presented as a 'we-girls-must-stand-together' feisty proto-feminist stance. In later series, in conjunction with the discourse of 'finding the forever home' this has taken on a woman-as-the-angel-of-the-hearth tone.

Backing Allsopp, as a solo presenter, between 2009 and 2013, in various projects centred on the home, was a strategic move by Channel 4. UK broadcasters, due to their admittedly different levels of public service remit, had been under scrutiny for some time for their treatment of female presenters and performers, as these women got into their forties and fifties.[7] The situation came to a head in 2010, when one of the female presenters on the BBC1 rural affairs show *Countryfile*, Miriam O'Reilly, brought an employment tribunal case against the BBC on the grounds of sexism and ageism. She had been replaced when the programme was moved from its Sunday morning BBC1 slot to a peak Sunday evening slot on its sister channel, BBC2.[8] In comparison, due to the popularity of *Location* and *Relocation*, Allsopp's career trajectory continued and continues upwards. A Nexis® search of national newspapers from 2007 to the present day demonstrates that these programmes and Allsopp's take up and enthusiastic use of the social media tool Twitter served and serves to ensure that she has had quite some visibility in the UK national press with regards to assessments of the type of femininity she embodies and the (gendered) views that she holds. All of this media coverage and self-presentation is arguably part of the labour to which Bennett refers, in maintaining, shaping and refining one's televisual image. In particular, journalists have picked up on her comments about the need for people to consume differently, which was, and continues today, to be a central tenet of austerity discourse. Bramall (2013) discusses the start of public debate about economic downturn. She pinpoints the date of Friday 24 April 2009 as significant, as the BBC2 flagship current affairs programme *Newsnight* led with the story that official figures from the Office of National Statistics had indicated that the British economy had shrunk 'at the fastest rate in 30 years' in the first three months of the year. This then led, Bramall writes, into a studio debate that strongly anchored the 'new age of austerity' in the post-World War II austerity era (2013, pp. 19–20). To underline the credibility of this comparison, two cultural commentators had been invited to discuss it – the historian, David Kynaston, who had written a book entitled *Austerity Britain, 1945–1951* and Allsopp, ahead of her new show of the time, *Kirstie's Homemade Home*. Bramall argues that Allsopp 'came out as a champion of the philosophy of "make do and mend", identifying it as the kind of "coping mechanism" people should turn to' (Bramall, 2013, p. 20). Earlier that year in an interview, Allsopp had been quoted as saying that as a nation we needed to have more of a sense of 'longevity' and heritage:

> In an average house I see an enormous turnaround of stuff. There are plenty of homes where nothing is more than five years old. What happened to the things that preceded them? What happened to the possessions of previous generations? It's almost like people had no parents or grandparents. Nothing has been passed on.
>
> (cited in Roux, 2009, p. 62)

In this way, the concept of make-do-and-mend becomes also about valuing things collected by and inherited down the generations of a family, thereby validating a sense of family presence and connection across the ages in the home and as part of the home. One could argue that this was a rather aristocratic viewpoint and, therefore, as Allsopp betraying her class background. However, in the last 10 to 15 years, there has been a huge increase in activity related to family history, as evidenced by the number of genealogy websites and range of reality TV programmes. The most notable of the latter, in the UK context, has been the BBC format series *Who Do You Think You Are?*, one of the 'landmark and flagship programmes for broadcasting reputation and audience share' being 'popular' and 'affecting' (Gray and Bell, 2012, p. 99). This ability to tap into populist sentiment was further demonstrated just before the *Newsnight* interview, where much had been made of Allsopp's horror and 'anger' at the 'profligacy' demonstrated by the MP expense claim scandal, and her talking about the need 'to differentiate between a luxury and a necessity' (cited in Thomson, 2009, p. 33). One particular article reporting her opinion demonstrates her faith in property as a means of security, whilst equally indicating the discourse of home ownership as integral to a person's life-cycle and their sense of self and not as a 'get-rich-quick-scheme'. This was the reason, she argued, for politicians' alienation from ordinary people:

> They [politicians] saw the property market as a cash cow. But most people weren't moving to make money, they were moving because their family was growing, or they were getting divorced, or retiring or changing jobs.
>
> (cited in Thomson, 2009, p. 33)

Furthermore, she bucked the trend of fuelling the intergenerational rift and blame-the-baby-boomer discourse, by stating that young first-time buyers needed to 'make sacrifices to get on the property ladder' and were expecting to achieve too many things with their finances – travel, university and home purchase (cited in Furness, 2013, n.p.). This discourse of 'cutting your coat according to your cloth' fitted in with the thrift and frugality messages of her ensuing television programmes and the increasing concerns being expressed by what was being termed in the UK press as, 'Britain's squeezed middle' (see, for example: Anon., 2011, n.p; Oborne, 2012, n.p.).

The general tone of the newspaper discourse regarding Allsopp is, with notable exceptions,[9] largely approving. In accounts of interviews, much is made of her open and friendly manner, and her lack of pretension despite the obvious material advantage. In particular, as *The Times* phrased it, her:

> exposing the below-stairs secrets of superwomen is applauded; put another way, that her television career and motherhood was and is only possible with a raft of domestic help, was seen as a further example of her pragmatism as well as an honesty and transparency in her relations with readers and television audiences which she has developed on screen.
>
> (Anon., 2013, n.p.)

In this way, it demonstrates what Jermyn identifies as a mode of celebrity-speak-in-interview discourse, the reflexive stance on the 'business of fame' (Jermyn, 2008, reworking Littler, 2004, pp. 13–14); one that gives the voice speaking it greater credibility and a position on the side of the ordinary woman and female experience rather than outside it.

Allsopp's performance of femininity and harnessing of feminist discourse in her arguments, however, does generate more ambivalence. For example, in a recent interview she talked, in particular, about young women's life stage planning and priorities:

> At the moment, women have 15 years to go to university, get their career on track, try and buy a home and have a baby. That is a hell of a lot to ask someone. As a passionate feminist, I feel we have not been honest enough with women about this issue.
>
> (Allsopp cited in Gordon, 2014, n.p.)

This was met with great criticism and concern, as female commentators, in particular, talked about her narrowing girls' goals down to husband, home and babies and downplaying higher education and careers as pathways to self-fulfilment and development.[10] However, a careful reading of her words demonstrates them to be more nuanced than the various critiques suggest. Her main point was that it was not a question of either/or, but that with a limited window of optimum fertility, the existence of 'time inequality' between men and women meant that for the latter, having children at a younger age biologically makes more sense (Allsopp cited in Gordon, 2014, n.p.). This, she admitted, was driven by a particularly personal perspective and experience, where having her own two children in her mid-to-late thirties required caesarean procedures in both cases and got her labelled as one of those women 'too posh to push'. The problem, of course, is that it requires firstly a certain social capital: networks that provide internships where one can prove oneself, and which lead to other job opportunities which can be moulded into a career, without the need for a degree as an entry qualification. Secondly, this ordering of priorities assumes a certain financial security which would allow women to stay at home to look after children, without needing a second income to enable the household to function, or leaving them vulnerable if the marriage or relationship was to end. It also does not recognise the more general difficulty of women entering the labour force without previous experience at an older age and the effect that this has on pensions and retirement planning.

In the same way, the privileging of the domestic sphere and the do-it-yourself 1940s and 1950s aesthetic and mood (as noticeable in the style and instrumentation of the musical interludes and in the visual grammatology) of the television programmes presented by Allsopp and discussed later in this chapter, divides opinion. The position and role of the woman in the home remains a contentious one, regarding issues of gendered dis/empowerment and self-determination. In recent years, the work of Lloyd and Johnson (2004), Brunsdon (2006) and Hollows (2006 and 2008), amongst others, has reflected on second wave feminism's relationship to the housewife and the domestic sphere; a historical relationship defined as 'a structure of othering' or 'dis-identity' (Brunsdon, 2006, p. 43). The critique of a post-feminist revalidation of the domestic continues in this mode. For some, it is seen as a retrograde step; a process of 'retreatism' (Negra, 2008, 5). Or as Mann writes, in her deconstructionist work *The Fifties Mystique*, where 'Distance has lent enchantment to the popular view of the life most girls and women led in the 1950s' and 'Younger women, exhausted by juggling jobs and children, are attracted by the idea of a pre-woman's liberation, full time homemaker's life' (Mann, 2012, p. 7). Coined by others as 'cupcake feminism' (Trussler, 2012, n.p.), from this political perspective it is seen as a soft-sell and soft-soap branding exercise to make feminist ideas more palatable to the next generation of women and the general public at large. It is not, according to Trussler, about consciously and therefore critically performing femininity as a form of masquerade:

on a relatively privileged woman, the sugar n' spice act counters
next to no expectations. It comes off more nostalgic than ironic.
These are symbols of rebellion that have lost their meaning.
They have been market researched, mass-produced and sold
back to us by Cath Kidston and Ephemera Inc.

(Trussler, 2012, n.p.)

In my discussion with colleagues at academic conferences and my observation of mainstream women's discussion forums such as Mumsnet (which
has a discussion strand entitled 'To like Kirstie Allsopp?'), women do seem
divided in their opinions regarding the presenter. This is particularly the case
if they see and present themselves as ascribing to feminist principles and
politics. On the one hand, whilst they may not like many of her views, there
is a cautious celebration of the fact, nevertheless, that as a woman in an inter-
net trolling age, where women's voices are still fighting to be heard and not
threatened, she is not afraid to use different media to articulate them. Equally,
whilst wary or sceptical of the 'angel of the hearth' image, there is more positive response to certain elements of her television persona. On the Mumsnet
string for example, women talk about her in many ways as a form of 'guilty
pleasure' (for example, Rowanhart: 'She is one of four Tories I secretly like';
LFCisTarkaDahl: 'I loathe Tories, really properly loathe them. But I have a
secret hankering to turn her. She is warm, funny and intelligent – I KNOW
I can turn her'; LaQueen: 'I luff her. Always strikes me as very straight, very
sensible [...] and with that alluring Head Girl vibe').[11]

Yet, the mode of address of *Kirstie's Homemade Home* and *Kirstie's Handmade Britain*, linked to Channel 4's professed intention to 'provide a platform
for the awkward squad in society' (Abraham, 2011, n.p.) and Allsopp's publi-
cised comments outlined above, articulates a limited critique of present-day
consumer capitalism. Celebrating craftsmen and artisanship, emphasising
localism and community and a limited form of green politics, with their
message of recycling and upcycling, the programmes tap into an ongoing
debate about alternative consumerism or 'alternative hedonism' (Thomas,
2008, p. 680). In this way, the programmes fit within the subgenre of lifestyle
programming that Thomas discusses, examining:

in what form these senses of dissatisfaction and alternative
desires might be circulating within texts and contexts accessed

by large and diverse audiences, audiences who would not necessarily have a green or anti-capitalist orientation [...] [explor-
ing] ambivalence and disquiet in relation to consumerism *from*
within.

(Thomas, 2008, p. 681)[12]

As a critique of the existing system, we can look to Dyer's (2002) utopian structures of feeling in entertainment formats, to consider why these
programmes and Allsopp's persona appear to have resonance and attrac-
tion, even as guilty pleasure for audiences at this time.[13] Writing about the
structural workings of entertainment, he talks about how 'entertainment
offers an image of "something better" to escape into, or something we want
deeply that our day-to-day lives don't provide' (Dyer, 2002, p. 20). This
utopianism functions at the level of 'sensibility' and 'affectivity': 'what it
would feel like rather than how it would be organised' (Dyer, 2002, p. 20).

The question then is, with the Allsopp recession programmes which
are here under analysis, what are the pleasures on offer? What are we as
viewers escaping from and to what? The key social tensions, inadequa-
cies and absences that Dyer identifies are scarcity, exhaustion, dreariness,
manipulation and fragmentation (2002, p. 26); all of which are debated
in periods of recession and austerity. If we take the 'from', then arguably
in a global financial recession and growing environmental crisis marked
by complex structures and abstract relations, one thing is a sense of a
'lack of control'. Linked to this is the sense of being manipulated. In
recent years in the UK, there have been various crises in authority, coin-
ciding with, or directly related to this period of austerity. The financial
sector, whilst argued by certain quarters to be key to a de-industrialised
UK economy, has demonstrated itself to be also one of its biggest threats.
There has been the scandal over politicians' expenses. The media too, as
the fourth estate, has been embroiled in crises of public trust and confidence. The BBC, as the main UK public service broadcaster, has been
accused of poor management both in terms of regulation and steward-
ship, present and historical, with the outcry over senior management
pay and redundancy packages and the unfolding stories of male talent
abuse of power, set off by the case of Jimmy Savile.[14] The unethical and,
at times, criminal behaviour of journalists working for certain sectors of
the press industry was highlighted for the public with the hearing of the

Leveson Inquiry running through 2011 and 2012. Equally, there is an insistent narrative of scarcity in our own personal lives, with shrinking household budgets, social mobility and horizons of opportunity, particularly for children and grandchildren, but also in the wider world. A sense of social isolation and fragmentation follows from disconnection from family and friends and from a sense of community, due to dual-earner, long work-hour and commuter cultures.

What we, as audience, are escaping to are Dyer argues, the 'utopian solutions' of 'abundance, energy, intensity, transparency, community' (2002, p. 20). *Kirsty's Homemade Home* and *Handmade Britain* offer energy and transparency, in particular through the figure of Allsopp herself. One of the key differences to her *Location/Relocation* persona is that Allsopp takes up the position of student in *Homemade Home* (series 1) and *Handmade Britain*. In the same way that Bell and Hollows argue about the process of 'ordinarinisation' of Eton- and Oxford-educated Hugh Fearnley-Whittingstall in the early series of *Escape to River Cottage* (2011, pp. 180–81), the image of the eager amateur enthusiast being guided by serious professional experts helps to de-emphasise the 'extraordinariness' of Allsopp's class privilege. In the first episode of *Homemade Home*, the audience is invited back to Allsopp's parental home. The establishing shots of the house exterior cannot hide the fact that this is not an average family property. However, the notion of the inherited ancestral home is immediately disavowed for a narrative of her parents' industry and enthusiasm, moving it from an aristocratic to a middle-class framing. In voiceover, Allsopp creates a picture of teamwork, careful design and clear purpose:

> This house is extraordinary because it's the culmination of 40 years work. My parents have been buying, making, collecting and moving all that time. They have lived in over 17 houses in that 40 years. They make a feature of items they've picked up at markets and auction rooms and the way they display them makes them look like priceless family heirlooms.
>
> ('Episode One', 2009)

The distancing of Allsopp from notions of elitism continues in the same opening episode in a sequence where she talks about the joys of skip diving. In an 'inside the Land Rover' sequence,[15] the audience is informed as to the key of successful skipping, which becomes a critique of wealthy throw-away consumerism. Driving down a country lane, she talks about going to 'upmarket areas … where people basically have more money than sense and are prepared to chuck out things which are perfectly good' ('Episode One', 2009). To underline this, we stop at a skip so that Allsopp, oblivious to becoming dripping wet and increasingly bedraggled, can fish a full length mirror out, proceeding to describe how she is going to transform and repurpose it. This encapsulates the 'all weathers/all seasons' down-to-business pragmatist mode of address of both the series and Allsopp's television persona. In a voiceover, laced with public service didacticism, we are told that before removing items from skips, by law one has to ask the permission of the skip hirer. Moving out of shot in order to do just that, Allsopp then returns and speaks directly to camera, saying, 'Yep! A total thumbs up … hopefully it wasn't because I'm that bird off the telly' ('Episode One', 2009). This sentence captures the tension that arises in placing Allsopp in the position of the 'ordinary person' participant in these first two shows: there is a level of televisual fame which she cannot avoid. However, via her phrasing, she manages to both familiarise and de-emphasise her celebrity by playing up the notion of being both recognised as a celebrity whilst not being recognised specifically. At the same time, her 'performance' of a working-class male vernacular manages an intriguing doubling effect of appropriation and misappropriation, distance and intimacy with the audience.

Central to Allsopp's 'ordinarinisation' are the frustrations expressed in her learning curves, which she experiences in *Homemade Home* and *Handmade Britain*. Audiences appear to read an authenticity into the enthusiasm and concentration that she brings to the crafts, and her delight in solving problems, and getting things to work and to fit. The sincerity of her persona, which seems to be such a draw for many viewers, is further underpinned by the more autobiographical and self-disclosing mode of these series. The narrative structure of *Handmade Britain* presents Allsopp learning a range of handcraft skills in order to enter different categories in regional County Shows and as a complete beginner in competitive crafting, going up against much more seasoned competitors. The show does much to build upon Allsopp's existing televisual presentation of self as knowing her own mind. However, there are numerous sequences of her flushed with effort and anxiety, hair dishevelled and face devoid of makeup, fretting over last minute finishing touches and presentation. These moments present a sense of self-effacement, lack of confidence and a certain vulnerability, which considerably softens, but does not eradicate the former 'Miss Bossyboots' persona. One particular episode in the series demonstrates this tension. Episode five adds a further variation to the programme structure by introducing the element of team work as opposed to individual competition, as Allsopp joins the newly formed Hampshire WI branch, the Disparate Housewives[16] to take part in the craft co-operative class. As much as the programme is about learning new crafting skills – needle felting, mosaic and silver work – it is also about Allsopp demonstrating, despite a clear urge to lead the group, an ability not to continually hold the limelight. Whilst the episode sets her up as pushing the theme of their entry – basing their three crafts on the children's book *The Secret Garden* – other parts of the narrative show her suggestions, whilst listened to very politely, ultimately rejected. The pattern for a mosaic mirror, which Allsopp is responsible for constructing in the group session with the expert, is judged as being too fussy and overcomplicated and is radically simplified by her two WI teammates, Louise and Katie. Furthermore, the rules of the competition only allow two out of the three in a team to undertake the final staging of the exhibits in the judging tent, and it is Allsopp who remains outside. Once again, her ideas for the staging, which she articulates in a rehearsal run-through, are not followed and although disquiet at their omission is voiced by her in omniscient narration, the decision to not do so is ultimately validated. Across the seven County Show episodes of the series, there is a balance of Allsopp's successes and failures, which through following the outcomes for her competitors, who are both female and male, is demonstrated to be the 'authentic' experience and outcome of these events. The metanarrative of the series is that such fairs are for everyone, cutting across class, celebrating individual ingenuity and offering community spirit even in economic downturn.

The narrative of *Homemade Home* series 1 (Channel 4, 2009) is one of abundance as she turns a dilapidated Devon cottage, through a process of recycling and upcycling, into a designer home.[17] Through the episodes,

Allsopp visits reclamation yards, antiques fairs and markets, auction houses and vintage shops to furnish her property. In episode one, the notion of 'connection' is strongly foregrounded – getting to know different sellers so that they know you and your tastes – 'If you're nice to them, they'll be nice to you and that is better than an army of personal shoppers' ('Episode One', 2009). In this way, consumption is presented as a thoughtful, non-antagonistic and non-alienating process. Spending time looking around these spaces is worth doing to find 'treasures' at low prices, but also in terms of significance, in discovering potential heritage and inheritance pieces, and the process is represented as a very pleasurable experience – all the more so for being unhurried, and considered. What is therefore being celebrated is an abundance of time – this is the luxury of time-out for the self to engage in making and creating. It may be 'other orientated' – Allsopp references her children as an appreciative audience or recipients of some of her endeavours – but it is also about a form of domestic 'management' based on taking time, rather than the more mundane and functional forms of house and homework.

That home in Devon then becomes the hub of her activity in *Handmade Britain*, developing a sense of continuity, connection and community identity with the television audience (on quite literally returning 'home' to Meadowgate). This sense of community is strengthened by the artisan experts who cross the threshold, welcomed as familiar faces and friends. It continues in *Handmade Britain*, as arts and crafts enthusiasts are introduced as serious but friendly competitors for places. Each of the County Shows is a visual celebration of energy, abundance, intensity and collective activity. There are high crane shots of milling crowds. Black and white film footage is intercut with the modern day to establish a sense of longevity, continuity and tradition, but also recognition of gradual change to these events across the years. Low angle shots and close ups of tables groaning with carefully grown, crafted and baked goods capture a sense of plenitude.

To conclude, these programmes hold in odd tension notions of community and collectivity on one side with neo-liberal individuation and 'responsible-self' discourses on the other. They exhort audiences to home-produce and support local trade whilst sitting at the centre of a large merchandising venture with high street corporate brands.[18] They are, arguably, the interior design/homemaker version of what Potter and Westall call 'veg-patch capitalism' (2013, p. 155). This, they argue, is a Coalition-devised 'austerity-led localism (that is) an extension of Thatcherite "small state" domestic self-management rhetoric coupled with a Blairite insistence on equal "opportunity for all" rather than actual socio-economic equality' (Potter and Westall, 2013, p. 162). Meadowgate is an upper-middle class retreat that speaks to cupcake feminist ideas referred to earlier in the chapter. This is a television 'stage' complete with Aga* and chickens in the back garden. Behind the scenes the alternative consumption and localist discourses which underpinned the series were challenged by reports, in the local and national tabloid press, of angry local residents questioning Allsopp's commitment to the vibrancy of village life. This was due to the house's actual status as a third home and holiday rental, rented out for £3,500 per week, particularly given that it is to be found in an area where affordable housing has been identified as a priority (see Salkeld, 2009, n.p.).

It says something about the power of television and the mechanism and resonance of the television personality, that despite many finding the politics problematic in terms of gender and more generally, these programmes 'worked' at an affective level. Evidence for this can be seen in comments from sites such as Mumsnet and by the fact that Channel 4 continued to commission these programmes for primetime mid-evening slots, even in a time of austerity from which broadcasting itself was not immune.

Channel 4, as a broadcaster, has shown in the past 15 years remarkable acuity and skill in developing front-of-screen-talent for its factual provision. Its successful partnership with Allsopp through boom and bust demonstrates the power of televisual modes of address – ordinariness, intimacy and sincerity. As examples of the makeover show, the greatest transformation at the heart of these series is making the Second Empire sofa maybe not look *but rather feel* as though it was made for a student flat.

Notes

1 Bennett has analysed the performance style of ITV light entertainer, Cilla Black; Woods analyses the value of sports presenter Clare Balding to both the BBC and Channel 4 in her coverage of the London 2012 Olympic and Paralympic Games. Holmes has urged a return to the archives to develop a more detailed historiographical approach, focusing in her 2011 article on the case of Sabrina, working in TV variety in the 1950s. More work has been done in the USA in this

area – see Becker (2004 and 2009) and Murray (2005) – and it appears to be a developing field with regards to Australian broadcasting history: see Bye (2009 and 2010) and Bonner (2007).

2 This push on the licence fee had already been hinted at by a previous CE, Mark Thompson, in his 2002 McTaggart lecture. This was a strategy no longer followed after Duncan. David Abraham, his successor, confirmed the channel's commitment as a public service broadcaster, but stated in his RTS 2011 speech that they would be 'putting away the begging bowl' (Abraham, 2011, n.p.).

3 The recognition of the value of partnerships and their longevity for branding purposes is demonstrated through the channel's use of golden-handcuff agreements with certain of its presenters. Oliver was one of these; a case widely reported in the trade press. Allsopp (with Spencer) has also been the subject of this, signing a three-year exclusivity agreement which was rapidly extended to six years when it became apparent that the BBC was attempting to poach the presenting duo (Parker, 2010, n.p.).

4 At the end of 2009 and through the beginning of 2010, as Britain started moving towards the General Election, a number of articles appeared in the British broadsheet newspapers, regarding 'the return of poshness to mainstream life'. Whilst referring to a new generation of politicians, Andy Beckett also focused on television, naming Hugh Fearnley-Whittingstall and Allsopp, in particular, as 'assets in what is usually considered the most populist of media, until recently dominated by self-made Britons and regional accents' (Beckett, 2009, n.p.). (This is arguably an overgeneralisation in that 'posh' people have always been a part of the television presenter landscape, with recent further examples being Trinny (Woodall) and Susannah (Constantine), the two Fat Ladies: Clarissa Dickson Wright and Jennifer Patterson, Nigella Lawson and Sophie Dahl.) Jenny McCartney for the *Telegraph* pushed the idea further by announcing this trend as 'new posh' rather than 'old posh'; the latter she describes as 'perceived as […] sneering, exclusive and arrogant […] barking ceaselessly of Britain needing to pull its socks up'. By contrast, the new posh, she argued, is defined as being 'humble, thoughtful, inclusive and keen to serve' and by 'rolling up (its) own sleeves and clearing up the mess': the rhetoric of 'we're all in this together' (McCartney, 2010, n.p.).

5 One clear 'recessionary misstep', Hamad argues, by the Allsopp/Spencer pairing was the series *Vacation, Vacation, Vacation* (Channel 4, 2011) where the emphasis was, despite a nod towards smaller budgets, largely extolling the pleasures of the luxury end of the holiday market. Unsurprisingly, the series was cancelled after eight episodes, on the basis that it had 'failed to resonate with audiences' (cited in Hamad, 2013, p. 247).

6 This included setting up the independent television production company Raise the Roof with Spencer in 2010. It is this company which now produces the programming they star in for Channel 4.

7 There are a number of cases in relatively recent UK broadcasting history – for example in the treatment of Moira Stuart, the first Afro-Caribbean female news-reader on British television, who had presented on almost every type of news bulletin for BBC Television since 1981. This ended in 2007, amid angry representation from supporters that this was because she had reached the age of 57. Then there was the replacement in 2009 of 66-year-old professional choreographer, Arlene Phillips, as a judge on the BBC format show *Strictly Come Dancing* (BBC1, 2004–present) by former contestant, 30-year-old Alesha Dixon. Some presenters left before they were 'sidelined', for example, BBC newsreader Anna Ford. The most public exit was by the main commercial broadcaster ITV's light entertainment doyenne, Cilla Black. She announced that she was quitting the Saturday night family entertainment dating show *Blind Date*, live on-air in 2003, after she became aware of ITV management's intention to reduce her role on the show.

8 O'Reilly brought the case as one of four female presenters, aged in their forties and fifties, who were dropped from the show. The Head of BBC Rural Affairs, Andy Thornham, was at pains to emphasise that this was about profile and reso-nance with peaktime audiences, as if this was a gender-neutral process and one of mere happenstance. The court found for O'Reilly on the basis of ageism and victimisation but not gender discrimination.

9 The main constituency is male journalists writing for the UK broadsheet, the *Guardian*.

10 Various female head teachers were cited in the press as condemning Allsopp's comments as 'throwback to the early 1950s' (Helen Fraser, CE of the Girls' Day School Trust, cited in Duggan, 2014, n.p. and cited again in Ellis-Petersen and Tran, 2014, n.p).

11 See <http://www.mumsnet.com/Talk/am_i_being_unreasonable/a1587575-To-like-Kirstie-Allsopp>.

12 This celebration of rural localism and the artisan has found further iterations in the documentary/challenge format and has also undergone a 'masculinisa-tion'. As part of its re-thinking of BBC2 afternoon scheduling in this period of cuts, and working with the resonance of its own television presenters, the Corporation had *Flog It* presenter, Paul Martin, front the series *Paul Martin's Handmade Revolution* (BBC2, 2012). In 2014, Channel 4 ran *Monty Don's Real Craft* on More4.

13 Others have used Dyer's model before me: Morris (2007) looking at the popu-larity of the makeover show in the UK from the end of the 1990s; Hollows (2003) in analysing the popularity of Nigella Lawson's cookery programmes and the escapist value of the domestic goddess persona.

14 Savile was one of the BBC's key television and radio personalities of the 1970s through to the late 1990s, particularly associated with youth programming, for example, *Speakeasy* (BBC Radio 1, 1969–1973), *Top of the Pops* (BBC1

1964–2004; BBC2 2005–2006), *Jim'll fix it* (BBC1 1975–1994, 1995, 2007). Having always presented himself as an eccentric figure in terms of appearance, dress and mannerisms, this persona turned into something much more threatening, when after his death he became linked in 2011 with accusations of child and adolescent abuse. Having worn the face of constancy, familiarity and intimacy for his viewers for so long, which Bennett (2010) identifies as key to the resonance of a television personality, the changing narrative about and characterisation of Savile was followed first by public disbelief and then a deep sense of disturbance and betrayal.

15 This is a stock sequence in television personality-led series, which underpins the notion of intimacy and familiarity, situating the audience as travelling companion and confidant.

16 This is, of course, a tongue-in-cheek play on the title of the US drama series *Desperate Housewives* (ABC, 2004–2012). As the Women's Institute has presented itself in recent years as balancing both tradition and change, one can easily understand why it would get involved in this particular television project.

17 Each episode saw Allsopp address a particular 'room' that makes up the home – episode 1: the kitchen; episode 2: the bathroom (in fact three); episode 3: the living room (in effect, two rooms, divided into grown up and child spaces); episode 4: the bedroom; and the final episode on the garden design.

18 Apart from the DVDs and books which follow from the television series, the Kirstie Allsopp brand includes a linens and wallpaper Home Living Range which is available online and also from middle-market retail stores such as House of Fraser, Next and Debenhams. Middle-class retailers Marks and Spencers ran a Kirstie Allsopp household utensil and ceramics gift and homeware range and Lakeland, too, sells Allsopp items: 'Reflecting Kirstie's flair for all things bright and beautiful, her gorgeous range of co-ordinating baking essentials range will add a homely touch to your cupcakes and preserves' (see http://www.lakeland.co.uk/p18048/Kirstie-Allsopp-Presentation-Range). Arts and crafts retailer Hobbycraft sells 32 different products in its Kirsty Allsopp line, from natural soap and lavender bombe-making kits to pinking shears.

Bibliography

Abraham, David. (2011). '"What we're 4": a speech given to the Royal Television Society'. 23 May. Available from: <http://www.rts.org.uk/speech-abraham-2011> [Accessed: 14 December 2014].

Anon. (2011). 'Taxation: squeezing middle Britain'. *Guardian*, 31 January. Available from: <http://www.theguardian.com/commentisfree/2011/jan/31/taxation-squeezing-middle-britain> [Accessed: 20 April 2015].

Anon. (2013). 'Kirstie Allsopp: Exposing the below-stairs secrets of superwomen'. *Sunday Times*, 24 March. Available from: <http://www.thesundaytimes.co.uk/ sto/comment/profiles/article1234469.ece> [Accessed: 27 August 2013].

Becker, Christine. (2004). '"Glamour Girl Classed as TV Show Brain": The Body and Mind of Faye Emerson'. *The Journal of Popular Culture*, 38/2, pp. 242–260.

—— (2009). *It's The Pictures That Got Small: Hollywood Film Stars on 1950s Television*. Middletown, Wesleyan University Press.

Beckett, Andy. (2009). 'Tory Chic: The Return of Poshness. Suddenly it Has Become Socially Acceptable – and Fashionable – to Dress, Sound, Play and Even Eat, Like the Upper Classes'. *Guardian G2*, 16 December. Available from: <http:// www.theguardian.com/uk/2009/dec/16/the-return-of-poshness> [Accessed: 27 August 2013].

Bell, David, and Hollows, Joanne. (2011). 'From *River Cottage* to *Chicken Run*: Hugh Fearnley-Whittingstall and the Class Politics of Ethical Consumption'. *Celebrity Studies*, 2/2, pp. 178–191.

Bennett, James. (2008). 'The Television Personality System: Televisual Stardom Revisited after Film Theory'. *Screen*, 49/1, pp. 32–50.

—— (2010). *Television Personalities: Stardom and the Small Screen*. London: Routledge.

Biressi, Anita, and Nunn, Heather. (2013). *Class and Contemporary British Culture*. Basingstoke: Palgrave Macmillan.

Bonner, Frances. (2003). *Ordinary Television: Analysing Popular TV*. London: Sage.

—— (2007). 'A Familiar Face: The Consequences of a Long Career on Screen'. *Australian Television History*, 26, pp. 91–111.

Bramall, Rebecca. (2013). *The Cultural Politics of Austerity: Past and Present in Austere Times*. Basingstoke: Palgrave Macmillan.

Brunsdon, Charlotte. (2006). 'The Feminist in the Kitchen: Martha, Martha and Nigella'. In: Joanne Hollows and Rachel Moseley (eds) *Feminism in Popular Culture*. Oxford: Berg.

Bye, Susan. (2009). 'Debating the Barrel Girl: The Rise and Fall of Panda Lisner'. *Media International Australia*, 131, May, pp. 117–126.

—— (2010). 'A Cruel Medium for a Woman: Female Personalities and the Early Days of Australian Television'. *Feminist Media Studies*, 10/2, pp. 161–177.

Duggan, Oliver. (2014). 'Kirsty Allsopp: Women Should Put Off University to Find a "Nice Boyfriend" and Have Babies'. *Telegraph*, 2 June. Available from: <http:// www.telegraph.co.uk/culture/tvandradio/10869202/Kirstie-Allsopp-Women-should-put-off-university-to-find-a-nice-boyfriend-and-have-babies.html> [Accessed: 25 March 2015].

Dyer, Richard. (2002). *Only Entertainment*, 2nd edition. Abingdon: Routledge.

Ellis-Petersen, Hannah, and Tran, Mark. (2014). 'Ignore "Patronising" Kirstie Allsopp's Advice, Teachers Tell Girls'. *Guardian*, 2 June. Available from:

<http://www.theguardian.com/tv-and-radio/2014/jun/02/teachers-round-on-kirstie-allsopp-over-babies-and-boyfriends-comments> [Accessed: 25 March 2015].

Furness, Hannah. (2013). 'Kirstie Allsopp: Getting on the Property Ladder has Never Been Easy'. *Telegraph*, 22 July. Available from: <http://www.telegraph.co.uk/finance/personalfinance/borrowing/mortgages/10194063/Kirstie-Allsopp-Getting-on-the-property-ladder-has-never-been-easy.html> [Accessed: 27 August 2013].

Glennie, Alasdair. (2014). 'Kirstie's My "Other Wife", Says Phil: *Location, Location, Location* Presenters Speak of Their Close Relationship'. *Mail Online*, 10 February. <http://www.dailymail.co.uk/tvshowbiz/article-2555467/Kirstie-Allsopps-wife-says-Phil-Spencer-Location-Location-Location-presenters-speak-close-relationship.html> [Accessed: 20 April 2015].

Gordon, Bryony. (2014). 'Kirstie Allsopp: "I Don't Want the Next Generation of Women to Suffer the Same Heartache"'. *Telegraph*, 1 June. Available from: <http://www.telegraph.co.uk/lifestyle/10868367/Kirstie-Allsopp-I-dont-want-the-next-generation-of-women-to-suffer-the-same-heartache.html> [Accessed: 29 November 2014].

Gray, Ann, and Bell, Erin. (2012). *History on Television*. London: Routledge.

Hamad, Hannah. (2013). 'Age of Austerity Celebrity Expertise in UK Reality Television'. *Celebrity Studies* 4/2, pp. 245–48.

Hollows, Joanne. (2003). 'Feeling Like a Domestic Goddess: Postfeminism and Cooking'. *European Journal of Cultural Studies*, 6/2, pp. 179–202.

—— (2006). 'Can I Go Home Yet? Feminism, Postfeminism and Domesticity'. In: Joanne Hollows and Rachel Moseley (eds) *Feminism in Popular Culture*. Oxford, Berg.

—— (2008). *Domestic Cultures*. Maidenhead: Open University Press.

Holmes, Sue. (2011). 'Whoever Heard of Anyone Being a Screaming Success for Doing Nothing? "Sabrina", the BBC and Television Fame in the 1950s'. *Media History*, 17/1, pp. 33–48.

Jermyn, Deborah. (2008). 'Still Something Else Besides a Mother? Negotiating Celebrity Motherhood in Sarah Jessica Parker's Star Story'. *Social Semiotics*, 18/2, pp. 163–176.

—— (2013). 'Past their Prime Time? Women, Ageing and Absence on British Factual Television'. *Critical Studies in Television*, 8/1, pp. 73–90.

Kirstie's Homemade Home. (2009–2010), Series 1 and 2, Channel 4, IWC.

Kirstie's Handmade Britain. (2011). Channel 4, Raise the Roof Productions.

Kirstie's Vintage Home. (2012). Channel 4, Raise the Roof Productions.

Kirstie's Fill Your Home for Free. (2013). Channel 4, Raise the Roof Productions.

Lloyd, Justine, and Johnson, Lesley. (2004). *Sentenced to Everyday Life: Feminism and the Housewife*. Oxford: Berg.

Littler, Jo. (2004). 'Making Fame Ordinary: Intimacy, Reflexivity and "Keeping it Real"'. *Mediactive*, 2, pp. 8–25.

Mangan, Lucy. (2011). 'TV Review: Great British Food Revival; Kirsty's Handmade Britain'. *Guardian*, 2 November. Available from: <http://www.theguardian.com/tv-and-radio/2011/nov/02/great-british-food-revival-review> [Accessed: 27 August 2013].

Mann, Jessica. (2012). *The Fifties Mystique*. Sheffield: The Cornovia Press.

McCartney, Jenny. (2010). 'The New Posh Takes Charge'. *Telegraph*, 15 May. Available from: <http://www.telegraph.co.uk/comment/columnists/jennymccartney/7728767/The-New-Posh-takes-charge.html> [Accessed: 27 August 2013].

Morris, Nigel. (2007). '"Old, New, Borrowed, Blue": Makeover Television in British Primetime'. In: Dana Heller (ed.) *Makeover Television*. London: I.B.Tauris.

Mumsnet. (2012). 'To like Kirstie Allsopp?' Available from: <http://www.mumsnet.com/Talk/am_i_being_unreasonable/a1587575-To-like-Kirstie-Allsopp> [Accessed: 14 December 2014].

Murray, Susan. (2005). *Hitch Your Antenna To the Stars: Early Television and Broadcast Stardom*. London: Routledge.

Negra, Diane. (2008). *What a Girl Wants? Fantasizing the Reclamation of Self in Postfeminism*. Abingdon: Routledge.

Nunn, Heather. (2011). 'Investing in the "Forever Home": From Property Programming to Retreat TV'. In: Helen Wood and Beverley Skeggs (eds) *Reality Television and Class*. Basingstoke: Palgrave Macmillan.

Oborne, Peter. (2012). 'Budget 2012: A Big Dangerous Moment on Tax – Will Osborne Live to Regret It?' *Telegraph*, 21 March. Available from: <http://www.telegraph.co.uk/finance/budget/9158109/Budget-2012-A-big-dangerous-moment-on-tax-will-Osborne-live-to-regret-it.html> [Accessed: 20 April 2015].

Ouellette, Laurie, and Hay, James. (2008). *Better Living Through Reality TV: Television and Post-welfare Citizenship*. Oxford: Wiley-Blackwell.

Parker, Robin. (2010). 'C4 Extends Phil and Kirstie Deal'. *Broadcast*, 15 January. Available from: <http://www.broadcastnow.co.uk/c4-extends-phil-and-kirstie-deal/5009698.article> [Accessed: 14 December 2014].

Philips, Deborah. (2005). 'Transformation Scenes: The Television Interior Makeover'. *International Journal of Cultural Studies*, 8/2, pp. 213–229.

Potter, Lucy, and Westall, Clare. (2013). 'Neoliberal Britain's Austerity Foodscape: Home Economics, Veg Patch Capitalism and Culinary Temporality'. *New Formations*, 80/81, pp. 155–178.

Roux, Caroline. (2009). '"Pink Walls and Chandeliers Don't Feel Right. We've Had Enough Frivolity": How Does Design Respond to a Bleak Economic Landscape? Philippe Starck, Sir Terence Conran and Kirstie Allsopp Debate the Future of Their Industries in These Lean Times'. *Guardian Weekend*, 10 January, p. 62.

Salkeld, Luke. (2009). 'The Angry Locals Who Aren't Sold on Kirstie Allsopp's Village Location'. *Mail Online*, 9 May. Available from: <http://www.dailymail.co.uk/tvshowbiz/article-1179323/The-angry-locals-arent-sold-Kirstie-Allsopps-village-relocation.html> [Accessed: 14 December 2014].

Thomas, Lyn. (2008). 'Alternative Realities: Downshifting Narratives in Contemporary Lifestyle Television'. *Cultural Studies*, 22/5, pp. 680–699.

Thomson, Alice. (2009). 'The Property Expert Who Would Find Herself Right at Home Cutting MPs' Expense Claims'. *The Times*, 11 April, p. 33.

Trussler, Meryl. (2012). 'Half-baked: The Trouble With Cupcake Feminism'. *The Quietus*, 13 February. Available from: <http://thequietus.com/articles/07962-cupcake-feminism> [Accessed: 27 August 2013].

Woods, Faye. (2013). 'Clare Balding: The Televisual Face of London 2012'. *Journal of Popular Television*, 1/1, pp. 137–142.

6

The Walking Dead and Gendering Zombie Austerity

Zach Finch

In an October 2013 interview with *Rolling Stone* magazine, Robert Kirkman, the co-creator of the comics and television series *The Walking Dead* (2010–present), stated: 'Apocalyptic storytelling is appealing when people have apocalyptic thoughts. With the global economic problems and everything else, a lot of people feel we're heading into dark times' (Peisner, 2013, p. 55). There is, and has been for several years, a wide cultural sentiment that crises are ongoing and a constant part of our daily lives. This feeling of impending doom has provoked a wide variety of responses from various groups in the United States and elsewhere. One of these responses is the desire to start over – or hit the reset button – on current economic policies and social institutions and formations. The global Occupy movement provides one example, which, among other things, seeks social and economic transformation that would eliminate the extreme inequality of wealth caused by global capitalism. Alternatively, neoliberals and right-wing advocates (such as the Tea Party movement in the USA) have responded with goals to reduce government debt and spending. They believe that government spending has caused the current economic crisis and that policies of austerity are the best possible solution. Such responses indicate that in times of crisis, ideological questions and contesting visions of the future of governments and social institutions can be, and should be, put to the fore.

Current social conditions and discourses are present in the forum of popular culture. In recent years, a tremendous number of texts devoted to post-apocalyptic narratives, subjects and ideas have populated all manner of media. All of them feature narratives of crisis and an overturned social order. Examples can be found in the films *28 Days Later* (Danny Boyle, 2002), *28 Weeks Later* (Juan Carlos Fresnadillo, 2007), *Land of the Dead* (George A. Romero, 2005), and *The Road* (John Hillcoat, 2009); the television shows *Revolution* and *The Walking Dead* (2010–present); and numerous stories in literature (*Plague Year* [2007] by Jeff Carlson; *The Maze Runner* [2009] by James Dashner), comics (*The Walking Dead* [2003–present], *Y: The Last Man* [2002–2008]), and video games (*The Last of Us* [2013], the *Resident Evil* series [1996–present], the *Left 4 Dead* series).

Though the post-apocalyptic narrative is not a new genre by any means, its popularity in recent years is significant because these works portray worlds in which the order of things has been changed or destroyed and what will replace it is as yet undetermined. Many scholars have written that we are currently at an ecological and economic threshold that requires new ideas and fundamental changes to ensure the very survival of the human species. Chris Harman describes capitalism as unsustainable when he writes: 'It gives a new character to old oppressions and throws up completely new ones. It creates drives to war and ecological destruction' (Harman, 2009, p. 11). Imagining a radically altered world, or a 'blank slate narrative' might be politically progressive in countering the 'facts' taken for granted in today's capitalism, which is often credited with causing many of the crises that face us today, such as climate change and severe forms of inequality. Citing anthropologist David Graeber, *Airship Daily* columnist John Powers writes:

> Graeber believes that neoliberalism, judged as a political project, has 'succeeded magnificently in convincing the world that capitalism – and not just capitalism, but exactly the financialized, semi-feudal capitalism we happen to have right now – is the only viable economic system'. As he sees it, the political project of neoliberalism is to ensure that 'under no conditions can alternatives, or anyone proposing alternatives, be seen to experience success'.
>
> (Powers, 2013, n.p.)

Zombie post-apocalyptic films are particularly worth looking at, given not just the number of these narratives in recent years but also their well-established precedents as allegories for current social anxieties and problems. Kyle Bishop points out that 'the human protagonists and the post-apocalyptic world they are forced to inhabit, provide the greatest insight into the cultural value of the zombie narrative' (2010, p. 206). As post-apocalyptic stories, many zombie narratives present something like an extreme form of austerity in their story-worlds: there is no (or very limited/primitive) government, no basic services and no infrastructure. At the same time, according to Powers, they also may present a potential for imagining a nearly clean slate for the surviving humans left in a world without capitalism and without the old institutions to enforce power structures (Powers, 2013, n.p.). The ways in which humans deal with that scenario (do they try to restore what was lost in the disaster, or do they attempt to forge a new, better society?) reflects on the debate in our own times with regard to equality and how society should be shaped going forward.

This chapter attempts to explain what austerity means in relation to *The Walking Dead* through the show's industrial practices, narrative and ideological positions. By depicting a severely regressed world, the series shows how austerity is not only an economic policy or set of business practices but reveals its ideological connections to patriarchy and traditional gender roles.

Austerity is one of the discourses to (re-)emerge in response to the economic crisis of 2008 and many scholars have spoken of its core ideas in terms related to zombies and the undead. In Europe and the USA, a variety of austerity practices and policies have been implemented to greater and lesser degrees. As defined by economist Mark Blyth, 'Austerity is a form of voluntary deflation in which the economy adjusts through the reduction of wages, prices, and public spending to restore competitiveness, which is (supposedly) best achieved by cutting the state's budget, debts, and deficits' (2013, p. 2). The idea that cutting government spending and reducing the social safety net as a way to promote growth is based on liberal economic ideas that began with Enlightenment philosophers such as John Locke, David Hume and Adam Smith. Their writings deal with the tension between a desire for markets free from government intervention and the necessity of governments to protect those same markets (Blyth, 2013,

p. 100). As Blyth points out, by the twentieth century, ' "cut the state" was the only answer deemed acceptable by the governing classes of the capitalist world' (2013, pp. 99–100). This position was tempered from the 1930s to the 1970s by Keynesian economic policies but, like a zombie, austerity policies have returned. Those advocating austerity generally do so from an ideological viewpoint that favours a top-down view of the world – that there are makers and there are takers, and the takers deserve the blame for economic crises because they use the bulk of expensive government services paid for by taxes on businesses and the wealthy. However, austerity practices are not limited to the public sector. Businesses downsize, reduce wages and benefits, and eliminate full-time positions in favour of a 'flexible' part-time workforce. Many studies, including Blyth's, show that in spite of austerity practices designed to promote growth, the exact opposite happens, and throughout the world austerity has brought with it 'class politics, riots, political instability, more rather than less debt, assassinations, and war' (Blyth, 2013, p. 229). Some scholars refer to austerity and several aspects of the economic crisis that began in 2007 in 'zombie' terms. Chris Harman, in his explanation of the root causes of the economic crisis, argues that '21st century capitalism as a whole is a zombie system, seemingly dead when it comes to achieving human goals and responding to human feelings, but capable of sudden spurts of activity that cause chaos all around' (Harman, 2009, p. 12). These 'sudden spurts' of chaos-inducing activity include mass unemployment, ecological disastersp and hunger (Harman, 2009, pp. 7–8). John Quiggin's book, *Zombie Economics*, refers to 'market liberalism' as the set of ideas behind policies that reject the 'role for the state in the provision of income security and services such as health and education' (Quiggin, 2010, p. 3). These 'market liberalism' ideas and their many forms are the 'zombie economics' Quiggin refers to; they are ideas proven wrong or ineffective in practice, yet they rise again from time to time and take the form of policy because the ideology behind them does not die.

It is in this environment – an era of renewed debate over the role of government in the economy and, fundamentally, the way society should be formed – that *The Walking Dead* is positioned. This chapter argues that the series' industrial practices and narrative elements display *The Walking Dead*'s (or, more properly AMC's) rhetoric of austerity (even if it is not truly austere in the sense of low budget movies and TV), and, closely related, the show's representations reinforce patriarchy and traditional gender roles. Simply, *The Walking Dead* is a text that reveals how the ideology of austerity is connected and intertwined with white male patriarchy and gender roles and, possibly, outright misogyny.

Cutting Back: *The Walking Dead's* Industrial and Narrative Austerity

The Walking Dead premiered on AMC on 31 October 2010, and the response was overwhelmingly positive from critics and viewers alike. Drawing upon zombie, action/adventure, and horror genres and conventions, the show is appealing to many audiences because of its emphases on action, moral dilemmas and suspense. For many viewers, imagining how one would react to survival scenarios in a post-apocalyptic world has a great appeal, as does the visual pleasure of the show's violence and gore. The series is based on the popular comic book of the same title, running from 2003 to the present, created by Robert Kirkman, and the artists Tony Moore and Charlie Adlard. Both tell the story of the Sheriff's Deputy, Rick Grimes (Andrew Lincoln), who wakes from a coma to find that the world has been overrun by zombies. In the comics and the television series, the story concerns Rick's attempts to survive, reunite with his family and interact with other survivors. The television pilot was ordered by AMC in January 2010 because of the popularity of the comics and Frank Darabont's commitment to direct the pilot and oversee the first season (Goldman, 2010, n.p.). To date, the series has been well-received and it has generated a loyal fan base, with its average episode viewership climbing from 5.97 million in season one to 8.99 million in season two, and 10.4 million in season three.

At first glance, *The Walking Dead* does not appear to engage in austere industrial practices. The series' narrative requires elaborate special effects, makeup and costumes in order to depict the survivors and their gory battles with the undead. Season one featured several panoramic shots of an abandoned Atlanta, recalling images from films such as *28 Days Later*, but also the wake of natural disasters such as Hurricane Katrina. As a featured series on AMC, *The Walking Dead* shared a lineup with shows such as *Mad Men*, *Breaking Bad* (2008–2013), and

The Killing. These award-winning series contain many of the characteristics Robert J. Thompson attributes to 'quality television' with their
acting and directing pedigrees, ensemble casts and emphasis on the
quality of the shows' writing (Thompson, 1997, pp. 13–16). Thus, it
would seem that *The Walking Dead*'s production budget and methods
should contrast with models of lesser means and ambitions, such as
many reality television shows, notorious for their specifically targeted
niche audiences and quick and cheap production strategies. However,
research into the production of *The Walking Dead* reveals a show
embracing austerity business practices, or at least a rhetoric of austerity, even though the show may be a much higher-budget production
than most television shows.

Fiscal downsizing is the first example of *The Walking Dead*'s austere
rhetoric and practice. The per episode budget decreased significantly
after season one in spite of the show's increased success. This falls in line
with practices of austerity that cut spending, even when something is
profitable in the hopes of creating even larger profit margins. More than
that, however, this also reflects the logics of recent global capitalism and
the downsizing across many industries. According to Peisner's article in
Rolling Stone, the budget was cut by $500,000 per episode from season
one to season two (Peisner, 2013, p. 58). Additionally, the 30 per cent
tax credit the show receives for shooting on location in Georgia goes
directly to AMC, and does not mitigate the budget cuts to production
(Ocasio, 2013, n.p.). According to AMC executives, these reductions are
not unusual. David Peisner writes that 'AMC president Charlie Collier
has asserted that pilot episodes usually cost more money and the Season
Two cuts were just the normal course of business' (Peisner, 2013, p. 58).
Like in other industries, practices of austerity during a time of profit have
become normal.

This austere stance has caused some consternation for those involved
with the series' production. Ocasio states that Frank Darabont was
fired after season one due to creative conflicts with AMC executive Joel
Stillerman, and because Darabont 'doesn't like to see the cast and crew
overworked and underpaid' (Ocasio, 2013, n.p.). Nellie Andreeva reported
on 1 December 2010 that AMC was considering entering season two of *The
Walking Dead* without a regular writing staff (this ended up being a threat

only) (Andreeva, 2010, n.p.). The labour conditions of shooting in Georgia during the summer are less than ideal as well, and Peisner goes on to point out: 'The cast and crew brave the heat, dodge the rain, navigate woods and grasslands teeming with hungry ticks, chiggers, mosquitoes, and endure the punishing schedule required to make a high-concept, action-packed, effects-heavy 43-minute film in eight days, and do this 16 times between May and November' (Peisner, 2013, p. 54). In the same article, cast member Norman Reedus comments on the difficult working conditions, recalling: 'We've had people come do the show and halfway through, they're like, "Fuck this! It's 120 degrees outside"' (Peisner, 2013, p. 54). Yet, in this article, these conditions are cited as reasons to celebrate the toughness of the cast and crew, who sacrifice for art, rather than protest against or to raise awareness of, labour conditions on the set of *The Walking Dead* (and probably on many other television shows and movies as well). This idea of sacrifice is in line with an ideology of austerity described by Blyth in which the many, especially workers at the lower end (much of the series' crew), must sacrifice proportionally more than those at the higher end (AMC executives) (2013, p. 8).

The production of *The Walking Dead* reflects some of the ways in which the show has embraced austerity as an industrial practice. These have their greatest impact on lower-level employees, such as the below-the-line crew (grips, production assistants, electricians, gaffers, etc.). Since most film and television budgets are calculated according to shooting days rather than a total number of labour hours, there is pressure to finish shooting on or ahead of the scheduled number of days estimated to complete an episode. For many film and television productions, the crew's sleep and rest are enemies of the budget. As Jonathan Crary describes in *24/7: Late Capitalism and the Ends of Sleep*:

> by the last decades of the twentieth century and into the present, with the collapse of controlled or mitigated forms of capitalism in the United States and Europe, there has ceased to be any internal necessity for having rest and recuperation as components of economic growth and profitability. Time for human rest and regeneration is now simply too expensive to be structurally possible within contemporary capitalism.
>
> (Crary, 2013, pp. 14–15)

Like the shuffling zombies on the show, the ideal crew member working on *The Walking Dead* would be immune to extreme heat and fatigue.

The Walking Dead's industrial practices and rhetoric position the series as austere (budget cuts, difficult working conditions, sacrifice by lower-level workers), but that is just one aspect of its relationship to austerity. The series' narrative takes place in a world that is austere in several other ways. As mentioned above, in the world of *The Walking Dead*, there is no government, no media and no official economic institutions. Various moral and psychological dilemmas are played out in addition to the basic struggle for survival under these primitive circumstances. The first season established the world on a large scale, as Rick awakens to discover his small Georgia town nearly deserted except for a few survivors. He travels to Atlanta, only to find it swarming with the undead. Eventually he meets up with a group of survivors that include his wife and son, and the group, under his leadership, makes their way to the Center for Disease Control (CDC). At the CDC, it is revealed that no help is coming and that their only options are suicide or the road. The first season utilised many set pieces, outdoor locations, special effects such as explosions, and hordes of cast members and CGI zombies.

During seasons two and three, many fans and critics commented that the reduced budgets for the show created a 'narrative atrophy' in terms of locations, set pieces and action that was 'not born of any plot necessity but the direct result of AMC's budgeting. Their fiscal austerity, if you will' (Pangburn, 2013, n.p.). The 'narrative atrophy' refers mainly to the boredom some viewers felt because almost all of the second season's action takes place on a farm where the group has taken refuge. Subplots dragged on, such as the search for the lost little girl, Sophia (Madison Lintz), and the love triangle between Rick, his wife Lori (Sarah Wayne Callies) and Rick's best friend and fellow deputy, Shane (John Bernthal). During the third season, filming locations were almost exclusively within the prison where Rick's group had taken refuge and the town of Woodbury, a nearby settlement run by the authoritarian character, the Governor (David Morrissey). In these ways, narrative atrophy was believed to be caused by the show's lower per episode budgets, revealing how industrial practices of austerity are connected to a series' narrative.

In the content of the stories themselves, the characters of *The Walking Dead* are seemingly forced to embrace austere practices in order to survive but, except for firearms, there is no consequential shortage of supplies. Food and water are rationed (though apparently never absent or compromised by spoilage, impurity, etc.), and the single most important commodities are weapons and ammunition. For instance, the group's goal for the entirety of episodes two and three of season one is to retrieve a bag of guns and ammunition Rick left behind in Atlanta. Surprisingly little screen time is given to the problems of procuring potable water and food. Throughout much of the series, it is assumed that Rick's group is able to scavenge enough supplies, and each of the locations they spend a significant amount of time at (the farm in season two and the prison in season three) are miraculously well-stocked with food. Even when they are missing an important necessity, such as baby formula in season three, the group quickly scavenges for a whole case.

Until season four, basic medical problems were virtually non-existent in *The Walking Dead*. Many of the characters seem to have superhuman tolerance for heat and resistance to disease. Most of the medical issues the series deals with are related to battle wounds and accidents, rather than common diseases that would kill people where modern medicine is not available. For example, Rick's and Lori's son, Carl (Chandler Riggs) is accidentally shot in the opening episode of season two, and the next two episodes are devoted to procuring medical supplies and the surgery performed by the farmer, Hershel (Scott Wilson). In the first episode of season three, Hershel is bitten on the leg by a zombie, yet he survives a hatchet-job amputation. In the season-long conflict between Rick's group at the prison and the Governor's at the nearby settlement, Woodbury, several people die of gunshot wounds and explosions, yet no one is shown to contract typhus, dysentery, cholera or influenza – all major killers before modern medicine and currently existent in places where medical resources are scarce. Thus, in showing a modified version of the difficulties of surviving in an austere world, such as *The Walking Dead*'s emphasis on weapons and combat rather than the traditional bare necessities, the austerity of their lives is not as austere as it seems because the characters do not seem to require as many of the basics as real-life humans. Ideologically speaking, it is fascinating given that in September 2013 more than 47.3 million US citizens received supplemental nutrition assistance, while *The Walking Dead* argues that the most important goods in a world of bare survival are weapons (US Department of Agriculture Food and Nutrition Service, 2013, n.p.).

White Males Back on Top in the Zombie Apocalypse

As shown above, *The Walking Dead* practices austerity in industrial terms and a form of austerity is present in its narrative elements, such as its parsimony of locations and the rules of survival. Its representations of characters and social structures also reveal some of the series' ideological underpinnings. Based on the content of the episodes, it may be concluded that the show promotes the naturalness of white male leadership, as well as old notions of gender roles. Such ideas are in line with an ideology behind austerity that says that those who need government services are weak and a burden on those who pay for the services. Since many of the perceived recipients of those benefits are women with children and minority groups who have suffered oppression and multiple forms of institutionalised inequality, the austerity of *The Walking Dead*'s narrative is something of a white male fantasy of a 'return' to power and traditional gender roles.

The naturalness of governance by white males is re-asserted in *The Walking Dead*'s post-apocalyptic world. In almost every social formation consisting of more than just a few survivors, the leader is a white male and this is assumed to be the 'natural' order of things. In the second episode of the first season, Rick encounters several members of the group of survivors that (unbeknownst to him at the time) include his wife and son, scavenging for supplies in an overrun Atlanta. When the group's racist leader, Merle Dixon (Michael Rooker), becomes unstable and threatens the life of an African American member of the group, T-Dog (Irone Singleton), Rick assaults Merle and takes over his position as the leader. After they rejoin the rest of the survivors, Rick assumes the leadership role, and this is largely unquestioned, even though he is a newcomer. His background as a sheriff's deputy also seems to give him additional credibility above the others, and in this way, the group clings to an older, patriarchal and pre-disaster notion of authority by automatically deferring to a representative of the old establishment of law and order. Writing about the comics, Gerry Canavan

142

argues that Rick Grimes is a 'synechdoche for pre-zombie social order' and that position is replicated in the television series (Canavan, 2010, p. 436). In *The Walking Dead*, the band of survivors bow to the familiar authority of law enforcement (one of the preeminent symbols and actors of the white male establishment power structure), even though the institutions of law and its enforcement have ceased to exist. Granted, Rick possesses intelligence, a firm moral compass, and skills in firearms and tactics, yet other characters in the group are endowed with many 'heroic' qualities. Glenn (Steven Yeun), for instance, is intelligent, proficient at procuring supplies and has a solid, moral sensibility. However, he is of Korean American heritage and his former employment in pizza delivery seems to relegate him (problematically) to the role of supporting player (both in the narrative of the series, but also, possibly, in Steven Yeun's status as an Asian American actor in Hollywood).

White males are also the leaders of other social formations in the series. When the group makes their way to the farm where the majority of the episodes in season two take place, they find that the leader of the small group already there is the owner of the farm, Hershel – a traditional, white male patriarch. Because the farm is his property (though the meaning of property and property laws is not seriously revised or discussed in *The Walking Dead* in spite of the fact that there are no institutions to enforce them), he gives the orders and the members of his group follow them. Also present is the authoritarian Governor, who figures prominently in season three. Though seemingly possessing no special skills such as Rick's law enforcement training or Hershel's medical knowledge, the Governor rules the small town of Woodbury because his talent seems to be his ruthlessness. Though each white male's leadership style and abilities vary, their positions of leadership go unquestioned for much of the series.

The storylines tend to pit the leaders' strategies against each other, with the members of the various groups as pawns. For example, in season two, Rick attempts to negotiate an arrangement for his group to stay on Hershel's land. Hershel wants them to leave as soon as everyone is healthy and able to travel. In episode six of season two, Hershel says to Rick: 'Let's keep this simple. I'll control my people, and you control yours'. The majority of season three's episodes focus on the violent and ongoing conflict between Rick's group at the prison and the Governor's group at Woodbury.

The supporting characters are mostly at the mercy of the plans of their leaders, who happen to be white males contesting for territorial domination and resources, much like the world before the undead takeover. If the utopian potential of the zombie apocalypse as articulated by John Powers lies in its ability to imagine better, future alternatives to capitalism and its accompanying power structures, *The Walking Dead*'s story envisions social formations that revisit and uphold white male patriarchy.[1]

Complementing the rejuvenation of white male power is the reinforcement of old gender roles, with a large dose of misogyny. Though later in the series several of the female characters are trained in firearms and become adequate in their use, the men are the primary hunters, protectors and fighters. The women's duties are almost exclusively domestic: they cook, do the laundry and care for the children. These tasks would have greater narrative importance if food was presented as extremely scarce or if illness and sanitation were bigger problems. Instead, these tasks are presented as mundane and as far less essential than the traditionally male activities of hunting and fighting. In season one, episode three, four of the female characters work together to do the group's laundry. In a rare moment questioning the gender roles of the group, Jacqui (Jeryl Prescott) (who ends up committing suicide by the end of season one) says 'Can someone explain to me how the women ended up doing all the Hattie McDaniel work?' Carol (Melissa McBride) replies, 'It's just the way it is'. Later in the scene, when Carol's husband, Ed (Adam Minarovich), becomes verbally and physically abusive, Shane attacks Ed to protect the females, but he does not help them with the laundry. Also, Shane's violent actions seem motivated as much by his frustration over losing Lori due to Rick's unexpected return as a sense of justice. When the incident is over, the women resume their work, and neither they nor Shane further question the division of labour.

The Walking Dead represents its female characters as morally, mentally and physically weaker than the men. In many cases they are liabilities rather than assets to the group. In the pilot episode, a flashback scene depicts a discussion between Rick and Shane before the zombie crisis. The differences between men and women are the subject of their talk. They conclude that women are wasteful and cruel, first through a joke that women are physically incapable of turning off lights, and, second, through

Rick's confession that earlier that day Lori had spoken harsh words to Rick in front of their son, Carl, questioning their marriage and Rick's commitment to the family. Throughout the first and second seasons, Lori is condemned for sleeping with Shane, even though everyone believed Rick was dead. This culminates in her death during childbirth early in season three which positions the tragedy as a punishment for her faithlessness to her (presumed dead) husband. Whether the baby was a product of the affair remains unclear.

In addition to their moral failings in this austere world of zombie crisis, women are usually represented as mentally unstable and physically weak. Andrea's (Laurie Holden) teenage sister, Amy (Emma Bell) is killed by a zombie in episode four of season one. During the attack, Amy is too terrified to fight back effectively; her physical weakness and inability to overcome her fear lead to her death. After Amy dies, Andrea becomes depressed and suicidal. Later, in season three, she becomes the Governor's lover, and her decision whether to stay with him and his group or leave causes the Governor's first attack on the prison. Throughout the latter episodes of season two and early in season three, Lori's pregnancy is a problem, and her medical needs hinder the group's ability to migrate; she becomes more or less baggage during the early portion of season three. Simon Abrams of *The Village Voice* writes that 'As in the comics, Lori provided Rick with a sense of normalcy rather than with anything like, say, practical aid' (Abrams, 2013, n.p.). Maggie was a helpful co-scavenger and Glenn's love-interest in season two and some of season three, but later in season three, as Abrams points out, 'Maggie (Lauren Cohan) wasn't given much to do after the Governor nearly raped her' (Abrams, 2013, n.p.). The trauma from this incident compromised her ability to be a productive member of the group for some of the third season. Michonne (Danai Gurira) is an exception to many of the depictions of women on the series because she is skilled with a katana blade and is probably the best hand-to-hand fighter of the group. However, she is mostly silent throughout and her lack of backstory in season three makes her something of an enigma and less a fully fleshed out character. Because of her fighting skill and mental toughness, Michonne does not fit into the series' neatly defined gender roles for women. This calls into question whether the writers are unsure how to portray a woman who does not easily fit into traditional gender roles.

These characterisations also stem from Robert Kirkman's source material and concepts. Recalling an interview with Kirkman, Abrams provides the reasoning behind the representation of women in *The Walking Dead*:

> I asked Robert Kirkman a tough question about his *Walking Dead* comic series, a question that now, after the TV adaptation's third season finale, is still resonant: Why are all the strong female characters either crazy or dead? His response, from issue No. 289 of *The Comics Journal*: 'I don't mean to sound sexist, but as far as women have come over the last 40 years, you don't really see a lot of women hunters. They're still in the minority in the military, and there's not a lot of female construction workers. I hope that's not taken the wrong way. I think women are as smart, resourceful, and capable in most things as any man could be ... but they are generally physically weaker. That's science.'
>
> (Abrams, 2013, n.p.)

According to *The Walking Dead*, women are often a liability in a world in which danger and death are ever-present and resources are scarce. Their moral, mental and physical weaknesses make it more difficult to survive in an austere world. At best, they do the traditional domestic chores assigned to women, and at worst they directly or indirectly cause death and destruction to the group through their mental 'weakness' (such as Amy's inability to overcome her terror) and physical infirmity.

The Walking Dead's essentialist portrayals of women also contribute to the show's reinforcement of gender roles. By displaying the seemingly inherent and biologically preordained weakness of women, the show's affirmation of patriarchy makes logical sense, thus reinforcing the 'naturalness' of male leadership. Women are *too* infirm to make the tough decisions necessary to protect the group; therefore, it is the 'duty' of the men to carry on and lead. In this way, *The Walking Dead* does not depict a do-over for civilisation, but rather a reinforcement of a conservative ideology that also advocates austerity in public and economic policies. In discourses supporting austerity, much of the blame is placed on those who use public services (and these are usually represented as women and minorities), and they state that 'everyone' (these same women, minorities and the entire working class) needs to make sacrifices to restore prosperity.

The Walking Dead's representations certainly advocate a reinforced patriarchal order and gender roles, but those ideological positions are undercut in several ways, too. For instance, the world that the characters inhabit is not an appealing one. Death is always a threat in the form of hordes of zombies that may strike at any moment, in spite of plentiful food and the characters' immunity to common diseases. The white male leadership of the groups often fails to protect them from the undead, too. In some cases, mistakes on the part of the leaders make the group more unsafe and unstable. For instance, in episode five of season two, Glenn learns that Hershel is keeping zombies locked in his barn because he believes they are sick people, rather than undead monsters. This puts everyone on the farm at risk and the resolution of this problem is a major point of conflict between Rick's group and Hershel's. At the end of season two, a horde of zombies attacks the farm and Hershel's ignorance of the threat of a potential zombie invasion leads to the deaths of several characters and a forced abandonment of the group's safe haven. In season three, the death of Lori unhinges Rick and he begins to hallucinate, compromising his ability to lead. The 'naturalness' of white male leadership may be apparent in the series, but the results of it are often negative.

At times, the series also seems to argue for democracy and a plurality of voices, including women's, within the social formations. As Rick's group escapes the chaos of the attack at the end of season two, Rick's leadership is questioned, but he declares: 'Get one thing straight: If you're staying, this isn't a democracy anymore' (season two, episode thirteen). Much of the third season is a battle between two absolute rulers, Rick and the Governor, and once again, the result is death and destruction for both groups. Near the end of season three, Rick changes his mind, saying: 'What I said last year, that first night after the farm – it can't be like that. It can't. What we do, what we're willing to do, who we are – is not my call. It can't be.' This leaves open the possibility of a more democratic social formation, and perhaps even a role for the women to take part in the governance of the group in season four. If the roles of the female characters are expanded or valued more, that would seriously question the gender roles on display in the first three seasons. But at the same time, this call to establish a more democratic group comes from the white male in charge, complicating this moment by reinforcing his authority to determine the kind of governance for the group. If *The Walking Dead* is a white male fantasy of power, then that power is often abused and shown to be destructive, but it is still the white male's to take or delegate. As of this writing, what a more democratic group would look like has not yet been determined by the series.

The Walking Dead is an exemplary austere television series. Its industrial practices reveal neoliberal economic logic, and the show's ideology is apparent in a narrative that presents an austere, but not anarchic, world in which patriarchy and gender roles have been reinforced. Thus, it seems that the series does not fulfil what John Powers describes as the progressive potential of the post-apocalyptic zombie narrative to imagine new and more equal social formations (2013, n.p.). In spite of the reinscription of patriarchy and gender roles, this world is not a peaceful and prosperous place. The social groups are dysfunctional in many ways, and the sheer amount of death seems to indicate that something is severely wrong with the way the new, post-apocalyptic society is ordered. Through *The Walking Dead*'s industrial, narrative and representational elements, it is possible to see how austerity is connected to patriarchy and gender roles, as well as how a 'reestablishment' of patriarchy and gender roles is not a path to a more just and peaceful human civilisation.

Note

1 *The Walking Dead* contrasts with some key zombie films like George Romero's *Night of the Living Dead* (1968) and *Dawn of the Dead* (1978), in that both feature African American men as capable leaders and survivors. In the case of *Night of the Living Dead*, the racism of the survivors in the farmhouse (most prominently displayed by Harry [Karl Hardman]) and the sheriff's posse proves deadlier than the shuffling zombies. These films are more overtly critical of racist power structures.

Bibliography

Abrams, Simon. (2013). 'Think *The Walking Dead* Has a Woman Problem? Here's the Source'. *Village Voice*, 3 April. Available from: <http://www.villagevoice.com/2013-04-03/film/the-walking-dead-woman-problem/> [Accessed: 10 December 2013].

Andreeva, Nellie. (2010). "*The Walking Dead*" Lets Go of Writers; Considers No Writing Staff for Season 2'. *Deadline Hollywood*, 1 December. Available from: <http://www.deadline.com/2010/12/the-walking-dead-lets-go-of-writers-considers-no-writing-staff-for-season-2/> [Accessed: 29 November 2013].

Bishop, Kyle William. (2010). *American Zombie Gothic: The Rise and Fall (and Rise) of the Walking Dead in Popular Culture*. Jefferson, NC: McFarland.

Blyth, Mark. (2013). *Austerity: The History of a Dangerous Idea*. Oxford: Oxford University Press.

Canavan, Gerry. (2010). "'We *Are* the Walking Dead": Race, Time, and Survival in Zombie Narrative'. *Extrapolation*, 51/3, pp. 431–53.

Crary, Jonathan. (2013). *24/7: Late Capitalism and the Ends of Sleep*. London: Verso.

Goldman, Eric. (2010). 'AMC Orders *Walking Dead* Pilot'. *IGN*, 20 January. Available from: <http://www.ign.com/articles/2010/01/20/amc-orders-walking-dead-pilot> [Accessed: 29 November 2013].

Harman, Chris. (2009). *Zombie Capitalism: Global Crisis and the Relevance of Marx*. London: Bookmarks.

Ocasio, Anthony. (2013). '"*The Walking Dead*": Why Frank Darabont was Fired & the Chaotic Aftermath'. *ScreenRant*. Available from: <http://screenrant.com/walking-dead-frank-darabont-amc-aco-127783/> [Accessed: 29 November 2013].

Pangburn, D.J. (2013). "*The Walking Dead*" is Suffering from AMC's Fiscal Austerity: How to Kill a Good Thing'. *deathandtaxes*, 5 March. Available from: <http://www.deathandtaxesmag.com/195196/the-walking-dead-is-suffering-from-amcs-fiscal-austerity-how-to-kill-a-good-thing/> [Accessed: 10 December 2013].

Peisner, David. (2013). 'Rick Grimes is Having Yet Another Very Bad Day', *Rolling Stone*, 1194, pp. 54–59.

Powers, John. (2013). 'The Political Economy of Zombies'. *Airship Daily*. Available from: <http://airshipdaily.com/the-political-economy-of-zombies/> [Accessed: 25 October 2013].

Quiggin, John. (2010). *Zombie Economics: How Dead Ideas Still Walk Among Us*. Princeton: Princeton University Press.

Thompson, Robert J. (1997). *Television's Second Golden Age: From Hill Street Blues to ER*. New York: Syracuse University Press.

US Department of Agriculture Food and Nutrition Service. (2013). 'Data and Statistics'. Available from: <http://www.fns.usda.gov/data-and-statistics> [Accessed: 10 December 2013].

7

Embodying Austerity: Food and Physicality in *The Hunger Games*

Erin Wyble Newcomb

Suzanne Collins's novel *The Hunger Games* (2010) pits the wealthy and gluttonous Capitol of Panem (and its inhabitants) against the impoverished and starving districts whose population depends on Panem for government and resources. The novel glorifies the struggle of its protagonist, Katniss Everdeen, who avoids the malnutrition of her community through skilled hunting and calculated law-breaking. The novel's titular event draws Katniss from her quiet existence on the periphery of her country into an arena where children must fight to the death to win wealth, fame and, of course, food for themselves and their communities. Much of the novel revolves around food – its surfeit or its lack, its quality, its emphasis in characters' daily lives. By establishing the Capitol as the enemy, Collins privileges austere consumption of food, elevating those characters whose existence hinges on the arrival of the next meal and whose bodies manifest the symptoms of persistent under-feeding and malnourishment. At one point during her training for the Hunger Games, Katniss outlines the steps she would need to take to recreate one of the meals in Panem; she concludes:

> What must it be like, I wonder, to live in a world where food appears at the press of the button? How would I spend the

hours I now commit to combing the woods for sustenance if it were so easy to come by? What do they do all day, these people in the Capitol, besides decorating their bodies and waiting around for a new shipment of tributes to roll in and die for their entertainment?

(Collins, 2010, p. 65)

Food differentiates between citizens like Katniss who value hard work, resourcefulness and purposeful time management, and 'these people in the Capitol' whose lives revolve around luxury, ease and frivolous self-gratification. Austerity, in the context of Panem, defines the virtuous poor (where virtue and poverty are one and the same) in opposition to the greedy elite. Whereas the novel emphasises class depictions of poverty that equate hunger with morality in order to encourage readers to identify with the oppressed people of Panem, viewers of the film gender those austere standards by evaluating the actress's body and finding her wanting (or, indeed, not wanting enough).

Critical reception of the 2012 film rendition of *The Hunger Games* challenges the cinematic representation of austerity by voicing the concern that the actress (Jennifer Lawrence) who plays Katniss did not adequately embody a starving protagonist. Amidst a chorus of reviewers who raise similar objections, Manohla Dargis of the *New York Times* asserts that Lawrence does not look 'hungry enough [...] for a dystopian fantasy about a people starved into submission' (2012, n.p.). In a comparable vein, Melissa Silverstein remarks:

> As of two days ago *The Hunger Games*' domestic gross was up above $173 million dollars. It will clearly be above $200 million before the weekend. It's a success so the nitpicking has started. We've seen [...] the racist tweets and now there are people complaining that Jennifer Lawrence looked a bit too healthy playing a character who was supposed to be poor and hungry.
>
> (Silverstein, 2012, n.p.)

Tying together the commercial juggernaut of the film and a feminist critique, Silverstein quips that 'This is beyond disgusting. Lawrence looks normal. Her male co-stars look even healthier (and have some seriously big muscles) yet no one thinks they are too healthy or big boned or big boobed or just plain old fat' (2012, n.p.). Silverstein recognises the gendered and racialised power dynamics influencing the reception of the film, and Elizabeth Lancaster sees the intersections as well, writing:

> This backlash about Lawrence's weight comes in the wake of the questioning of Rue's race in the film. The pre-teen is played by Amandla Stenberg, who is African American. In recent days her casting was the subject of racially fuelled criticism by a handful of moviegoers who have suffered their own backlash.
>
> (2012, n.p.)

While I do not deal specifically with the character of Rue or the racist reception of her casting, I think it speaks volumes that audiences respond to these actresses' bodies in an attempt to police and subvert the interpretation of Collins's novel (where, not incidentally, Rue is described as dark skinned on page 126).

I argue that the gendering of austerity in the film illustrates a reification of starving bodies that mirrors the spectacle of the Hunger Games themselves in Collins's original text; the clamour for accuracy that seeks to diminish the actress's physical form is akin to the voyeurism that prompts the Capitol's affluent, indulgent residents to find pleasure in the violent oppression of the Games' contestants. The criticism of Lawrence's body demonstrates that viewers are doubly watching *The Hunger Games*: as audience to the film and as citizens who enforce standards of austerity without recognising the extent to which the spectators best identify with the Capitol's extravagance. Shannon Mortimore-Smith compares the audience(s) not just to the Capitol but to the Gamemakers – those responsible for the direct manipulation of the Tributes within the arena: 'these millions, with one hand planted firmly on the remote control and the other buried in a bowl of buttered popcorn, continue to influence the outcomes of those they observe' (2012, p. 159). Mortimore-Smith says viewers are 'insulated by their own apathy and far from any "real" danger or consequences' and support the continued spectacle 'through their "sponsorship" of the advertisers who fuel this programming' (2012, p. 159). Audiences, says Mortimore-Smith, do not consume passively, even if (or perhaps especially when) the primary exchange for entertainment is our attention. Audiences actively interpret, constructing and deconstructing the meaning as they read and watch.

In this chapter, I structure my argument in three parts: defining the relationship between austerity and consumption in *The Hunger Games* novel, illustrating the movement from consumption as spectacle for audiences of the film and within the novel, and, finally, demonstrating the transformation of bodies into products also ripe for audiences' consumption. Using feminist theories of embodiment, I analyse the gendering of austerity where starvation (or the appearance of starving) signifies feminine virtue, reflecting the oppressive nature of the Capitol's regime back upon the audiences whose appetite for emaciated female forms seems insatiable.

Austere Consumption

Early in Collins's novel, Katniss describes her hometown as 'District Twelve. Where you can starve to death in safety' (2010, p. 6), and despite the heroine's fear that her rebellious words might be overheard, she later repeats 'Starvation's not an uncommon fate in District Twelve' (2010, p. 28). Once in the Capitol, Katniss calculates her ability to recreate one of the feasts:

> I try to imagine assembling this meal myself back home. Chickens are too expensive, but I could make do with a wild turkey. I'd need to shoot a second turkey to trade for an orange. Goat's milk would have to substitute for cream. We can grow peas in the garden. I'd have to get wild onions from the woods. I don't recognize the grain, our own tessera ration cooks down to an unattractive brown mush. Fancy rolls would mean another trade with the baker, perhaps for two or three squirrels. As for the pudding, I can't even guess what's in it. Days of hunting and gathering for this one meal and even then it would be a poor substitution for the Capitol version.
>
> (Collins, 2010, p. 65)

The text's title emphasises food relationships, and Katniss delineates the consumption hierarchy here, where the Capitol glories in luxury and surfeit and the outlying districts struggle for survival against imminent and ever-present starvation. Food defines Katniss's life and times and serves for the audience as a kind of moral compass wherein the Capitol's lifestyle of ease contrasts with the Districts' work ethic; austere consumption signals moral fortitude as opposed to frivolity.

That assumed relationship between food consumption and personal morality exists outside Collins's work as well. In 'The "Fine Reality of Hunger Satisfied": Food as Cultural Metaphor in Panem', Max Despain asserts that Collins envisions 'gastronomy as the essential descriptor of society and culture' (2012, p. 69). Further, he writes, by '[t]apping into the complex contemporary guilt Americans feel about indulgence, abundance, and weight gain, Collins can count on her readers to find the Everdeen family's hand-to-mouth existence as unfamiliar as the hovercraft in her narrative' (2012, p. 70). Based on this interpretation, it seems clear that Collins means to align the audience of her novel and the film with the audience of the Games themselves – a sort of meta-commentary on spectatorship. As Despain implies, an audience who can purchase books and film tickets shares more in common with the Capitol than Katniss's District Twelve; at the same time, just because audiences share the values and practices of the Capitol does not mean they fail to recognise the virtuousness implied by Katniss's consumption. *The Hunger Games* as novel and film asks us to root for Katniss and apply the same standards of austerity to the actress who embodies the protagonist as the Capitol does to the Districts. Despain concludes that in the penultimate scene with the berries, 'Collins clings to this theme of the poisonous quality of food' (2012, p. 71), yet the relationships between the Capitol and the Districts, as well as between the audiences real and fictional, remain fraught with contradictions about consumption. Katniss wins the Hunger Games by abstaining from the poisonous berries, and audiences laud that self-control as morally exemplary even as most (like the Capitol) fail to practice it.

The privileging of austere consumption in both Katniss's victory and Collins's real-life audiences shows up in the backlash against Jennifer Lawrence's body, where audiences assume that bodies correlate directly to food consumption practices; says feminist theorist Susan Bordo, 'The body – what we eat, how we dress, the daily rituals through which we attend to the body – is a medium of culture. [...] The body may also operate as a metaphor for culture' (1993, p. 165). Reviewers who criticised Lawrence's body engage in two levels of cultural critique, where her body gets read as too full in a context of food abundance and where the culture itself is both too full and insatiably hungry; at the same time that the critics impose an austere view of consumption, they highlight the cultural failures to maintain the intertwined standards of austerity and morality. That cultural gluttony gets inscribed on Lawrence's body, demanding a kind of verisimilitude from her performance that is illusory and always unsatisfying. The irony of audiences critiquing Lawrence's form surfaces in the film reviews and the even more contemporary issue of leaked nude photos of the actress, where despite finding her body wanting, the image of it becomes a product to consume – and audiences always want more. *Vanity Fair*'s November 2014 cover features Lawrence proclaiming 'It's my body, and it should be my choice'. In the novel and the film, as well as their surrounding marketing, consumption becomes spectacle as *The Hunger Games* becomes a brand, and a household name, along with its players.

Spectacle and Consumption

Take, for instance, the *Covergirl* campaign accompanying the release of the second film, *Catching Fire*, which advertises '12 districts. 12 looks. 1 exquisite collection. Choose your district' (Long, 2013, n.p.). Consider also the bump in book sales Andy Lewis attributed to the film: 'Publisher Scholastic announced today that there were 36.5 million copies of the bestselling trilogy in print, a 55 percent jump from the 23.5 million copies in print at the start of 2012' (2012, n.p.). By the summer of 2012, John Gaudiosi reported that:

> Although author Suzanne Collins only wrote three books, her Hunger Games trilogy has been able to zap the magic out of J.K. Rowling's seven-part Harry Potter franchise on Amazon.com. Taking into consideration print and digital Kindle book sales combined, *The Hunger Games*, which are much shorter reads than the Potter books, have captivated a wider range of fans around the globe.
>
> (Gaudiosi, 2012, n.p.)

Amidst sales of products like *The Unofficial Hunger Games Cookbook* (by Emily Ansara Baines, 2011), film-inspired Barbie dolls and an increased interest in archery (Hood, 2013), the marketing juggernaut spawned by Collins's work illustrates the range of players in this capitalistic (and Capitol-istic) frenzy. The spectacle of consumption surrounding the products of *The Hunger Games* as novel and film mirrors the spectacle of consumption imposed by the Capitol regime. As Katniss describes:

> To make it humiliating as well as torturous, the Capitol requires us to treat the Hunger Games as a festivity, a sporting event pitting every district against the others. The last tribute alive receives a life of ease back home, and their district will be showered with prizes, largely consisting of food. All year, the Capitol will show the winning district gifts of grain and oil and even delicacies like sugar while the rest of us battle starvation.
>
> (Collins, 2010, p. 19)

Collins's use of the verb 'show' here plays interestingly with the idea of spectacle, and the contrast between the delicacies given to the winning districts and the consumption practices of the book and film audiences demonstrates their clear alignment with the Capitol citizens' appetite for luxury goods; by contrast, the districts' awe of sugar seems beyond austere.

It is no wonder, given that context, that Katniss seems obsessed with food throughout the novel. She acknowledges a pre-meal 'basket of rolls […] would keep my family going for a week' (Collins, 2010, p. 55) and says her favourite part of the Capitol experience is '[t]he lamb stew' (Collins, 2010, p. 127). Her own understanding of consumption is set against her awareness of differences in Capitol culture, explaining:

> The arenas are historic sites, preserved after the Games. Popular destinations for Capitol residents to visit, to vacation. Go for a month, rewatch the Games, tour the catacombs, visit the sites where the deaths took place. You can even take part in reenactments. They say the food is excellent.
>
> (Collins, 2010, p. 145)

While this quotation demonstrates Katniss's grim humour and the apathy of the spectators she must please as her sponsors, it also bears an eerie resemblance to the practices of audiences outside the text and film, who also role play and purchase their way into the dystopian narrative. That gulf between the priorities of the Capitol and the districts extends to interpretations of bodies as well. Katniss discloses '[t]hey do surgery in the Capitol, to make people appear younger and thinner' whereas in District 12, 'looking old is something of an achievement since so many people die early' and '[a] plump person is envied because they aren't scraping by like the majority of us' (Collins, 2010, p. 125). Katniss takes it as given that her embodiment is part of the spectacle of the Hunger Games, because 'the best-looking tributes always seem to pull more sponsors' (Collins, 2010, p. 59), and so her training regime incorporates appealing to the Capitol's standards of beauty without the lifelong supply of Capitol resources. Readers and filmgoers seem to apply similar prescriptions for characters' actions and appearances, thus layering the spectacle with consumption of the food, the texts and the represented bodies.

That representation and critique of Lawrence's size takes on a gendered component as some critics respond to the space her character occupies in relation to her male counterparts. Linda Holmes quips 'Going by the traditional Hollywood rules, make no mistake: Peeta is a Movie Girlfriend' a gendered mashup she calls 'rather delightful' (2013, n.p.). Jeffrey Wells, meanwhile, claims that:

> Lawrence seems too big for Hutcherson. She's a fairly tall, big-boned lady (I've been in a hotel room with her) who's maybe 5'8", and he seems to be something like 5'7". Male romantic figures have to be at least as tall as their female partners, and we all know most girls like guys to be at least a little bit taller, so Lawrence and Hutcherson don't seem like a good fit.
>
> (Wells, 2012, n.p.)

Here Wells highlights the romance of the film, missing or ignoring that the romance is staged and Katniss herself spends much of the storyline preoccupied with their survival as opposed to their romantic 'fit'. Perhaps Wells, like the Capitol audience, gets caught up in the star-crossed lovers angle that Katniss exploits when she muses 'One kiss equals one pot of broth. It's not the sort of thing I can blurt out, either. To say my thoughts aloud would be tipping off the audience that the romance has been fabricated to play on their sympathies and that would result in no food at all' (Collins, 2010, p. 296). The aesthetic arguments about the pairing of Katniss and Peeta distract from the context of survival and violence, and audiences within the story and outside it seem eager to gobble up a love triangle in lieu of a narrative that offends and challenges the commodification and consumption of gendered bodies.

In their tellingly titled piece "'She's More Like a Guy" and "He's More Like a Teddy Bear": Perceptions of Violence and Gender in *The Hunger Games*', Nancy Taber, Vera Woloshyn and Laura Lane discuss their studies of adolescent girls reading the series. They state that 'three out of the four participants believed that girls do not fight and are more likely to be interested in romance than violence' (Taber, Woloshyn and Lane, 2013, p. 1030) and that 'the girls appeared most comfortable when the characters enacted stereotypical gendered behaviors in the book' (p. 1034). These authors indicate the ways that readers can resist messages that defy hegemonic codes, choosing instead to emphasise the aspects of texts that reinforce rather than challenge audiences' ideologies. In another essay, the same authors team up to analyse the ways that Katniss as a character defies audiences' gendered expectations: 'her female body marks her as a woman with elements of emphasized femininity while her actions encompass elements of hegemonic masculinity' (Woloshyn, Taber and Lane, 2013, pp. 151–152). Katniss's gendered ambivalence creates a marketing problem for her Hunger Games prep team, and Woloshyn, Taber and Lane assert '[i]n order to gain audience approval and sponsorship, she needs to adopt a feminine, romantic orientation as the object of heterosexual desire' (2013, p. 157). These authors problematise that role within the text and I would extend their argument by adding that viewers of the film seem to come up against the same problem as readers and citizens of the Capitol – that Katniss takes up too much space. Emphasising the romantic storyline repositions Katniss not as protagonist but as object, and dismissing Lawrence's body as 'too big' for her part suggests a larger cultural problem with powerful womanhood or femininity that demands visibility while eschewing traditional gender roles. The problem, then, with Katniss or Lawrence is not that either is too big or too powerful, but that each disrupts hegemonic masculinity; the woman who takes up too much space is a problem not because of her consumption, but because of her womanhood.

Bordo outlines the problem of associating the female with the body (and thus the male with the mind) in *Unbearable Weight*, concluding:

> The body as animal, as appetite, as deceiver, as prison of the soul and confounder of its projects: these are common images within Western philosophy. This is not to say that a negative construction of the body has ruled without historical challenge,

or that it has taken only one form, for the imaginal shape of the body has been historically variable.

(Bordo, 1993, p. 3)

Elspbeth Probyn takes Bordo's premise into a post-modern context where 'the feminine body, fragmented and processed through the simulacrum of the media scene, has become the metaphor for all bodies', and, further, 'bodies, not as flat surfaces, but as ever-changing, embodied subjectivities' (1987, pp. 350, 357). These feminist theorists gender the interpretation of bodies like Lawrence's, asking audiences to reevaluate what it might mean to impose austerity on the physical form of a female lead. Katniss's – or Lawrence's – body becomes problematic for multiple audiences who imagine and interpret her body as a medium for conveying a controversial message. As Allison Layfield writes:

> In relation to *The Hunger Games*, this search for the 'naked self' is further complicated by the layers of audiences who 'watch' Katniss progress through the games. There is the Panem audience, consisting of viewers in the different districts from which the tributes are collected. Then there are the actual readers of *The Hunger Games* novels, who watch the games through Katniss's perspective and 'see' the filming of the games through written description. Finally, there are the viewers of *The Hunger Games* film adapted from the first novel. For each of these groups, the 'real' Katniss is determined by distinctly different layers of representation.
>
> (Layfield, 2013, n.p.)

Layfield problematises nakedness, watching, seeing and reality itself, illustrating that each is deferred and constructed within a network of always-mediated images. While Layfield's project centres on 'identity construction' and *The Hunger Games* as a product of reality television, her discussion of audience implicitly alludes to Jean Baudrillard's concepts of the simulacrum, where the 'hyperreality' of signs, images and simulation take the place of the material; says Baudrillard in *Simulacra and Simulacrum*, '[i]t is a question of substituting the signs of the real for the real (1994, p. 2). Yet many feminists question what happens when an image of the body (the hyperreal) displaces the significance of the material body.

In 'Beating the Meat/Surviving the Text, or How to Get Out of this Century Alive', Vivian Sobchack asserts '[t]he sense of the body that Baudrillard privileges, then, is sense as it is amputated from its origins in material existence' (1995, p. 207). Sobchack proclaims 'Pain would remind [Baudrillard] that he doesn't just *have* a body, but that he *is* his body', a reminder that she sees as central to human feeling and morality – 'based on the lived sense and feeling of the human body not merely as a material object one possesses and analyzes among others, but as a material subject that experiences its own objectivity' (1995, p. 213; emphasis in original). Victoria Grace reads Baudrillard differently in an attempt to redeem the theorist's utility for feminist theories. She writes:

> In Baudrillard's terms, power, meaning, and reality are illusory. This does not mean that the real is a figment of our imaginations! In fact, possibly the 'reality' of the real is so unbearably not a figment of our imaginations that we attempt to render it bearable (apparently controllable) through ideologically reducing the metamorphosis of the real (the play of illusory appearances) to a transcendent instance. It is then truly of the order of illusion. To dissolve power and meaning through the reversion of their illusion is to dissolve ontology of any essence; to return it to the symbolic order of appearances.
>
> (Grace, 2000, p. 192)

Sobchack and Grace both strive (albeit in distinct ways) to reconcile Baudrillard's concept of hyperreality with materiality. It is telling that Sobchack invokes pain while Grace references (lack of) control and (un) bearability – two traits that often elude bodies and that are particularly assigned to female bodies; the 'bearable' and 'unbearable' that Grace describes relate to the title of Bordo's seminal work on the body as 'unbearable weight' (Grace, 2000, p. 192). Vivienne Muller applies Baudrillard directly to *The Hunger Games*, querying 'is there a danger that the texts become what they condemn, a simulacrum that eventually fails to move beyond its own terms of reference?' (Muller, 2012, p. 62) Or, to relate that question specifically to how audiences of *The Hunger Games* read gendered bodies, what does it mean for spectators to say Katniss is not 'hungry enough'?

Unlike her multiple audiences, Katniss never forgets that she is part of a mediated spectacle; in Collins's novel, she shows continual (and savvy) awareness of the cameras within and beyond the area – a strength that helps her survive. At one point during the Games, she admits 'I'm glad for the cameras now. I want sponsors to see that I can hunt, that I'm a good bet because I won't be lured into traps as easily as the others will by hunger' (Collins, 2010, p. 164). Katniss cites her lack of hunger as an asset in a contest predicated on the idea that the hunger of others makes good entertainment. Critic Shannon Mortimore-Smith writes:

> Like many young adult viewers today, the futuristic Capitol citizens who reside in the pages of Collins's cautionary tale are intentionally oblivious to the power of their gaze. Whether caught up in the 'drama' of reality television or Panem's games, both real and fictional audiences alike are ensnared by the remarkable pageantry that accompanies each spectacle.
>
> (2012, p. 164)

Given the reception of the film, I would extend Mortimore-Smith's argument to adults as well, suggesting that the allure of imposing austerity on others' consumption is a temptation that draws audiences into forgetting the ways that the images of Katniss and Panem obscure material conditions of human bodies with appetites. As Mortimore-Smith continues, '[r]elishing their claim over the lives of those they view, twenty-first-century audiences – consumed with their next media fix – fail to recognize that they, too, have become hostages to the entertainment they watch' (2012, p. 165). We may be what we eat, and we are, Mortimore-Smith asserts here, likewise consumed by what we consume. Mortimore-Smith advocates a critical reading stance for audiences, just as Katniss develops an oppositional gaze where she positions herself actively for the cameras instead of passively being a pawn in the Games.

The problem, even with that kind of critical reading (a point where I wholeheartedly agree with Mortimore-Smith), is that both the fictional Katniss and the real Lawrence illustrate the ways that interpretation is not always controllable. Helen Day points out that 'Katniss's strength comes from recognizing that she is always a part of the Hunger Games', yet realises that '[s]imulation, in this series, is always a temporary state: the real can be hijacked, but it always returns' (2012, pp. 174, 176). That tension between simulation and reality exists outside the text as well, where the fixed image of Lawrence's body and the text of *The Hunger Games* always exist in interpretive relationship to the embodied human Jennifer Lawrence and multiple audience interpretations of novel and film. Should *The Hunger Games* prove to have staying power in popular culture, the passage of time will only exaggerate the distinction between the unchanging film and the aging of Lawrence. Day states that '[i]n *The Hunger Games* trilogy, image is manipulated by everyone, used to disguise the real, hijack the real, reveal the real, and finally become the real' (2012, p. 177). Here Day points out the ways that Katniss's fictional fate is influenced by politics and 'the next power-hungry leader' (2012, p. 177) yet audiences also witness an accelerated, conclusion storyline for a character whose life moves faster than real time. It seems, then, that audiences long to be satisfied by Katniss and her storyline even as the film stars remain in the same timeframe as their spectators; Katniss as character speeds past Lawrence and the audiences in an effort to sate viewers' and readers' desire for closure – and in the process, Katniss's image becomes a product for audiences to consume.

Consumable Bodies

In *Technologies of the Gendered Body: Reading Cyborg Women*, Anne Balsamo explains '[g]ender, like the body, is a boundary concept. It is at once related to physiological sexual characteristics of the human body (the natural order of the body) and to the cultural context within which that body "makes sense"' (1996, p. 9). The simulation scenarios in Collins's work play with ideas of real and hyperreal, often dissolving (at least as far as audiences are concerned) the bodily boundaries of an actress/character like Lawrence/Katniss. Yet the problem that Baudrillard's work reveals (or perhaps too often conceals) about the hyperreal is that the boundaries of material bodies always exist already, even if, as Balsamo points out, those bodies are subject to culture-laden interpretations. In this section, I argue that Collins's language in *The Hunger Games* prepares readers for consuming Katniss's body in ways that do not (and perhaps cannot, given the medium) appear in the film. Privileging the first-person narration of the novel gives audiences access to the ways that Katniss sees herself and her body as food for the audiences in reflections only suggested by the movie. Audiences of both novel and film, however, treat Katniss as consumable, devouring her story and her embodied image as their due; it is not surprising, given that both Katniss and Peeta bear edible names (if only in a homophone) and live in the nation of Panem, which references the bread from the ancient Roman tradition of bread and circuses. Many critics, especially Muller (2012), Hannah Trierweiler Hudson (2010), Mortimore-Smith (2012), Day (2012) and Andrew O'Hehir (2012) work explicitly with the relationship between the gladiatorial references and contemporary audiences. I turn my attention here to the transformation of a character and an image which becomes a product for audiences to consume – a kind of bingeing that assumes it is free to look and to critique as if there are no material consequences. It is just that there are always material consequences.

Several examples in Collins's novel suggest Katniss's edibility. First, Katniss explains her name:

> Tall with leaves like arrowheads. Blossoms with three white petals. […] Small, bluish tubers that don't look like much but boiled or baked are as good as any potato. 'Katniss,' I said aloud. It's the plant I was named for. And I heard my father's voice joking 'As long as you can find yourself, you'll never starve'.
>
> (Collins, 2010, p. 52)

Though her father refers here to the literal practice of foraging for food, the project of finding herself occupies Katniss throughout the series – especially as her body and image become coopted for the Games. Even when she contemplates winning The Hunger Games, she muses '[m]ost of [my life] has been consumed with the acquisition of food. Take that away and I'm not really sure who I am, what my identity is' (Collins, 2010, p. 311). She uses language of eating ('consumed') to describe the trajectory of her life, but her sense of self and her identity shift with her roles in the Games and afterward as she wonders what a life without hunger looks like (Collins, 2010, p. 311). For Katniss and many of her fellow Tributes, hunger is a daily staple, the very stuff of life. Indeed the divide between the hungry and the well-fed separates citizens within the districts and Tributes within the Games; says Katniss, '[t]hat the Careers have been better fed growing up is actually to their disadvantage, because they don't know how to be hungry' (Collins, 2010, p. 208). In the earlier example where Katniss wants to showcase her hunting skills for the camera, she sees hunger as a trap, a way of making fools. Here, Katniss acknowledges being hungry as a path to critical consciousness, a way of knowing oneself and regarding the world (and the systemic oppressions of Panem and The Hunger Games) with cunning and discernment. The shared history of austere consumption can make Tributes and citizens desperate, and it can make them wise; the former serves as entertainment for the multiple audiences of *The Hunger Games* while the latter threatens class privileges within and beyond Collins's texts.

Katniss's philosophising on hunger pairs with many references to her body as figurative food. When she arrives in the Capitol for training, she rationalises, 'I'm stuffing myself because I've never had food like this, so good and so much, and because probably the best thing I can do between now and the Games is put on a few pounds' (Collins, 2010, p. 44). This statement calls to mind an animal being prepared for slaughter, an image Collins seems to intentionally play with during Katniss's pre-Games evaluation: 'Suddenly I am furious, that with my life on the line, they don't even have the decency to pay attention to me. That I'm being upstaged by a dead pig' (Collins, 2010, p. 101). The Gamemakers will literally eat the pig, but Katniss and her body are primed for consumption as well, her appearance made palatable for audiences who hunger for scenes of violence. Referring to the hair-removal process of her pre-Games makeover, Katniss recalls feeling 'like a plucked bird, ready for roasting' (Collins, 2010, p. 61). During the parade, Katniss reflects on her 'Girl on Fire' costume, thinking 'I'm not convinced I won't be perfectly barbecued by the time we reach the city's center' (Collins, 2010, p. 67). The Games begin with the Tributes encircling 'The Cornucopia', that ubiquitous symbol of Thanksgiving for Collins's US audiences, on whom the irony of a horn of plenty and an allusion to a holiday of gluttony in a sporting event with starving children ought not to be lost. A fire in the arena prompts Katniss to proclaim 'my throat and nose are burning […] my lungs begin to feel as if they are actually being cooked' (Collins, 2010, p. 171). These figurative examples of cooking Katniss or body-as-food appear throughout Collins's novel, strengthening my argument that within the context of the Games and Panem, the body becomes a product to consume. Audiences crave the images of Katniss's body as well as the work that her body achieves – shooting arrows, parading through the city, evading and fighting her way through the arena. As the Games advance and Katniss approaches victory, her application of food-metaphors to other Tributes increases as well, illustrating the way that she and the other players become enmeshed in a system that regards them as a feast.

When Katniss and Peeta (himself a bread product) team up to seek out their remaining 'enemy' Cato, Peeta calls the mission 'a piece of cake' and Katniss responds '[n]ext time we eat, it will be in the Capitol' (Collins, 2010, p. 327). The fateful meeting takes place, of course, at The Cornucopia, where in the penultimate scene Cato lies within the horn while the District Twelve Tributes hold onto its upper surface. Katniss describes the scene thus:

> the real nightmare is listening to Cato, moaning, begging, and finally just whimpering as the mutts work away at him. After a very short time, I don't care who he is or what he's done, all I want is for his suffering to end. [...] No viewer could turn away from the show now. From the Gamemakers' point of view, this is the final word in entertainment.
>
> (Collins, 2010, p. 339)

When Katniss mercifully kills Cato a couple of pages later, she calls him 'the raw hunk of meat that used to be my enemy' (Collins, 2010, p. 341). The climactic scene of the Games involves a Tribute literally being eaten, and, given Katniss's speculation that the mutts are cyborg hybrids of the previously dead Tributes' bodies, the scene features Tributes eating a Tribute. Children consume each other for the entertainment of audiences who, in turn, consume this spectacle while embellishing their bodies and gorging themselves on abundant food. It is no wonder, then, that in a context that imposes starvation and grotesque consumption on its most disenfranchised citizens (poor, malnourished children) Katniss's victory and rebellion come in the form of a refusal to eat. At the end of Chapter 25, she and Peeta stage the ingestion of poisonous berries to force the Capitol to allow two winners, and, when the announcer concedes, they spit out the faux food. Eating in The Hunger Games is essential and dangerous, and food – its quality, lack and relationship to the body – signifies social position. Katniss embodies and subverts the food culture of Panem, by becoming an(other) body for the audiences to consume and by refusing the toxic patterns of consumption made available to her in the Games. Even the act of killing Cato resists the ideology that the Tributes and their bodies (to which they are reduced) are food for the audiences to binge and purge.

These concepts show up differently in the film version of *The Hunger Games* because audiences lose Katniss's internal perspective. And, instead of imagining the appearance of Katniss and the world of Panem, audiences of the film see the forms of Lawrence and her fellow actors. The shift from imagining Katniss's body to reading Lawrence's physical form means that moviegoers offer interpretations of the text dependent on a material body, at least as mediated by a screen. That screen plays a tremendous role in critical consumption of Lawrence-as-Katniss. L.V. Anderson says '[t]he fact that a woman's shape deviates slightly from the stick-thin figures that populate the silver screen does not make her "big"', and the author wonders why the same standards are not applied to Lawrence's male co-stars (Anderson, 2012, n.p.). Olivia Fleming agrees, asserting that Lawrence's 'body type, while not mirroring her more starved looking peers, differing ever so slightly from the current Hollywood norm, is lean, fit and slender – perfect for the professional hunter which she plays in the film' (2012, n.p.). Fleming, too, cites sexism in the backlash against Lawrence, and both Anderson and Fleming fall back on genetic arguments – chalking bodily diversity amidst starvation up to genes. These reviewers work against a writer like Dargis, who protests '[a] few years ago Ms. Lawrence might have looked hungry enough to play Katniss, but now, at 21, her seductive, womanly figure makes a bad fit for a dystopian fantasy about a people starved into submission' (2012, n.p.) To be fair, Dargis calls the larger issue 'disengaged performance"' (2012, n.p.), but the language all three reviewers use to evaluate Lawrence's body is telling. Both Anderson and Fleming hedge on their assertions of sexism, falling back on a vaguely scientific (and unsubstantiated, at least in their articles) claim about human genetics. Dargis, meanwhile, sees Lawrence's womanhood as the problem – implying that the womanliness of her body is itself the issue, the female body that demands attention.

Alexandra Le Tellier gets closest to my argument when she sees the strength of Katniss's character at odds with some viewers' sexism and 'the court of public opinion and its sometimes destructive power to determine someone else's fate' (2012, n.p.). Or, as Bordo writes in more academic language:

> What the body does is immaterial, so long as the imagination is free. This abstract, unsituated, disembodied freedom […] glorifies itself only through the effacement of the material praxis of people's lives, the normalizing power of cultural images, and the continuing social realities of dominance and subordination.
>
> (Bordo, 1993, p. 275)

The rulers of Panem understand food regulation as a weapon and a tool of oppression; they understand how to render the bodies of the disenfranchised as fodder for consumption, as well as how to control and manipulate the images and materiality of those bodies to sustain their regime. Katniss and Lawrence, in the resistant roles they play across multiple textual mediations, threaten the regime that imposes austerity on their embodied subjectivities – by acts from hunting illegally in the woods to playing the starring role in an action film. Each act asserts their respective and conflated assertions of the right to exist, to take up space, to consume even as they themselves are being consumed.

Bibliography

Anderson, L.V. (2012). 'Jennifer Lawrence is not "Too Big" to Play Katniss'. *Slate*, 3 March. Available from: <http://www.slate.com/blogs/browbeat/2012/03/23/jennifer_lawrence_s_body_not_skinny_enough_to_play_katniss_.html> [Accessed: 19 August 2014].

Balsamo, Anne. (1996). *Technologies of the Gendered Body: Reading Cyborg Women*. Durham, NC: Duke University Press.

Baudrillard, Jean. (1994). *Simulacra and Simulation*. Ann Arbor: University of Michigan Press.

Bordo, Susan. (1993) *Unbearable Weight*. Berkeley: University of California Press.

Collins, Suzanne. (2010). *The Hunger Games*. New York: Scholastic.

Dargis, Manohla. (2012). 'Tested by a Picturesque Dystopia'. *New York Times*, 22 March. Available from: <http://www.nytimes.com/2012/03/23/movies/the-hunger-games-movie-adapts-the-suzanne-collins-novel.html?_r=0> [Accessed: 19 August 2014].

Day, Helen. (2012). 'Simulacra, Sacrifice and Survival in *The Hunger Games*, *Battle Royale*, and *The Running Man*'. In: Mary F. Pharr and Leisa A Clark (eds) *Of Bread, Blood, and The Hunger Games*. Jefferson, NC: McFarland & Co.

Despain, Max. (2012). 'The "Fine Reality of Hunger Satisfied": Food as Cultural Metaphor in Panem'. In: Mary F. Pharr and Leisa A Clark (eds) *Of Bread, Blood, and The Hunger Games*. Jefferson, NC: McFarland & Co.

Fleming, Olivia. (2012). 'Was Jennifer Lawrence Too Fat for *The Hunger Games*? Critics Believe Actress Should Have Looked "More Hungry"'. *Mail Online*, 28 March. Available from: <http://www.dailymail.co.uk/femail/article-2121740/Was-Jennifer-Lawrence-FAT-Hunger-Games-Male-critics-believe-actress-looked-hungry.html> [Accessed: 19 August 2014].

Gaudiosi, John. (2012). 'Hunger Games Trilogy Beats Harry Potter Series to Become All-Time Bestselling Book Series'. *Forbes*, 17 August. Available from: <http://www.forbes.com/sites/johngaudiosi/2012/08/17/hunger-games-trilogy-beats-harry-potter-series-to-become-all-time-bestselling-book-series/> [Accessed: 19 August 2014].

Grace, Victora. (2000). *Baudrillard's Challenge: A Feminist Reading*. New York: Routledge.

Holmes, Linda (2013). 'What Really Makes Katniss Stand Out? Peeta, Her Movie Girlfriend'. *NPR*, 25 November. Available from: <http://www.npr.org/blogs/monkeysee/2013/11/25/247146164/what-really-makes-katniss-stand-out-peeta-her-movie-girlfriend> [Accessed: 19 August 2014].

Hood, Grace. (2013). 'More Girls Target Archery, Inspired by "The Hunger Games"'. *NPR*, 27 November. Available from: <http://www.npr.org/2013/11/27/247379498/more-girls-target-archery-inspired-by-the-hunger-games> [Accessed: 19 August 2014].

Hudson, Hannah Trierweiler. (2010). 'Sit Down with Suzanne Collins'. *Instructor*, 120/2, n.p.

Lancaster, Elizabeth. (2012). 'Was Jennifer Lawrence Too "Curvy" to Play Katniss in "Hunger Games"?' *MTV.com*, 28 March. Available from: <http://www.mtv.com/news/1681998/hunger-games-jennifer-lawrence-weight/> [Accessed: 19 August 2014].

Layfield, Allison. (2013). 'Identity Construction and the Gaze in *The Hunger Games*'. *The Looking Glass: New Perspectives on Children's Literature*, 17/1. Available from: <http://www.lib.latrobe.edu.au/ojs/index.php/tlg/article/view/389/382> [Accessed: 30 April 2015].

Le Tellier, Alexandra. (2012). '"Hunger Games": Star's "Baby Fat" Shouldn't Eclipse the Film's Message'. *Los Angeles Times*, 28 March. Available from: <http://articles.latimes.com/2012/mar/28/news/la-ol-hunger-games-jennifer-lawrence-weight-20120328> [Accessed: 19 August 2014].

Lewis, Andy. (2012). '"Hunger Games" Movie Fuels Sharp Rise in Book Sales'. *The Hollywood Reporter*, 28 March. Available from: <http://www.hollywoodreporter.com/news/hunger-games-twlight-book-sales-versus-jennifer-lawrence-josh-hutcherson-305457> [Accessed: 21 December 2014].

Long, Heather. (2013). 'Total Misfire: Brands Like Covergirl and Subway Miss Point of Hunger Games'. *Guardian*, 22 November. Available from: <http://www.theguardian.com/commentisfree/2013/nov/22/hunger-games-catching-fire-covergirl-subway-nerf-ads> [Accessed: 7 November 2014].

Mortimore-Smith, Shannon R. (2012). 'Fueling the Spectacle: Audience as Gamemaker'. In: Mary F. Pharr and Leisa A Clark (eds) *Of Bread, Blood, and The Hunger Games*. Jefferson, NC: McFarland & Co.

Muller, Vivienne. (2012). 'Virtually Real: Suzanne Collins's *The Hunger Games* Trilogy'. *International Research in Children's Literature*, 5/1, pp. 51–63.

O'Hehir, Andrew. (2012). '"The Hunger Games": A Lightweight Twi-pocalypse'. *Salon*, 20 March. Available from: <http://www.salon.com/2012/03/20/the_hunger_games_a_lightweight_twi_pocalypse/> [Accessed: 19 August 2014].

Pharr, Mary F., and Clark, Leisa (eds) *Of Bread, Blood, and The Hunger Games*. Jefferson, NC: McFarland & Co.

Probyn, Elisabeth. (1987). 'Bodies and Anti-Bodies: Feminism and the Post-Modern'. *Cultural Studies*, 1/3, pp. 349–360.

Ross, Gary. [Dir.] (2012). *The Hunger Games*.

Silverstein, Melissa. (2012). 'Hunger Games Backlash: Jennifer Lawrence Doesn't Look Hungry Enough'. *Women and Hollywood*, 29 March. Available from: <http://blogs.indiewire.com/womenandhollywood/hunger-games-backlash-jennifer-lawrence-doesnt-look-hungry-enough> [19 August 2014].

Sobchack, Vivian. (1995). 'Beating the Meat/Surviving the Text, or How to Get Out of this Century Alive'. In: Mike Featherstone and Roger Burrows (eds) *Cyberspace/Cyberbodies/Cyberpunk: Cultures of Technological Embodiment*. Thousand Oaks, CA: SAGE Publications.

Taber, Nancy, Woloshyn, Vera, and Lane, Laura. (2013). '"She's More Like a Guy" and "He's More Like a Teddy Bear": Girls' Perceptions of Violence and Gender in *The Hunger Games*'. *Journal of Youth Studies*, 16/8, pp. 1022–1037.

Vanity Fair. (2014). 'Cover Exclusive: Jennifer Lawrence Calls Photo Hacking a "Sex Crime"'. *Vanity Fair*, November. Available from: <http://www.vanityfair.com/hollywood/2014/10/jennifer-lawrence-cover>. [Accessed: 6 February 2015].

Wells, Jeffrey. (2012). 'Hunted, Not Haunted'. *Hollywood Elsewhere*, 20 March. Available from: <http://www.hollywood-elsewhere.com/2012/03/hunted-not-haun/> [Accessed: 19 August 2014].

Woloshyn, Vera, Taber, Nancy, and Lane, Laura. (2013). 'Discourses of Masculinity and Femininity in *The Hunger Games*: "Scarred", "Bloody", and "Stunning"'. *International Journal of Social Science Studies*, 1/1, pp. 150–160.

8

'I Want What Everyone Wants': Cruel Optimism in HBO's *Girls*

Ruth Charnock

In 'One Man's Trash' (season two, episode five of HBO's *Girls*), Hannah Horvath, an aspiring writer who is working, reluctantly, as a barista at her friend's café, goes around to a stranger, Joshua's, house to confess to a misdeed. She has just met Joshua, briefly, when he came into the café to complain that the staff there had been dumping their trash in his can. Despite, or perhaps because of the tenor and brevity of this meeting, after a very brief confession by Hannah, the pair have sex. Hannah stays at Joshua's house for two days, where the pair, variously, read the newspapers, play naked table-tennis, cook steaks and have sex. Towards the end of the episode, Hannah passes out in Joshua's shower. He rescues her and takes her to his bedroom, where he dries her hair. Hannah starts to cry, telling Joshua (among other things): 'I just want what everyone wants' (season two, episode five). The next morning, Joshua leaves for work before Hannah wakes up. She eats breakfast alone, reads the newspaper, and takes the trash out. The episode ends with Hannah walking away from Joshua's house. We never see or hear about Joshua again.

In this chapter, I will focus on 'One Man's Trash' and *Girls* more broadly as important artefacts for thinking through some of the questions, contradictions and controversies raised by popular culture's response to twenty-first-century austerity. My reading of *Girls* will be primarily, although not solely, directed by cultural theorist Lauren Berlant's concept of cruel optimism, a notion which, she argues, has fundamentally shaped and continues to shape a collective Western fantasy of the good life and its impossibility within the present economic, social and cultural climate. I will then go on to argue that 'One Man's Trash', in particular, exemplifies the set of feelings, objects and scenes that attend cruel optimism. Underlying this consideration is the contention that Berlant's theory of cruel optimism offers a vital set of tools for understanding and unpacking the feeling of the contemporary – not only in popular culture but also in the genres of the lived everyday. Specifically, *Girls*, in its representation of four women in their mid-twenties living in New York, indexes a particular kind of cruel optimism – that which attends the white, Western Millennial,[1] just out of university and newly on the job-market. Whilst *Girls*, for many critics, fails as any kind of encompassing take on twenty-first-century austerity, predicated as it is on the lived experiences of an arguably privileged group, the media furore surrounding the show (and, not least, that which has attended its creator Lena Dunham who also stars in the show), suggests that it has hit a cultural nerve, worthy of exploration. *Girls*, whilst it is undoubtedly narrow in its cultural focus, and perhaps, too, in its audience demographic, raises a series of crucial questions regarding both the construction of austerity within popular culture and, more specifically, the contemporary experience of millennials.

Girls might seem an unlikely topic within a collection on austerity and popular culture. After all, in its depiction of four white, privileged (and sometimes parentally bankrolled), middle-class bohemian, twenty-something girls living in Brooklyn, the programme is hardly at the coalface of the Great Recession. Yet, what it does offer is one version of millennial experience, as Dean J. DeFino suggests:

> This generation came of age with a strong sense of entitlement, self-confidence, and assertiveness – not to mention a natural impatience towards the values and conventions of previous generations – only to reach their 20s and face desperate economic conditions (the Great Recession), dissipated revolutions (Occupy Wall Street) and the depressing realization that Twitter

and Facebook may actually make one less capable of finding meaningful relationships.

(DeFino, 2014, p. 190)

DeFino captures much of the spirit of *Girls* here although it is doubtful throughout how 'desperate' the economic conditions that the girls of *Girls* face really are, since, with the exception of Marnie, all of the female characters (and Adam of the male characters) in the programme receive financial support from their family members (DeFino, 2014, p. 190). Furthermore, a recent infographic suggests that the show's characters live way beyond their means and could not sustain the lifestyles they appear to on the wages they earn.[2] In this sense, although *Girls* has frequently been read as anti-aspirational in contrast to its spiritual older sister *Sex and the City* (1998–2004) – with *New York Times*'s Frank Bruni drawing attention to *Girls* 'bleak' depictions of sex[3] and relationships, and 'dull' colour palette, describing it as '*Sex and the City* in a charcoal gray Salvation Army overcoat' – *Girls* does fantasise a life for its characters that in real economic and material terms, they would not have access to (Bruni, 2012, n.p.).

Girls, then, stands in a complex relationship with its characters' romantic and economic aspirations, and with the very fact of aspiration itself. Yet, as DeFino identifies above, all four central characters are preoccupied by the attainment and experience of meaningful work. The programme plays on the bathetic dulling of expectations that attends particularly Marnie's and Hannah's forays into the world of work. In this, as I shall discuss in more detail in a moment, *Girls* enacts the attenuation of millennial ambition that characterises many popular cultural depictions of the contemporary graduate.[4] This attenuation, as I will argue below, is symptomatic of the complex relationship to contemporary fantasies of the good life that characterises cruel optimism. In particular, 'One Man's Trash' throws into relief Hannah's dawning perception of her own precarity in comparison with others sharing the same city.

Girls and the Millennial

Following the subprime mortgage crisis of 2007 and banking crisis of 2008, when *Girls* aired for the first time on 15 April 2012, it was within a 'bust culture', as Kirk Boyle and Daniel Mrozowski describe it, 'inflected by diminishment, influenced by scarcity, and infused with anxiety' (Boyle and Mrozowski, 2013, p. xi). According to their diagnosis, in 2013, America was 'in the midst of a distinct cultural formation' characterised, they argue by '[an MTV dramedy][5] about recent college graduates who refer to "Occupy" and the "1%", and who struggle to pay off student loans, afford rent, and find and keep work' (Boyle and Mrozowski, 2013, p. ix). Of these issues, the Occupy movement and the 1% go unmentioned by *Girls* thus far – a silence criticised by several detractors of the series. J. Maureen Henderson has pilloried *Girls* for misrepresenting millennials:

> Millennials may get a bad rap when it comes to philanthropy but 75% of them donated to charity in 2011 and 63% of them volunteered in some capacity. [...] You know, when they're not planning spur-of-the moment weddings to investment bankers or ingesting crack at warehouse parties in Bushwick.
>
> (Henderson, 2013, n.p.)

Henderson acerbically refers here to two scenes as examples of *Girls'* lack of realism when it comes to the demographic it purports to represent. Other critiques of *Girls* have skewered it on its whiteness, the absence of references to real economic hardship in the show, and the lineage of its actors.[6]

Many of the critiques and criticisms of *Girls* revolve around issues of representation. Martha Nussbaum has commented that 'Dunham's show takes as its subject women who are quite demographically specific – cosseted white New Yorkers from educated backgrounds – then mines their lives for the universal' (Nussbaum, 2012, n.p.). However, in this chapter, I will not be arguing for *Girls* as a universal representation of lived experience under austerity, or even as a universal representation of millennial experience. Such broad strokes threaten to elide the demographic specificity of *Girls* – both its characters and its target audience – and it is important to hold onto this specificity in order to avoid obscuring the show's position on austerity politics and culture. This position is nuanced, particularly in its consideration of inter-generational experiences of the Great Recession.

Whilst *Girls* is not exemplary of a 'universal' experience of austerity (as if such a thing could be possible), it does access a specifically twenty-first century phenomenon: that of the so-called 'Boomerang Generation'. Out of university, onto a flailing and unrewarding job market, the notion of children either returning home to live with their parents or relying on them for financial support (as in *Girls*) crops up frequently in contemporary austerity narratives. A 2014 *New York Times* article states that, in the USA: '[O]ne in five people in their 20s and early 30s is currently living with his or her parents. And 60 percent of all young adults receive financial support from them' (Davidson, 2014, n.p.). As *Girls* creator Lena Dunham commented in an interview for *Channel 4 News*: '[this] is the first generation of Americans who can expect to do worse than their parents did. So I wanted to [...] talk about these girls, barely out of college, full of hope and met with very little' (2014, 3.21). One of the things that 'One Man's Trash' performs is this generational divide – not between Hannah Horvath and her parents but, rather, between Hannah and a man whom, age and status-wise, belongs much more to *Girls'* predecessor and influence, *Sex and the City*,[7] than in *Girls'* stock of characters. I will suggest that the genre of life-style represented by Joshua in this episode casts *Girls* as profoundly in dialogue with *Sex and the City* as a pre-recessional fantasy that *Girls* can touch but not possess. Furthermore, the gender politics of this episode suggest a postfeminist fantasy of surrender to the richer, older man. As I will now discuss with regards to Lauren Berlant's 'cruel optimism', Joshua represents a version of the good life that Hannah wants but cannot have.

Cruel Optimism

In Berlant's work, the 'good life' translates as the set of fantasies, more often than not collective but also, sometimes, intensely personal, that structure what it means to have a meaningful, sustaining and sustainable life. Generally put, Berlant's assertion in *Cruel Optimism* is that the fantasies of the good life that emerged, particularly in America in the postwar period, are increasingly unrealisable. This 'fraying of the fantasies of the good life' is due, in Berlant's formulation, to the 'lived precarity of this historical present' (Berlant, 2011, p. 196), a present characterised by the diminution of fantasies of 'upward mobility, job security, political and social equality, and lively, durable intimacy' (2011, p. 3). *Girls* has a tumultuous relationship with its own fantasies of the good life. Sometimes, the series appears unable or, at least, *unwilling* to imagine a happy future for its central characters. Other times, as in 'One Man's Trash', *Girls* proffers the possibility and proximity of an attainable good life, only to whip it away, undermine it, ironise its potential or shame and punish its characters for thinking that they could achieve it.

Anyone who desires to improve the conditions of their life and believes that such improvements are attainable is engaging in optimism. But what makes optimism cruel, Berlant argues, is:

> [w]hen something you desire is actually an obstacle to your flourishing. It might involve food, or a kind of love, it might be a fantasy of the good life, or a political project. It might rest on something simpler, too, like a new habit that promises to induce in you an improved way of being.
>
> (Berlant, 2011, p. 1)

Optimism generated by the objects Berlant suggests here is not *necessarily* cruel. It could be that one's optimism in a political project comes good or that a kind of love really *does* work out better than the ones that have come before. The affirmation of optimism by result, of course, relies on a certain ability and willingness to endure the present, to live in hope that things will improve.

Optimism becomes cruel, Berlant argues, 'only when the object that draws your attachment actively impedes the aim that brought you to it initially' (2011, p.1). To use two examples from Berlant, a relation of optimism would become cruel when the political project manifests as impossible to realise, and the harder you work at it, the more impossible it becomes. Or, the relationship that you thought was the one you had always hoped for turns out to be the one that eviscerates you even more than the others. And yet, you hold on, now hoping against yourself that your optimism will come good and result in a good life. For Berlant, then:

> Optimism is cruel when the object/scene that ignites a sense of possibility actually makes it impossible to attain the expansive transformation for which a person [...] risks striving; and, doubly, it is cruel insofar as the very pleasures of being inside a relation have become sustaining regardless of the content of the relation, such that a person or a world finds itself bound to a situation of profound threat that is, at the same time, profoundly confirming.
>
> (Berlant, 2011, p. 2)

176

In other words, cruel optimism happens or is happening when the very conditions of the thing or person you want bar you from getting what you want from it or them. And yet, you stay anyway, 'bound', as Berlant intones (rightfully) ominously, 'to a situation of profound threat that is, at the same time, profoundly confirming'.

Crucially, Berlant temporalises the affective structure of cruel optimism: it is a feeling for our times – times that take their shape, she argues, from the 'fraying fantasies' of good life that I referred to a moment ago regarding what it means to have a good life:

> The set of dissolving assurances [...] includes meritocracy, the sense that liberal-capitalist society will reliably provide opportunities for individuals to carve out relations of reciprocity that seem fair and that foster life as a project of adding up to something and constructing cushions for enjoyment.
>
> (Berlant, 2011, p. 3)

Girls, I will be a suggesting in a moment, is structured from the stuff of these fraying fantasies. As such, it belongs to but also comments on what Berlant describes as 'the emergence of a precarious public sphere': 'An intimate public of subjects who circulate scenarios of economic and intimate contingency and trade paradigms for how best to live on, considering' (Berlant, 2011, p. 3). Berlant captures the spirit of *Girls* here. The phrase 'how best to live on' forms an uncanny palimpsest to Season Two's tagline: 'living the dream, one mistake at a time' (2013).

The Impasse of 'One Man's Trash'

As a series, *Girls* is not always certain about 'how best to live on'. For the most part, it is immersed in its depiction of the precarity of its four main characters' lives – in particular, that of Hannah, who styles herself as if not 'the voice of her generation then at least a voice of a generation' (Dunham, 2012). For the first three seasons, at least, *Girls* depicts its characters' fraying fantasies of the good life. Crucially, in the pilot, Hannah's parents cut off her allowance, telling her 'we can't keep bankrolling your groovy lifestyle' (Dunham, 2012). Hannah's response characterises the sense of expectancy tinged with disappointment and bathos that defines the programme. High on opium tea, sweating in her parents' hotel room, she tells them: 'I am so close to the life that I want, to the life that you want for me – so, for you to just end that right now …?'. Whilst Hannah aligns the life she wants with the life her parents want for her, there is actually little sense in the series as a whole that any of the characters have substantially imaginable futures – especially not futures that look like those their parents might have had at the same age.

Nowhere is the inter-generational dynamics of cruel optimism more in evidence than in 'One Man's Trash'. It exists curiously apart from both the formal structure and plot-line of the rest of the season. Whilst an episode of *Girls* will, typically, take a digest of all its central characters, 'One Man's Trash' features a brief initial appearance by misanthropic Ray and then focuses solely on Hannah and one-off character Dr Joshua (Patrick Wilson). Narratively, the episode never gestures beyond itself and, in a further departure for the series, the majority of the episode takes place in one setting: Dr Joshua's glossy, recently remodelled brownstone, lingered over lovingly from the outside as Hannah approaches the house towards the beginning of the episode. The house and its accoutrements function as particular objects of optimism throughout the episode, although their cruelty is always imminent as the end of the episode, analeptically, reveals.

'One Man's Trash' begins in Ray's café where Hannah is working. An increasingly ruffled Dr Joshua enters the café to complain that they have been dumping their trash in his can. The ever-truculent Ray denies that this could be possible, as Hannah watches on. As Joshua storms out of the café, Hannah tells Ray that he has been a 'dick' and leaves herself ('One Man's Trash', season two, episode five). We next see Hannah approaching what will turn out to be Joshua's house. He answers the door, she tells him there is something she needs to talk to him about, he invites her in – with a demonstration of slight unwillingness by Hannah who comments that she does not want to 'get into a Ted Bundy situation' – a comment that registers her vulnerability in entering the house of a stranger. Yet Hannah's curiosity about the inside of Joshua's house (a brownstone, of which Hannah later comments 'I didn't even know houses like this existed in my neighborhood') overrules her speculation that he might be a psychopath. Of course, this speculation has already been neutralised itself by the uttering – irony here, as throughout *Girls*, works to both take the sting out of the characters' own sense of their precarity and to amplify this precarity for the audience.

So it is in 'One Man's Trash' where, throughout the episode, we are always waiting for the fall. Hannah's misfortune has been so enshrined by this point that to expect she would fare otherwise in this episode would be to read the show, ostensibly, against its own genre of feeling. I do not mean to suggest here that the viewer *does* expect Joshua to be Ted Bundy mark two but, rather, that the genre of *Girls*, to this point, has never been a romance. And yet the fact after that formally, this episode sets itself apart from the rest should be read, I argue, as the extension of the possibility that, in this episode, things might be different for Hannah. Whilst previous episodes play out the encounters, scenes and economics of cruel optimism, 'One Man's Trash' is initially purely optimistic, in both content and form.

Regarding the difference of this episode, I would like to posit two things: firstly, that 'One Man's Trash' works as a kind of impasse within the series. Secondly, that the episode proves to be the most cruelly optimistic of all, precisely *because* it momentarily allows both Hannah and the viewer a respite from the sometimes brutal precarity of the everyday that otherwise marks the series. 'One Man's Trash' slavishly indulges a version of the good life, a version that Hannah did not even know she wanted. It makes this life appear attainable to Hannah right up to the point that, in an excruciating *cri de coeur*, she admits she wants it. And then, unsummarily, irrevocably, humiliatingly, the promise of this life and the episode itself dissolves.

I mentioned above that we should consider 'One Man's Trash' as an impasse: a useful concept for theorising the structure of the present. As Berlant employs it in *Cruel Optimism*:

> The impasse is a stretch of time in which one moves around with a sense that the world is at once intensely present and enigmatic […] [I]t may be that, for many now, living in an impasse would be an aspiration, as the traditional infrastructures for reproducing life – at work, in intimacy, politically – are crumbling at threatening pace. The holding pattern in 'impasse' suggests a temporary housing.
>
> (Berlant, 2011, pp. 4–5)

'One Man's Trash', in its depiction of Hannah's aspirations but also through its temporal, scenic and relational structuring, constitutes itself as just such an impasse – retaining throughout this sense that Joshua's world is 'at once intensely present and enigmatic'. Whilst it particularises its objects of fantasy and the encounter between Hannah and Joshua, the episode retains a timeless quality – refusing to index the present as a thing always slipping away until, horribly, it all disappears at once. After Hannah enters Joshua's house, the episode surrenders itself to a continuous present – accentuated by Joshua's decision to take a day off work: a decision which he presents casually, further inscribing the episode's lax attention to time and its shaping by, and of, labour. In an episode driven by both the content and feeling of aspiration, Joshua's place proves to be Hannah's own version of Berlant's 'temporary housing' – housing which, as the episode unfolds, appears to offer the promise of permanent accommodation: the long-term mortgage, rather than the short-term let (Berlant, 2011, pp. 4–5).

Joshua invites Hannah in. After exchanging pleasantries, Hannah moves into her confession: it is *she* who has been dumping the café's trash in Joshua's can. She is contrite, he is bemused:

HANNAH: I did it. I do it. Put trash places it legally shouldn't go. It's kind of like my vice.

JOSHUA: Why?

HANNAH: I think it actually makes a lot of sense if I describe it to you, which is that Ray leaves work early and I'm supposed to take out the trash. But I lost my dumper key and you saw for yourself what a total fucking dick he can be. […] So I started looking for places to put it. And your house – it was close enough but it was also far enough and I really like what the outside looked like so … You know: that's how it started.

JOSHUA: So you're just trying to save your own ass.

HANNAH: Honestly, I think it's just that I've never had my own trash-can so it's just hard for me to imagine how frustrating that would be to have someone else's trash in there. But I know now.

('One Man's Trash', season two, episode five)

What are the politics and erotics of fly-tipping? As this moment plays out, Hannah's initial justification for 'her vice' is work-related: she fly-tips to avoid her boss' ire – Ray is 'an ass' ('One Man's Trash', season two, episode five). But Hannah's fly-tipping exceeds this explanation. She specifically picked out Joshua's house because she 'really liked what the outside looked like'. Hannah's illicit dumping, then, should be read as both sabotage of and homage to Joshua's life – a life which has accrued its own domestic trash can, unlike Hannah's own. There is something about the effluvia of the city and the mixing of private and commercial waste as a comment on what Berlant calls the 'intimate public' of contemporary life that I can only point to here. Instead, I will read Hannah's vice as a fantasy of owned property and the daily gestures that maintain it.

Shortly after her confession, Hannah kisses Joshua and they have sex for the first time, on Joshua's lovingly depicted marble kitchen counter. Hannah's impulsivity here, we might argue, is just the latest manifestation of her fantasy of proximity to Joshua's lifestyle. As she says 'everything that [Joshua] appear[s] to have [...] is very nice' ('One Man's Trash', season two, episode five). But this is also a moment in which the show itself opens into a different kind of fantasy. Mostly populated by men who are either in their mid-twenties, like Hannah's sometime boyfriend, the sadistic, repugnant yet compelling Adam, and older men like her boss Ray, in his mid-thirties, who spends most of the second season homeless and misanthropic, the arrival of the forty-something Dr Joshua augurs a new genre of man for the series: financially solvent, in a caring rather than commercial or dubiously artistic profession, and, apparently, straightforward in his desires. Age-wise, lifestyle-wise, he belongs much more to *Sex and the City* than to *Girls*. His self-assurance, his solvency (represented by his household accoutrements which both Hannah and the camera fixate upon) represent, as Dean J. DeFino puts it 'a deep generation divide' between the two programmes. Unlike Hannah's generation, '[Carrie Bradshaw's] generation is self-assured because they have already achieved career success. When they graduated from college in the yuppie heyday of the late 1980s, opportunities were everywhere' (DeFino, 2014, p. 190). The episode aligns Joshua's economic security with his emotional security, a security that invites Hannah into a full performance of her economic and emotional insecurity. Joshua and Hannah's relationship is founded on their economic difference and the gendering of this difference leads to the episode's climactic scene: when Hannah faints in Joshua's shower and he rescues her from it.

Joshua's home, structured as an impasse, is a place of domestic and economic retreat for Hannah, away from what she perceives as the hardships of her own life, and also functions as a movement away from the shared apartments and stark bathrooms that characterise the show's usual domestic scenes. Lovingly, lingeringly, the camera catalogues Joshua's things – spending much more time, for example, looking at his fridge and his fruitbowl than at his body. This is not to say that Joshua's obvious physical appeal is overlooked in this episode; rather, that once it has been established, the camera indulges in objects that more obviously structure Hannah's desire for Joshua's life. In this manner, 'One Man's Trash' works as a fantasy of retreat into an idealised, upper middle class domesticity – a staple of postfeminist popular culture, as Diane Negra theorises: 'postfeminist concepts such as "retreatism" (the pull back by affluent women to a perfected domesticity) take distinct shape as class and race fantasies' (Negra, 2009, p. 9). Importantly in this episode, Hannah walks out of her job at the café to go to Joshua's house. When, at the end of the episode, Joshua says he has to go to work, Hannah expresses surprise. 'One Man's Trash' allows Hannah her retreatist fantasy but also critiques it as both unrealistic and unobtainable.

Related to this, the episode also suggests that Hannah cannot function within Joshua's life(style). Towards the end, Hannah collapses in Joshua's wet room and is rescued by him. The shower's extravagance, the level of domestic and physical pleasure it promises is in accordance with the rest of Joshua's objects which are all, as Hannah puts it, 'so nice' ('One Man's Trash', season two, episode five). Joshua's shower also stands in contrast to Hannah's bath – a regular location within the programme and one which is rarely indexed as a site of pleasure. This moment is both a faint and a swoon. Physically and psychologically, Hannah is rendered increasingly vulnerable throughout season two, plagued, in particular, by a recurrence of her teenage OCD. Luckily, here, there is a doctor in the house – allowing the episode to continue in its vein of optimism where, instead of Hannah's vulnerability inviting harm or indifference, it invites rescue by a handsome professional. Swooning, Hannah surrenders to her desire to be absorbed, fully surrounded and encompassed by Joshua's domestic objects. The swoon registers the desirability of the shower, as well as Hannah's inability to, quite literally, withstand this desirability. To swoon *in* the shower is also to swoon *at* the shower. In keeping with my reading of this episode as an impasse, Hannah's swoon further registers as a moment of inert, suspended and willed passivity in the face of objects that seem to hold out the promise of a better life.

The shower scene further registers Hannah's vulnerability as a female in Joshua's house – not because he might be a serial killer (the episode never takes this possibility seriously) but, rather, because she is powerless in the face of his wealth and all that it seems to promise. But Hannah's physical vulnerability is predicated, albeit tangentially, on her economic precarity. That is to say, the moment in the shower suggests that, because Hannah is so starved of the kind of luxury offered by Joshua's shower, she cannot comport herself safely within it. The scene both underlines the stereotypical gendering of Hannah and Joshua's roles throughout this episode and their economic inequality. Crucially, Hannah's swoon allows a scene of rescue, with Joshua functioning as a classic romantic hero. In this way, the episode performs a postfeminist fantasy of female surrender, an abdication of agency to a powerful, wealthy and erotic male. It is this fantasy that Hannah is vulnerable to, and the ramifications of this vulnerability that are felt when she confesses it to Joshua.

'I Want What Everyone Wants': Hannah's Confession

Following Dr Joshua's rescue, the pair are next pictured in his bedroom – Hannah supine, her head in his lap while he towel-dries her hair. Again: so far, so optimistic – the moment registers as one of promising intimacy, a promise further validated by Joshua's insistence that Hannah must call him if she ever feels faint again. Whilst *Girls* is not a show devoid of tenderness, this is the first time that such tenderness plays out between Hannah and a man she is sleeping with – tenderness more commonly imagined in the show as something that only happens in female friendships, if anywhere.

This scene of paternalistic care, so outside *Girls'* typical genre of relationship, initiates the tipping point in 'One Man's Trash': the moment where optimism becomes cruel optimism. It is not enough for Hannah to accept Joshua's tenderness, she also has to editorialise it:

HANNAH [CRYING]: Please don't tell anyone this, but I want to be happy.

JOSHUA: Of course you do, of course you do. Everyone does.

HANNAH: Yeah, but I didn't think that *I* did. I made a promise such a long time ago that I was going to take in experiences, all of them, so that I could tell the people about them and maybe save them but it gets so tiring trying to take in all the experiences for everybody – letting anyone say anything to me. Then I came here and I see you. And you've got the fruit in the bowl and the fridge with all the stuff, the robe and you're touching me in a way that […] and I realize that I'm not different, you know? I want what everyone wants, I want all the things. I just want to be happy.

('One Man's Trash', season two, episode five)

'I want what everyone wants', Hannah tells Joshua. But it is more accurate to say that she wants what Joshua appears to *have*: a version of the good life with, as Hannah says, 'the fruit bowl and the fridge with the stuff – the robe'. This 'stuff', as I have been suggesting throughout this chapter, structures Hannah's desire and, arguably, our own in this episode – much more than Joshua himself ever does. In this scene, but throughout the episode, Hannah does most of the talking, ensuring that, as I gestured towards earlier, Joshua remains more one-dimensional an object of desire than his shower, fruit-bowl or fridge. The decision to characterise Joshua in this way becomes clear at this point in the episode: whilst a fridge cannot reject you, a man can. That is, Joshua's one-dimensionality up this point has ensured that neither Hannah, nor the viewer, has to deal with his difference from her fantasy of the good life she could have with him. As an optimistic object, he retains his potential right up until the moment that Hannah deconstructs this potential by fully naming it as such. That is, in admitting to her optimism about her future life with Joshua, Hannah's optimism becomes cruel.

The greater the optimism, the crueller it will feel when this optimism comes to naught. But this is also a scene that deals in shame: whilst Hannah might be too absorbed in her confession to realise that she is being slowly, irrevocably rejected by Joshua, the viewer is not. The camera cuts to Joshua's face at points throughout Hannah's monologue. Initially, he displays concern, then paternalistic sympathy, then, ultimately, a combination of contained disgust and incomprehension. Whilst the majority of 'One Man's

Trash' revels, then, in the fantasy of an inter-generational good life, here, this fantasy ruptures when it becomes clear that Joshua is both unprepared and unwilling to commiserate with Hannah's account of herself as an artist who suffers experiences 'so that [she] can tell the people about them and maybe save them' ('One Man's Trash', season two, episode five). The sheer excess of feeling in Hannah's speech – an excess performed by its length, intensity and the freight of its clichés: particularly Hannah's insistence that she wants to 'feel it all' – turns this from a scene of intimacy into a scene of abject desire. Furthermore, the episode wants the viewer to feel *as* abject (if not more) than Hannah here regarding the conventionality of her fantasy of the good life. The fact of Hannah's confession that she 'wants what everyone wants' is intended to stand in contrast to the rest of the show which, up to this point, appears to have shunned or ironised such conventional desires. But, in a double blow, the viewer is also made to feel the full cruelty of their *own* optimism in the episode's genre here – where it seems, up to this point, like this might be the relationship that works out. As I argued at the beginning of my reading, the episode is structured as an impasse, in order to make the viewer set aside everything that they know about *Girls* so far – in order, that is, that this episode *feels* optimistic before it becomes cruel. Arguably, then, the show wants to punish, upbraid or, at the very least, remind viewers (or at least those viewers that identify with Hannah) of their mistake. Girls like Hannah don't get to have guys like Joshua, or share their lives.

As Berlant writes of cruel optimism, 'the scene that ignites a sense of possibility actually makes it impossible to attain the expansive trans-formation for which [...] a person risks striving' (Berlant, 2011, p. 4). In admitting to Joshua that 'I just want what everyone wants – to be happy', Hannah makes the mistake of assuming that Joshua will give her what she wants, even if she admits to *why* she wants it. She also forgets, for a moment, which television show she is in, one in which as part of a gen-eration characterised by precarious living, she can have no purchase on the good life, or at least not this version of it. In keeping with the genre of cruel optimism then, Hannah misreads this scene as one of possibility, not realising that in admitting to Joshua the full extent of her desire for the good life, a good life that she believes he represents, she makes its attain-ment impossible.

Joshua's face closes, he tells Hannah that he is tired and needs to go to work tomorrow. When she wakes up in the morning he is gone. Hannah runs her hand along the suits in his wardrobe, makes toast, reads the *New York Times*. This time around, these domestic rituals are drained of their potential. And yet, the episode continues to index Joshua's objects of desire in a succession of frames accompanied by wistful, jazzy music. In a wry return to the episode's premise Hannah takes out Joshua's trash as she leaves.

Conclusion: *Girls'* Cruel Optimism

To conclude: *Girls*, and particularly 'One Man's Trash', consistently represents the fraying of old fantasies of the good life: the permanent job, the mortgage, the long-term, nurturing relationship and financial solvency for its twenty-something characters. Whilst the programme has been criticised for the entitlement of its actors and what has been seen, on occasion, as a smug, insular hipsterised vision of millennial precarity, I have argued that *Girls*, and in particular this episode, indexes the complexity of cruel optimism and its sustainment as a contemporary affect. In this respect, *Girls* is an important cultural artefact for thinking through discourses regarding the Boomerang Generation, white, Western privilege and the attenuation of fantasies of the good life. If Hannah Hovarth is rendered abject, embarrassing and irritating when she confesses to Joshua that she just 'want[s] what everyone wants' then, I have argued, it is also the viewer's own optimism that is rendered cruel. And if, as Adam Phillips says, 'the myth of potential makes mourning and complaining feel like the realest things we ever do', then 'One Man's Trash' is far from disposable (2013, p. 2).

However, as I have gestured towards throughout, this cruel optimism is also profoundly gendered in the episode, working along the lines of the precarious female who would be rescued by the secure male. Throughout the rest of *Girls*, Hannah is on, by and large, the same economic plain as the other characters: male and female. Yet, in 'One Man's Trash', her emotional and economic precarity is gendered, with Dr Joshua functioning as the older, male and financially solvent foil to this precarity. However, the promise that he seems to proffer is rendered as impossible, suggesting that *Girls* cannot imagine a financial or emotional milieu for its characters beyond its own, problematic version of austerity. Optimism, here writ as a fantasy of power showers, older male doctors, unpunished days off work, brownstones and pristine kitchens, becomes cruel as soon as Hannah invests in it. Wanting 'what everyone wants' renders her unable to have it. As such, 'One Man's Trash' is cruelly optimistic in imagining a life beyond austerity.

Notes

1 This designation is not without its detractors but for a comprehensive explanation of the term, see: Neil Howe and William Strauss, *Millennials Rising: The Next Great Generation* (2000). The term 'precariat' is also in current usage but applies to a wider demographic than that considered in this chapter.

2 See, 'Why aren't the Girls broke?' *Daily Mail*, <http://www.dailymail.co.uk/femail/article-2907164/They-debt-NYU-fees-stints-rehab-girls-Girls-live-way-means-season-season.html>.

3 Significantly, the depiction of the sex between Hannah and Joshua in 'One Man's Trash' is much less bleak, both in its camera-work and tone, than many of Hannah's other sexual encounters throughout the show. The pilot episode, for example, depicts her body starkly: on her front with her tights pulled down as her love interest, Adam, penetrates her from behind in a dingy apartment.

4 *Frances Ha* (2012) sends its central character, who has ambitions to be a dancer, firstly to the reception desk of the dance company she wants to work for, and then back to her old college as a waitress.

5 *Underemployed*, which aired in 2012.

6 See, for example: Carroll, 2012; Suebsaeng, 2012; Holmes, 2012.

7 Martha Nussbaum gives some sense of *Girls'* complex relationship with *Sex and the City* in a *New York Magazine* piece, where she describes how references to *Sex and the City* are banned on the set of *Girls*, but adds that 'despite the denials at HBO and by the show's creators [...] *Girls is* a post *Sex and the City* show' (Nussbaum, 2012, n.p.).

Bibliography

Abraham, Tamara. (2015). 'Why Aren't the Girls Broke? From Cosy Brooklyn Rentals to Tuition and Stints in Rehab, How TV Characters Live Way Beyond Their Meager Means'. *Daily Mail*, 12 January. Available from: <http://www.dailymail.co.uk/femail/article-2907164/They-debt-NYU-fees-stints-rehab-girls-Girls-live-way-means-season-season.html> [Accessed: 13 January 2015].

Berlant, Lauren. (2011). *Cruel Optimism*. Durham, NC: Duke University Press.

Boyle, Kirk and Mrozowski, Daniel. (2013). *The Great Recession in Fiction, Film and Television*. Lanham, MD: Lexington Books.

Bruni, Frank. (2012). 'The Bleaker Sex'. *New York Times*, 31 March. Available from: <http://www.nytimes.com/2012/04/01/opinion/sunday/bruni-the-bleaker-sex.html?_r=2&scp=1&sq=Frank%20Bruni%20%22Girls%22&st=Search&> [Accessed: 14 January 2015].

Carroll, Rebecca. (2012). 'White Girls, Big City: What HBO's New Show Misses'. *The Daily Beast*, 20 April. Available from: <http://www.thedailybeast.com/articles/2012/04/20/white-girls-big-city-what-hbo-s-new-show-misses.html> [Accessed: 15 January, 2015].

Channel 4 News. (2014). Interview with Jon Snow and Lena Dunham. Channel 4, 20 January. Available from: <https://www.youtube.com/watch?v=w3flbO2bQbc> [Accessed: 15 January 2015].

Davidson, Adam. (2014). 'It's Official: The Boomerang Kids Won't Leave'. *New York Times*, 22 June. Available from: <http://www.nytimes.com/2014/06/22/magazine/its-official-the-boomerang-kids-wont-leave.html?_r=0> [Accessed: 15 January 2015].

DeFino, Dean J. (2014). *The HBO Effect*. New York: Bloomsbury.

Dunham, Lena [Dir.]. (2012). 'Pilot', *Girls*. HBO. 12 March.

——— (2013). 'One Man's Trash', *Girls*, HBO, 2 May.

Henderson, J. Maureen. (2013). 'How HBO's Girls Gets Everything About Millennial Life, Like, So Totally Wrong'. *Forbes*, 13 January. Available from: <http://www.forbes.com/sites/jmaureenhenderson/2013/01/13/how-hbos-girls-gets-everything-about-millennial-life-like-so-totally-wrong/> [Accessed: 14 January 2015].

Holmes, Anna. (2012). 'White "*Girls*"'. *The New Yorker*, 23 April. Available from: <http://www.newyorker.com/culture/culture-desk/white-girls> [Accessed: 15 January 2015].

Negra, Diane. (2009). *What a Girl Wants?: Fantasizing the Reclamation of Self in Postfeminism*. Oxford: Routledge.

Nussbaum, Martha. (2012). 'It's Different for "*Girls*"'. *New York TV*, 25 March. Available from: <http://nymag.com/arts/tv/features/girls-lena-dunham-2012-4/> [Accessed: 15 January 2015].

Phillips, Adam. (2013). *Missing Out: In Praise of the Unlived Life*. London: Penguin.

Suebsaeng, Asawin. (2012). '"Girls": What the Hell was HBO Thinking?', *Mother Jones*, 11 April. Available from: <http://www.motherjones.com/mixed-media/2012/04/tv-review-girls-hbo-lena-dunham> [Accessed 13 January 2015].

9

Baring the Recession: Sexual Sensationalism and Gender (A)politics in Contemporary Culture

Stéphanie Genz

'We live in a time of deep foreboding, one that haunts any discourse about justice, democracy, and the future', Henry Giroux notes in his account of the 'Disimagination Machine', emphasising that 'market discipline now regulates all aspects of social life' (Giroux, 2013, p. 257). Giroux is uncompromisingly scathing in his attack on neoliberalism and free-market fundamentalism that in his eyes sustain deregulated 'casino capitalism' and give rise to a pseudo-Darwinist, survival-of-the-fittest world ruled by the need to accumulate capital and get ahead in the cut-throat game of self-interest. In this new historical conjecture marked by recessionary politics and austerity measures, freedom and equality have become unaffordable luxuries for the vast majority of the population as 'the corporate state replaces the democratic state' and commitment to social bonds are turned over to market forces (Giroux, 2011, p. 593). Giroux is adamant that what we are seeing in the harsh climate of the post-2008 economic downturn amounts to a breakdown of democracy symptomised by the disappearance of critical thought, the realm of the social, public values and any consideration of the common good. In its place, the recessionary era is characterised by predatory corporatism, obsessive investment with self-interest and a 'narcissistic

189

hyper-individualism that radiates a new sociopathic lack of interest in others' (Giroux, 2013, p. 260).

The post-millennium has undoubtedly been troubled by a seemingly interminable economic crisis and the ensuing atmosphere of austerity and anger at corporate greed, the rollback of opportunities and transfer of risk to culture at large. The current political and cultural moment is also complexly gendered, fears abounding that we are witnessing 'the end of men' (see Rosin, 2010) and a concomitant 'rise of women' (see Barrow, 2012), a trend not borne out by economic reality and rising numbers of unemployed women. As Anna Bird, the Fawcett Society's Head of Policy and Campaigns, has warned, 'the impact of austerity has brought us to a tipping point where, while we have got used to steady progress towards greater equality, we're now seeing a risk of slipping backwards' (Bird qtd in Davies, 2011, n.p.).

In this chapter, I want to parse out the interplay of economic insecurity and gender by focusing on a prominent contemporary discourse of sexual sensationalism that has emerged in a number of guises, both in popular culture as well as in more politicised quarters where it is encapsulated by a sexualised form of activism – what I label 'boob and bust' politics – to address gendered inequalities. From FEMEN's 'topless Jihad' against sex tourism and religious institutions in the Ukraine to the now worldwide 'SlutWalk' movement to challenge sexual violence, sexualised feminist politics have erupted in many different locations, re-appropriating the topless female body as a means for political expression and activism. Popular culture has witnessed a similar shift towards sexual licentiousness and aggressive physicality that reflects the immediacy of our times with citizens sharply divided by their rank/class and access to capital. The sexual sensationalism on show for example in historical/fantasy television series like *Game of Thrones* (2011–), *The Borgias* (2011–2013) and *The Tudors* (2007–2010) speaks to the stark realities of a post-2008 world in which well-being and security are no longer guaranteed by the neoliberal, meritocratic mantra of a free-market economy that is meant to provide everyone with the right to make profits and amass personal wealth. At the same time, I argue that popular television series such as these do not deny or refute sexism – by rendering it 'imperceptible' as some second-wave feminists in the 1970s argued (see Frye, 1983) – in their unapologetic and humourless depiction of hetero-sexist norms and sexual violence. This is emblematic of a contemporary dialectic of, what I call, sexist liberalism and liberal sexism that complicates (and possibly invalidates) optimistic articulations of (female) entitlement and empowerment, favoured by both neoliberal and postfeminist rhetoric (see Genz, 2009). As I go on to investigate, the liberal sexism/sexist liberalism on show also raises interesting questions about the nature of visibility itself and its relation to critique whereby making a political issue 'visible' or 'speakable' might not be enough as an act of emancipation and political awareness.

Austerity Neoliberalism and *Boob and Bust* Politics

Grounded in the idea of the free, possessive individual, neoliberalism's critical and political potential has long been discussed by a range of commentators.[1] For Zygmunt Bauman, for example, neoliberalism's reliance on hyper-individualism inevitably results in an atomised society that has ceded the notion of collective citizenship and social responsibility:

> individual men and women are now expected, pushed and pulled to seek and find individual solutions to socially created problems and implement those solutions individually [...] This ideology proclaims the futility [...] of solidarity: of joining forces and subordinating individual actions to a 'common cause'.
>
> (Bauman, 2008, p. 88)

In the same vein, Henry Giroux maintains that the regime of 'economic Darwinism' under neoliberalism relies on an ethos of anti-intellectualism and ignorance to both 'depoliticise the larger public while simultaneously producing the individual and collective subjects necessary and willing to participate in their own oppression' (Giroux, 2011, p. 165). In this reading, the 'cheerful robot' comes to be seen as a metaphor for the systemic construction of 'a new mode of depoliticised and thoughtless form of agency' that reduces civic responsibility to banal acts of consumption (Giroux, 2011, p. 165). The end result is a 'politics of disimagination' that generates a politically inert mass of 'uniformed customers, hapless clients, depoliticised subjects, and illiterate citizens' who are unable to 'think critically, imagine the unimaginable, and engage in thoughtful and critical dialogue' (Giroux, 2013, pp. 263–264).

The production of civic passivity and political illiteracy has been amplified under the strain of the post-2008 recession that mobilises ideas of self-sufficiency and self-responsibilisation in order to convince the individual consumer-citizen of the economic necessity and moral obligation to bear the burden of the financial crisis (see Clarke and Newman, 2012). As Jeremy Gilbert has examined, neoliberal politics of austerity turn people away from larger forces by 'secur[ing] consent and generat[ing] political inertia' in a bid to convince and console austerity-weary citizens that the sense of perpetual competition and insecurity that pervades recessionary cultures is natural and that frankly, there is no point in fighting the inevitable (Gilbert, 2013, p. 15). Here, survival – or, in Gilbert's words, 'feeding one's children and keeping them out of relative poverty' (Gilbert, 2013, p. 14) – becomes an achievable but highly demanding task that keeps most social actors too busy to engage in any substantive political challenge to the norms. The general cultural mood is summed up by the notions of 'disaffected consent' and 'resigned compliance' where consent is conditional, grudging and disengaged, rather than enthusiastic (Gilbert, 2013, pp. 13, 18).[2] This has led to an intensification of neoliberal enterprise culture where citizens are called upon to share sacrifice, shoulder the economic downturn and the responsibility for economic uplift and (self-)improvement.[3]

While our current era might thus be described as 'post-political' in some ways – characterised by self-responsibilisation rather than social responsibility – it has nonetheless produced distinct forms of social and political action that re-engage with critical thinking and the language of reform and activism. Against the backdrop of global cut-backs, bailouts and austerity measures, macro-political protests are growing, not just pursuing an anti-capitalist vein that highlights the self-serving and avaricious practices of the 'masters of capital', typified by the widely reviled image of the 'greedy banker'. The present climate of global crisis and uncertainty has also generated a range of specifically gendered revolts that adopt a 'boob and bust' politics that make explicit use of the female body to call attention to political and social issues that pertain to women's bodies (sexual violence and discrimination, prostitution, sex trafficking etc.). The reasoning that underlies these gendered body protests can clearly be traced back to a postfeminist logic that argues for the subjectifying potential of the (post)feminine body and makes a case for 'sexual micro-politics' that allows individual women to express their sexuality in a politically relevant manner (Genz, 2006, p. 339).[4] As I have discussed in previous work, sexual micro-politics seek to 'redistribute the dimensions of female agency by reworking the systems of sexual and economic signification', making room for *femmenists* who 'stage a sexualization of the feminist body in order to construct a new femininity (or, new femininities) around the notions of autonomy and agency' (Genz 2006, p. 345). Here, the female body is seen as a billboard that becomes available for a reappropriation and resignification, what Judith Butler refers to as 'subversive citation from within' (Butler, 1995, p. 135).[5] At the time, I remained hesitant whether these sexualised micro-politics could be replicated on a macro-political level, whether the female body could be used as a political tool to rewrite patriarchal scripts for women as a collective.

In some ways, these questions have now been taken up by 'boob and bust' political movements like the Ukrainian activist group FEMEN and the global SlutWalk phenomenon. These bare-chested protests employ the body as gendered political capital to unmask distinctively female crises in the context of an increasingly imbalanced global society. The SlutWalk movement in particular has magnified these postfeminist debates on a macro-political scale, spreading around the globe from its original manifestation in Toronto in 2011 where the ill-advised comments of a Canadian police officer during a routine 'personal safety' visit to a university campus – suggesting that 'women should avoid dressing like sluts in order not to be victimized' – galvanised local women to organise an activist protest against 'slut-blaming' ideology that implicates the victim of sexual violence (Ringrose and Renold, 2012, pp. 333–343). This kind of sexualised activism seeks to effect a positive re-evaluation of sexual promiscuity and/or sex work through a mobilisation of the 'slut' persona – connected with a whole category of words associated with female sexuality ('tart', 'slag', 'whore' etc.).[6] In order to disrupt the sexualising gaze upon the female body, SlutWalkers dress up in sexually provocative clothing – fishnets, stockings and suspenders, bras, corsets, short skirts – scrawl messages on their bodies and carry placards declaring 'Don't Tell Us How to Dress' and 'I am Not a Slut but I Like Having Consensual Sex'. SlutWalk Toronto's official T-shirt proclaimed 'My body is not an insult', thus underlining women's choices to express sexual agency and freedom over gendered politics of sexual violence. As Ringrose and Renold explain, one of the goals of the SlutWalk as a collective movement is to 'push the gaze off the dress and behaviour of the victim of sexual violence back upon the perpetrator, questioning the normalisation and legitimisation of male sexual aggression' (Ringrose and Renold, 2012, p. 334). In this sense, 'boob and bust' politics is not unlike other kinds of sexual politics that centre on the reclamation of words, the term 'queer' as an emblem of pride and visibility being the most notable in this respect.[7]

Founded in 2008 in Kyiv, Ukraine, FEMEN heighten the theatrical and performative dimensions of these sexual body politics through carefully managed and staged topless protests which they brand 'sextremism'.[8] Echoing SlutWalk's *body as manifesto* tactics and message, activists argue that they are reclaiming their naked bodies and 'defend[ing] with their breasts sexual and social equality in the world' (qtd in O'Keefe, 2014, p. 8). Comprised mostly of university-educated women, FEMEN has received copious international media coverage, with French Magazine *Madame Figaro* for example ranking founding member Inna Shevchenko on their 2012 Women of the Year list. While the initial focus of the group was on sex tourism and the sex industry in Ukraine, recent protests have expanded their reach – addressing a range of issues from the wearing of the hijab to women's exclusion from economic decision-making – and courted media visibility, notably in the case of organised publicity stunts, such as outside the home of former International Monetary Fund head Dominique Strauss Kahn where they posed as sexy chambermaids. As has been noted by commentators, FEMEN protests are sexually overt and activists bare their breasts to capture the attention of the mainstream media (see O'Keefe, 2014). FEMEN's sextremist methods recover the naked female body as an instrument of patriarchy – where it is 'used by man's hands in fashion industry, in sex industry and in advertisements' – and engage in a resignification of sexual stereotypes whereby 'we are making a sign that it's back now to its rightful owner, to women' (Larssen qtd in O'Keefe, 2014, p. 10).

In addition, FEMEN also positions itself explicitly as an updated, sexy and smart version of feminism: as the movement's co-founder Shevchenko has stated, 'classic feminism no longer works. It is, if you excuse me, impotent' (qtd in Glass, 2012, n.p.). Unsurprisingly, feminist critics have reacted with ire to such pronouncements, highlighting the pitfalls of sex-tremist logic that employs the nude body as a means of protest. As Theresa O'Keefe has recently argued, 'FEMEN need the male gaze; they explicitly seek to capture it. They take the commodification and objectification of women's bodies and use it to sell a message' (O'Keefe, 2014, p. 10). In this sense, FEMEN's topless protesting needs to be differentiated from other forms of nude feminist activism – such as Nigerian women's naked demon-strations to challenge colonialism (see Ekine, 2001) – that make subversive use of the naked female body to disrupt social taboos. By contrast, in the case of FEMEN, the naked breast is not taboo but an integral component of women's sexualisation in many Western countries. As such, 'FEMEN's per-formance of nudity [...] rests on the premise that breasts deemed worthy of sexualisation, deemed desirable according to dominant norms, are the only breasts that can be rendered visible' (O'Keefe, 2014, p. 11). Related to this, another point of contention has been the obvious hetero-normative appeal of FEMEN activists who are typically white, young and in possession of a slim and trim body. The movement's public face undoubtedly consists of a group of conventionally attractive women who self-exhibit and flaunt their bodies instrumentally to attract media attention and desire. While on their website FEMEN activists describe themselves as 'fearless and free Amazons' who are 'physically and psychologically ready to implement the humanitar-ian tasks of any degree of complexity and level of provocation', they also champion a striking 'pop star look' (Zychowicz, 2011, p. 218) – wearing lit-tle beyond make-up and a vinok, the traditional Ukrainian garland of flow-ers – that is easily commodifiable and digestible for mainstream tastes and imagination.[9] This aligns these macro-political protests with sexual micro-politics where individual women exert their consumer agency to achieve empowerment 'by using their bodies as political tools within the parameters of a capitalist economy' (Genz, 2006, p. 345).[10]

So, what are we to make of this type of 'boob and bust' politics that employ sexual sensationalism and manipulate nudity as exhibitionistic performance? Do contemporary sexualised forms of body protest amount to what Giroux calls 'the return of the social question' that nourishes a sense of critique, civic courage and collective struggle (Giroux, 2011, p. 598)? Or, do they represent a politics of conformity emblematic of a predatory sexism that interpellates women as sexual subjects who, in order to be *visible*, need to be visually appealing?[11] Clearly, sexualised macro-politics demand careful investigation on a number of fronts, specifically in relation to norms of hetero-corporeality and the performance of the sexy female body (see O'Keefe, 2014); the mix of feminist language and rejection of the feminist label; the reclamation of patriarchal signifiers of abuse (like 'slut') that might be beyond redemption;[12] a facile and decontextualised universalism that associates nudity with liberation and insists that all women will be liberated by going topless;[13] the failure to account for the structural and intersectional nature of women's oppression; the inherent limitations and exclusivity of these movements for example in terms of their predominant Whiteness (see Nguyen, 2013); and the celebritisation and branding of the political realm that requires political actors to be media savvy and eye-catching (see Drake and Higgins, 2006). Thus, while 'boob and bust' politics might not necessarily introduce a new political language and generate a 'radical imagination' that creates 'modes of agency that are critical, informed, engaged, and socially responsible' (Giroux, 2013, p. 265), they nonetheless allow us to think beyond the intellectual vacuum of neoliberal individualism that cultivates political inertia and illiteracy. As Giroux allows, 'it is precisely through the indeterminate nature of history that resistance becomes possible and politics refuses any guarantees and remains open' (Giroux, 2014, p. 265). Yet, at the same time, in these circumstances it might no longer be enough to expose and *make visible* the practices of (patriarchal) subjugation and victimisation, as *visibility* as a tool of (political) critique becomes questioned and questionable. In a culture shaped by the need for intense and perpetual excitement, the spectacle of sexy politics acts as an apt barometer of the changing conditions of sex and sexual politics. Here, we might need to re-think Foucault's suggestion that 'the mere fact that one is speaking about it [sex] has the appearance of a deliberate transgression' as transgression itself becomes highly sexualised and marketable (Foucault, 1978, p. 6).

Moreover, the confidence around resignification – that a history of patriarchal domination and sexual victimisation could be reclaimed and given a new meaning – that underlie 'boob and bust' politics is wavering in the context of our contemporary age of uncertainty riddled with debt, doubt and destitution. If late twentieth- and early twenty-first-century neoliberal culture was marked by optimism, entitlement and the opportunity of prosperity, then indisputably such articulations have become more doubtful and less celebratory in a post-2008 recessionary environment where the neoliberal mantra of choice and self-determination is still present but becomes inflected with the experiences of precarity and risk and the insistence on self-responsibilisation.[14] In a climate of austerity, this changing affective state implies that the trust in sexual resignification as a political tool needs to be tempered, specifically by an awareness that these are also extraordinarily sexist times in which sexism is at once hypervisible and not seen. In the following section, I will further investigate contemporary modes of sex(ism) and their relation to sexually sensationalist popular culture.

Gotta Fuck and Post-Sexism

'I'm not going to fight them, I am going to fuck them', Petyr Baelish (aka 'Littlefinger') notes in the first season of the HBO drama *Game of Thrones* (2011–, season one, episode four), exemplifying the series' explicit use of sex as a means of power and survival employed by both male and female characters. Adapted from George R.R. Martin's international bestselling epic fantasy novels, the television series' pornographic fusion of violence and sexuality has struck a cultural nerve with audiences worldwide, with *Game of Thrones* officially becoming the most-watched HBO series of all time in 2014. Here, sex is everywhere and everyone has sex, so much so that the series seems to revolve around a 'gotta fuck' mandate whereby sex is ubiquitous and compulsory. One explanation for the series' success can undoubtedly be found in the spectacle of violence and sex that satisfies audiences' need for heightened sensations and voyeuristic viewing pleasures that are unconstrained by a moral compass. More importantly however, Martin's fantasy *speaks to us* because it is a poignant social commentary grounded in sexual/sexist, economic, cultural and political conditions. Despite the fantasy setting, *Game of Thrones* is overtly presentist in its engagement with social matters like gender and sexuality and economic fears of bankruptcy. The series is laden with socio-political themes including issues of power and gender politics and it works within a value system based on contemporary Western cultural, political, aesthetic and economic factors. In this context, we need to investigate 'fucking' as a carnal strategy that can be employed as a way of survival and doing politics.

In some ways, *Game of Thrones*' established formula of sex and violence can be seen as emblematic of a wider cultural shift that allows for a broadening of sexual narratives and more permissive attitudes to sex. Variously termed 'pornographication', 'porno chic' (McNair, 1996, 2002) and 'raunch culture' (Levy, 2006), the sexualisation of culture has been discussed at length by media scholars who highlight 'the extraordinary proliferation of discourses about sex and sexuality across all media forms' (Gill, 2007, p. 151).[15] This also aligns the HBO series with other contemporary historical/fantasy texts like Showtime's *The Tudors* (2007–2010) and *The Borgias* (2011–2013) that are typified by sexual sensationalism and violent physicality. *Game of Thrones* in particular has been famed for its *sexposition* sequences in which expository dialogue is accompanied by nudity, most notably in season one, when King's Council member (and bordello owner) Littlefinger instructs two prostitutes in their art of pleasure while comparing his own casuistry to theirs (season one, episode seven). For some critics, such scenes have a narrative function: 'For the viewer, the sex scenes guarantee that our eyes will not be glazing over with too much information; for the narrative, sexposition suggests the power that even sex workers may have over the most influential of men' (Wells-Lassagne, 2013, p. 421). From this perspective, *Game of Thrones* manages to avoid sliding into pornography and circumnavigates charges of trivial sexism by using nudity and violence in a 'non-gratuitous' manner.

While *Game of Thrones* can clearly be located as part of an expanding 'pornosphere' – in which an accelerating flow of sexual information has led to a 'less regulated, more commercialized, and more pluralistic sexual culture' (McNair, 2002, p. 11) – it also parades a liberal, at times blasé, attitude towards sexism that begs to be acknowledged. In my eyes, the series exhibits a form of *sexist liberalism* that can easily slide into *liberal sexism* that is blunt and unsentimental in its portrayal of sexual abuse, physical violence and torture.[16] Indeed, we would be hard pressed to deny that our sexually sensationalist times are also extraordinarily sexist and 'everyday sexism' is institutionalised and normalised in culture.[17] Despite the ubiquity and commonplaceness of sexist representations, values and practices, becoming aware and politicising sexism has become an increasingly tricky project as sexism itself is no longer clearly delineated by a particular set of actions and attitudes towards women. As Sara Mills has commented, 'the nature of sexism has changed over the last 15 years because of feminist campaigns over equal opportunities, so that there now appears to be less overt sexism' (Mills, 2003, p. 90). Sexism and anti-sexism have become entangled and confused with ideas around political correctness and 'an excessive attention to the sensibilities of those who are seen as different from the norm' (Mills, 2003, p. 89). The post-recession years in particular have seen a reinvigoration of types of sexism – 'new sexism' (Benwell, 2007); 'enlightened sexism' (Douglas, 2010); 'postfeminist sexism' (Gill, 2011); 'critical sexism' (Ahmed, 2013) – that belie assumptions of gender equality and sexual freedom. Sexism nowadays takes many different forms and is often disguised by an ironic tone and postmodern reflexivity which, in Susan Douglas' words, allow for an 'enlightened' sexist stance that wears 'a knowing smirk', is immune from criticism and is 'feminist in its outward appearance' (Douglas, 2010, pp. 14, 10).

If we adopt Marilyn Frye's definition of sexism as 'cultural and economic structures' that 'create and enforce the elaborate and rigid patterns of sex-marking and sex-announcing which divide the species, along lines of sex, into dominators and subordinates' (Frye, 1983, p. 19), then *Game of Thrones* is clearly sexist. Female characters especially are dehumanised as sexual objects, mutilated or physically hurt – the lowborn prostitute Ros who is tortured and murdered by mad boy-king Joffrey in season three being the most obvious example here. The lives of most male and female characters are structured around a 'gotta fuck' mandate that typically posits men as the subjects of the 'fuck' and women as its object. Here, sexism is overt and undisguised and sex is often depicted as painful, most commonly exercised by men upon women and as such, symptomatic of male supremacy that trades in power and violence. Rape in particular is depicted with complacency and smug indifference as a common weapon and efficient instrument of power used in times of social unrest and war but also as a means to cement kinship relations between men and their families. Inequality is clearly sexualised in this context whereby male characters are often considered to have a right of sexual access to female characters while sexual violence and coercion are also eroticised, notably in the case of Cersei's rape by her brother in season four. Following the death of their eldest son born out of their incestuous relationship, Jaime forces himself on his sister next to Joffrey's dead body, her repeated pleadings ('It's not right') nullified by his nonchalant answer 'I don't care' (season four, episode three). Not only is this scene disconcerting because of its morbid nature but it also invests rape with sexual qualities that makes violence appear sexy – responding to viewer criticisms, director Alex Graves claimed that the assault became 'consensual by the end' (Sepinwall, 2014, n.p.). Here, the viewer is invited to partake in a well-rehearsed defensive sexual script whereby 'no' means 'yes' and women 'are up for it' in the end. In this scenario, men are sexually assertive and experienced while women are more reluctant and threatened by unwanted sexual attention.

In particular, unmarried adolescent girls are targeted for rape or other forms of sexual violence: while Sansa Stark epitomises these fears for most of the televised seasons, the inevitability of women's sexual submission is made explicit in the case of Daenerys Targaryen whose privileged birth does not protect her from being sold to a warlord and used for sex (albeit sanctioned by matrimony). Daenerys' example can also be read through a well-rehearsed sex-positive postfeminist script around sexual subjecthood that interprets femininity and sexuality as a potential source of female agency and power (see Genz, 2009). After enduring repeated sexual assaults at the hands of her warrior husband, she seeks advice from a handmaiden on how to pleasure him. 'The Dothraki take slaves like a hound takes a bitch', the girl counsels her, 'Don't make love like a slave. In this tent, he belongs to you' (season one, episode two). Similar sex advice is delivered by a number of characters, from pimp Petyr Bailish's directive to his prostitutes to make male customers feel 'better than other men' (season one, episode seven) to Cersei's blunt tuition to a newly menstruating Sansa Stark that 'tears aren't a woman's only weapon. The best one's between your legs. Learn how to use it' (season two, episode nine). In this way, women are instructed to 'fuck their way out of everything' and use sex instrumentally as a source of power (season two, episode nine).[18]

At times, this 'gotta fuck' agenda is defused and masked by being channelled through a hetero-conservative script of romance, marriage and patriarchal kinship mandates that command women to be fertile and bear (male) 'fruit'. The red sorceress Melissandre for example gains control over Stannis Baratheon and his army by promising him a son and heir and later advising his cooperative but 'unproductive' (i.e. unable to birth a male offspring) wife, 'It's only flesh. It needs what it needs' (season four, episode seven). In Daenerys' case, the initial suggestion of marital rape is superimposed by a more romantic idea of sexual love where men are happy for women to be 'on top'. As rape is sanctioned by marriage, women might have no choice but to embrace their victimisation and find pleasure in objectification. Here, a case could be made for 'positive' objectification or sexual subjecthood but ultimately such hetero-conservative, postfeminist readings around female sexual agency and desire are suspended and cut short by Khal Drogo's death that leaves an inexperienced Daenerys struggling to become a ruler in her own right.

In our haste to simplify these narrative developments and construe *Game of Thrones*' treatment of sex as a continuation of well-established sexual scripts and gender politics, we could interpret what we are seeing here as the same old story of sexual and sexist discourse: sex is a means of power employed by both men and women whereby men use rape as a threat and women seek to acquire a form of sexual power that allows them to transcend their object status. Yet, the knot of sex, power and victimisation secured by a hetero-normative grid is not as tightly fastened as it initially appears. What might start out as a gendered conflict between female victims and male aggressors is increasingly complicated as the gender binary of strength and vulnerability becomes blurred. In *Game of Thrones*, both male and female characters endure suffering, sexual violation and dismemberment, Theon Greyjoy's castration and psychological abuse in season three being the most prominent example. Also, the series' commitment to the visualisation of sex(ism) could be read as a nod to critical/political stances that endeavour to make visible the structures of sexist patriarchy and its effects on both men and women. This strategy was employed by second-wave feminists in particular for whom sexism had to be seen and named as a problem because, as Marilyn Frye suggests, many 'would not see that what I declared to be sexist was sexist' (Frye, 1983, p. 17). Here, the awareness of sexism is irrevocably tied to the possession of a feminist consciousness and the awakening from a state of victimisation and oppression to one of emancipation.

If, as Sara Ahmed (2013) writes, 'complicity is a *starting point*', then *Game of Thrones* might be seen as part of a critical project to underscore our implications in the world that we critique. The series undeniably makes sexism visible by baring the various forms of oppression that it takes and exposing the underlying power hierarchies of gender and sexuality. Importantly, sexism in *Game of Thrones* does not rely on humour to make it palatable, nor is it hidden under the veil of postmodern nostalgia where style replaces substance.[19] The type of liberal sexism/sexist liberalism on show does not need elaborate demystification through layers of ironic representations, nor complex decoding of discursive ambiguity. On the contrary, this is sexism visible for all, uncompromising, confrontational and humourless in its relentless portrayal of sexist abuse.[20] The tactic of 'making visible' also aligns this popular culture text with 'boob and bust' politics that attempt to reconstruct the sexualised female body as a site of political engagement. At the same time, both politicised and popular versions of sexual sensationalism pose a range of questions in relation to the nature of visibility itself and its critical/political potential. *Game of Thrones*' hyperbolic visualisation of sex and violence appears daringly cutting-edge as it challenges us to face sex(ism) head-on. Yet, this can amount to what Ahmed calls 'critical sexism' whereby sexist structures and logic are reproduced by 'critical subjects who do not see the reproduction [of sexism] because of their self-assumed criticality' (Ahmed, 2013, n.p.). Sexism and its inherent violence are not denied or refuted in this case – or made 'imperceptible' as second-wave feminists like Frye argued – and yet, they are manipulated to such an extent that 'making it perceptible' and visible might no longer suffice as an act of political awareness, critically engaged and socially responsible agency. In this sense, sexual sensationalist politics and culture allow for a mode of criticality that is potentially complicit with the reproduction of sexist norms and practices it sets out to criticise. Here, the act of naming and visualising sexism does not undo the problem but recreates it in a *liberal sexist* guise. The dialectic of liberal sexism and sexist liberalism thus points towards a complex intellectual, cultural and political space that does not necessarily foreclose visibility and criticality, interpellating us as critical consumers while simultaneously limiting the scope and potency of that critique. In my eyes, this need not amount to a moral blindness and intellectual coma whereby we are becoming numb to the pernicious effects of sexism – what Giroux calls the 'death of critical thought' (2011, p. 167) – yet it highlights the cultural, political and ideological challenges that any form of substantive contemporary critique of gendered, sexist, class and economic power dynamics has to face. While bared and paraded before our media-savvy and critically astute eyes, sexism is nonetheless *dealt with* and thus paradoxically comes to be seen as *less* of a problem.

Notes

1 Propagated prominently by the Thatcher and Reagan regimes of the late 1970s and 1980s, neoliberal ideas, policies and strategies have incrementally gained ground globally – 'setting the pace', as Hall puts it, by 're-defining the political, social and economic models and governing strategies' (Hall, 2011, p. 708). Market discipline and rationale irrevocably entered all aspects of social life under 'Third Way' politics in the 1990s that promoted particular types of entrepreneurial, competitive and commercial behaviour in citizens.

2 As Gilbert notes:

> Put crudely, perhaps the most commonplace relation to capitalist realism – or neoliberal ideology – in the contemporary world is an explicit rejection of its norms and claims accompanied by a resigned compliance with its demands. We know that we don't like neoliberalism, didn't vote for it, and object in principle to its exigencies: but we recognise also that unless we comply with it, primarily in our workplaces and in our labour-market behaviour, then we will be punished […] and will be unlikely to find ourselves inhabiting a radically different social terrain.
>
> (Gilbert, 2013, p. 13)

3 As the former British Prime Minister David Cameron, for example, put it in 2010:

> We are all in this together, and we will get through this together. We will carry out Britain's unavoidable deficit reduction plan in a way that strengthens and unites the country. […] So yes, it will be tough. But we will get through this together – and Britain will come out stronger on the other side.
>
> (Cameron, 2010, p. 5)

4   Of course, the sexualisation of the female/feminist body also has to be contextu-
    alised within wider feminist debates, particularly the 1970s 'pornography wars'
    that saw 'pro-' and 'anti-sex' feminist camps sharply divided over how to inter-
    pret the sexualised female body. For more on this see Genz (2009).

5   At the time, I used the example of the American designer and activist Periel
    Aschenbrand whose T-shirt campaigns follow the logic of sexual micro-politics.
    As Aschenbrand summarises her mission statement:

> We should reject renting our bodies as billboard space for odious
> companies and use them instead to our advantage, to advertise
> for shit that matters. [...] We should use our tits to make people
> think about the things no one is making them think about.

> (Aschenbrand qtd in Genz, 2006)

6   SlutWalk's modus operandi is to 'challenge the word slut and other degrading words
    around sexuality and sexual assault in their current mainstream use' and to '(re)ap-
    propriate the word slut to use it in a subversive, self-defining, positive, empowering
    and respectful way'. As the organisers of the original Toronto SlutWalk put it:

> We are tired of being oppressed by slut-shaming; of being
> judged by our sexuality and feeling unsafe as a result. [...] No
> one should equate enjoying sex with attracting sexual assault.
> We are a movement demanding that our voices be heard.

    See <http://www.slutwalktoronto.com/satellite/organize>. Also see Attwood
    (2007) for a mapping of the shifting meanings of the term 'slut' over time.

7   This is what Judith Butler calls 'a reversal of effects' in which the repetition of in-
    jurious speech becomes the 'constitutive possibility of being otherwise' (Butler,
    1997, pp. 14, 102). Here, 'the word that wounds becomes an instrument of resist-
    ance [...] a repetition in language that forces change' (Butler, 1997, p. 163).

8   According to FEMEN's website, sextremism is a:

> fundamentally new form of women's feminist actionism. [It] is
> female sexuality rebelling against patriarchy and embodied in
> the extremal political direct action events [...] Sextremism is
> the woman's mockery of vulgar male extremism and its bloody
> mayhems and a cult of terror.

9   See O'Keefe (2014, pp. 10–11). Anna Hutsol, the creative mastermind behind
    FEMEN, openly admits that the group employs a PR strategy by limiting the
    cast of performers to sustain their celebrity status and boost their marketability.
    More controversy was added in 2013 when filmmaker Kitty Green's documen-
    tary about FEMEN revealed Victor Svyatski as a former 'consultant' who selected
    which women would participate in the group's topless protests.

10 As Hutsol explains the branding strategy and market appeal of FEMEN: 'I think if you can sell cookies in this way [through mass appeal] why not also push for social issues using the same method? I don't see anything wrong with that' (qtd in Zychowicz, 2011, p. 221).

11 For more on sexual subjecthood, see Genz (2009).

12 See Dines and Murphy (2011). As Nguyen notes:

> T-shirts, buttons, and posters proclaiming, 'This is what a slut looks like' seek to reclaim the insult 'slut' through inversion, but, I argue, they leave in place the structure of subjugation. [...] Is it possible for a woman to be a 'kind slut,' an 'intelligent slut,' or a 'generous slut'? [...] To answer the insidious charge of women's essential sexual promiscuity with the declaration 'Yes, we are sexual!' is not much of a rejoinder. [...] In essence, inversion leads not only to reaffirmation but also to normalization.
>
> (Nguyen, 2013, p. 160)

13 As Kapur notes in an Indian context, the SlutWalk:

> can be articulated as a form of feminism 'lite'. 'Lite' because they do not claim to bring about a transformation in the form of some 'big bang' moment. Nor do they advocate a distinct theoretical position. They are situated as techniques of critique, not only of dominant attitudes towards women's sexuality, but also of some segments of the feminist movement's complicity in reinforcing a sexually-sanitised understanding of female subjectivity.
>
> (Kapur, 2012, p. 12)

14 See Gilbert (2013). This changed affective regime has had an effect on post-feminist popular culture at large and its depiction of female characters. For instance, Lazar's suggestion that 'the postfeminist subject [...] is entitled to be pampered and pleasured' needs to be problematised in the context of a post-recession environment that no longer guarantees (economic) success and reward to even the most hard-working individuals (Lazar, 2009, p. 372). In this sense, where for example in the case of late twentieth- and early twenty-first-century heroines, failing might have been conceived as a 'virtue' (see McRobbie, 2009) – epitomised by the professional ineptness and persistent blundering of Helen Fielding's Bridget Jones – such under-achievement and incompetence are no longer held up as endearing signs of female identification and imperfection but now turn out to be equivalent to economic suicide as countless, qualified professionals compete in an ever more aggressive and merciless job market.

15 While the sexualisation of culture has been widely theorised, debate continues over whether it represents a loosening of sexual norms or the mainstreaming of subordination for women. See, for example, Levy (2005).

16 See Genz (2016). *Game of Thrones* exploits what Duschinksy calls the 'liberal loophole' whereby 'systematic forms of oppression are reduced to the question of whether a citizen has or has not given meaningful consent' (Duschinsky, 2013, para. 2.1). In this way, focus can be shifted from the brutal power disparities and structural inequalities that define and demarcate the playing field to the individual competitors who choose to engage in a game that potentially oppresses and subjugates them.

17 See for example Laura Bates' website 'The Everyday Sexism Project' (<http://everydaysexism.com/>) that collates women's routine experiences of prejudice and harassment.

18 In my eyes, this does not amount to a sex-positive agenda that defines sexuality as emancipatory and *empowering*. Rather, as Simone de Beauvoir among many others has argued, women can use sex as a tool to achieve a *powerful* social standing (de Beauvoir, 1997, p. 141).

19 This distinguishes liberal sexism from other types of 'new' or 'enlightened' sexism characterised by an ironic tone and postmodern reflexivity that provide immunity from criticism (see Benwell 2007; Douglas 2010).

20 The notion of permissive sexual liberalism was repudiated most recently in the series by the bleak and uneroticised depiction of Sansa Stark's off-camera rape by her psychopathic husband Ramsay Snow in season five, underlining the sexual/sexist abuse suffered by women in a hetero-patriarchal social order.

Bibliography

Ahmed, Sara. (2013). 'Critical Racism/Critical Sexism'. *Feminist Kill Joys*, 19 December. Available from: <http://feministkilljoys.com/2013/12/19/critical-racismcritical-sexism/> [Accessed: 5 August 2014].

Attwood, Feona. (2007). 'Sluts and Riot Grrrls: Female Identity and Sexual Agency'. *Journal of Gender Studies* 16/3, pp. 233–247.

Barrow, Becky. (2012). 'Women Workers Bearing the Brunt of Rising Job Losses as Twice as Many Men Keep Jobs'. *Daily Mail*, 16 February. Available from: <http://www.dailymail.co.uk/news/article-2101796/Women-workers-bearing-brunt-rising-job-losses-twice-men-jobs.html> [Accessed: 10 July 2014].

Bauman, Zygmunt. (2008). *The Art of Life*. London: Polity.

Benwell, Bethan. (2007). 'New Sexism: Readers' Responses to the Use of Irony in Men's Magazines'. *Journalism Studies* 8/4, pp. 539–549.

Butler, Judith. (1995). 'For a Careful Reading'. In: Seyla Benhabib, Judith Butler, Drucilla Cornell and Nancy Fraser (eds) *Feminist Contentions: A Philosophical Exchange*. New York: Routledge.

—— (1997). *Excitable Speech: A Politics of the Performative*. New York and London: Routledge.

Cameron, David. (2010). 'We Must Tackle Britain's Massive Deficit and Growing Debt'. *The Conservative Party*, June. Available from: <http://www.conservatives. com/News/Speeches/2010/06/David_Cameron_We_must_tackle_Britains_ massive_deficit_and_growing_debt.aspx> [Accessed: 1 March 2015].

Clarke, John and Newman, Janet. (2012). 'The Alchemy of Austerity'. *Critical Social Policy* 32/3, pp. 299–319.

Davies, Lizzy. (2011). 'The Rubber Gloves are On: Marchers to Fight for Women's Rights Amid Cuts'. *The Fawcett Society*, 18 November. Available from: <http:// www.theguardian.com/society/2011/nov/18/fawcett-march-womens-rights- amid-cuts> [Accessed: 10 July 2014].

de Beauvoir, Simone. (1997 [1949].) *The Second Sex*. London: Vintage.

Dines, Gail and Murphy, Wendy. (2011). 'SlutWalk is Not Sexual Liberation', *Guardian*, 8 May. Available from: <http://www.theguardian.com/commentisfree/ 2011/may/08/slutwalk-not-sexual-liberation> [Accessed: 18 March 2015].

Douglas, Susan. (2010). *The Rise of Enlightened Feminism: How Pop Culture Took Us from Girl Power to Girls Gone Wild*. New York: St. Martin's Griffin.

Drake, Philip and Higgins, Michael. (2006). '"I'm a Celebrity, Get Me Into Politics": The Political Celebrity and the Celebrity Politician'. In: Su Holmes and Sean Redmond (eds) *Framing Celebrity: New Directions in Celebrity Culture*. New York: Routledge.

Duschinsky, Robbie. (2013). 'Childhood, Responsibility and the Liberal Loophole: Replaying the Sex-Wars in Debates of Sexualisation?'. *Sociological Research Online* 18/2, 7. Available from: <http://www.socresonline.org.uk/18/ 2/7.html> [Accessed: 22 July 2014].

Ekine, S. (2001). *Blood Sorrow and Oil: Testimonies of Violence from Women of the Niger Delta*. Oxford: Centre for Democracy and Development.

FEMEN website. Available from: <http://femen.org/about> [Accessed: 18 March 2015].

Foucault, Michel. (1978). *The History of Sexuality Volume 1: An Introduction*. New York: Pantheon Books.

Frye, Marilyn. (1983). *The Politics of Reality: Essays in Feminist Theory*. Trumansburg, NY: Crossing Press.

Genz, Stéphanie. (2006). 'Third Way/ve: the Politics of Postfeminism'. *Feminist Theory* 7/3 pp. 333–353.

Genz, Stéphanie. (2009). *Postfemininities in Popular Culture*. Basingstoke: Palgrave Macmillan.

—— (2016). '"I'm Not Going to Fight Them, I'm Going to Fuck Them": Sexist Liberalism and Gender (A)politics in *Game of Thrones*'. In: R. Schubart and A. Gjelsvik (eds) *Women of Ice and Fire: Gender, Game of Thrones and Multiple Media Engagements*. New York: Bloomsbury.

207

Gill, Rosalind (2007) *Gender and the Media*. Cambridge: Polity.

—— (2011) 'Sexism Reloaded, Or, It's Time to Get Angry Again'. *Feminist Media Studies* 11/1 pp. 61–71.

Giroux, Henry. (2011). 'The Disappearing Intellectual in the Age of Economic Darwinism'. *Policy Futures in Education* 9/2, pp. 163–171.

—— (2013). 'The Disimagination Machine and the Pathologies of Power'. *Symploke* 21/1–2, pp. 257–269.

—— (2014). 'Neoliberalism and the Machine of Disposability'. *Truth Out*, 8 April. Available from: <http://www.truth-out.org/opinion/item/22958-neoliberalism-and-the-machinery-of-disposability> [Accessed: 6 June 2014].

Glass, Katie. (2012). 'Sisters of the Revolution! Time to Blow Your Tops'. *Sunday Times*, 8 April. Available from: <http://www.thesundaytimes.co.uk/sto/Magazine/Features/article1008102.ece> [Accessed: 13 January 2015].

Hall, Stuart. (2011). 'The Neo-Liberal Revolution'. *Cultural Studies* 25/6, pp. 705–728.

Kapur, Ratna. (2012). 'Pink Chaddis and SlutWalk Couture: The Postcolonial Politics of Feminism Lite'. *Feminist Legal Studies* 20, pp. 1–20.

Lazar, Michelle M. (2009). 'Entitled to Consume: Postfeminist Femininity and a Culture of Post-Critique'. *Discourse and Communication* 3/4, pp. 371–400.

Levy, Ariel. (2006). *Female Chauvinist Pigs: Women and the Rise of Raunch Culture*. London: Pocket Books.

McNair, Brian. (1996). *Mediated Sex: Pornography and Postmodern Culture*. London: Arnold.

—— (2002) *Striptease Culture: Sex, Media and the Democratisation of Desire*. Abingdon: Routledge.

McRobbie, Angela. (2009). *The Aftermath of Feminism: Gender, Culture and Social Change*. Thousand Oaks, CA: Sage.

Mills, Sara. (2003). 'Caught between Sexism, Anti-Sexism and "Political Correctness": Feminist Women's Negotiations with Naming Practices'. *Discourse Society* 14/1, pp. 87–110.

Nguyen, Tram. (2013). 'From SlutWalks to SuicideGirls: Feminist Resistance in the Third Wave and Postfeminist Era'. *Women's Studies Quarterly* 41/3–4, pp. 157–172.

O'Keefe, Theresa. (2014). '"My Body is my Manifesto!" SlutWalk, FEMEN and Femmenist Protest'. *Feminist Review* 107, pp. 1–19.

Ringrose, Jessica and Renold, Emma. (2012). 'Slut-shaming, Girl Power and "Sexualisation": Thinking Through the Politics of the International SlutWalks with Teen Girls'. *Gender and Education* 24/3, pp. 333–343.

Rosin, Hanna (2010) 'The End of Men'. *The Atlantic*, July/August. Available from: <http://www.theatlantic.com/magazine/archive/2010/07/the-end-of-men/308135/> [Accessed: 1 February 2014].

Sepinwall, Alan. (2014). 'Review: *Game of Thrones* – "Breaker of Chains": Uncle Deadly?', *Hit Fix*, 20 April. Available from: <http://www.hitfix.com/whats-alan-watching/review-game-of-thrones-breaker-of-chains-uncle-deadly> [Accessed: 20 September 2014].

Wells-Lassagne, Shannon. (2013). 'Prurient Pleasures: Adapting Fantasy to HBO'. *Journal of Adaptation in Film & Performance* 6/3, pp. 415–426.

Zychowicz, Jessica. (2011). 'Two Bad Words: FEMEN and Feminism'. *The Anthropology of East Europe Review* 29/2, pp. 215–227.

Index

Index

Index

Index

Storey, John 7
survival 36–37, 54, 70, 78, 83, 102, 106, 134–135, 137, 140–142, 146, 148, 154, 158, 161, 162, 189, 192, 197–199

Tasker, Yvonne 3, 8, 48
'television personality' 112, 124
Thatcher, Margaret 17, 20, 27, 87, 88, 91–96, 99

unemployment 2, 3, 10–11, 19, 45
see also employment

'veg-patch capitalism' 123–124, 131
Victorian 1, 9, 17–18, 20, 23, 27, 37
vintage culture 10, 65–73, 80–82
virtue 12, 152, 154, 205

Walden, Brian 27
Walker, Alan 27
Walking Dead, The 11–12, 133–149

wartime 10, 65, 67, 71, 72, 74, 75, 76, 77, 80, 81, 82
Waters, Catherine 17
Waters, Melanie 8
Welfare State, the 4, 19, 37
white male 12, 47, 50, 53, 59, 137, 143–148
see also race
Wilson, A. N. 1–2
Wollstonecraft, Mary 34, 36
women
see femininity, gender, motherhood
workhouse, the 19, 20, 28, 29–30, 31, 33

Young Ones, The 11, 87, 91–98, 103, 105

zombies 11–12, 135, 135–136, 137, 140, 141, 142–145, 147–148